Dynamics of Economic Spaces in the Global Knowledge-Based Economy

T0270976

This book addresses how economic spaces dynamically change within the context of the global knowledge-based economy. Specifically, it centers the discussion on integrated views of understanding and conceptualizing dynamic changes of global economy under the global megatrends of globalization, knowledge-based economy, information society, service world, climate change, and population aging. Focusing on East Asia, especially on Korea, it deals with case studies regarding the processes and patterns of these global dynamics, looking at economic spaces of various spatial scales and types of economic actors.

This book develops a theoretical model for understanding and analyzing the dynamics of economic spaces that are being reshaped within the larger global economy. It also emphasizes the analysis of empirical studies at the levels of firm, region, and state by considering an evolutionary perspective over time. In developing its theoretical framework, this book examines regional resilience, intangible assets, service innovation, path dependence, and other notions related to the evolution of economic spaces, and incorporates these elements into real-world case studies.

The integrated theoretical framework examined here contributes a new perspective on spatial disparities in the global economy. An integral model of service innovation; the integration of path dependence and regional resilience; the interaction between firm and region for the accumulation of intangible assets; and the roles of governments and global firms: these are all essential to understanding the dynamics of economic spaces in East Asia. The theoretical model and case studies in this book suggest policy implications for developing countries, especially in the Asian and African regions, with regard to regional development and innovation policies.

Sam Ock Park is Professor Emeritus, Department of Geography, Seoul National University, and Chair Professor, Department of Public Administration, Gachon University, South Korea.

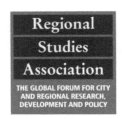

Regions and Cities

Series Editor in Chief:
Susan M. Christopherson, *Cornell University, USA*

Editors:
Maryann Feldman, *University of Georgia, USA*
Gernot Grabher, *HafenCity University Hamburg, Germany*
Ron Martin, *University of Cambridge, UK*
Martin Perry, *Massey University, New Zealand*

In today's globalised, knowledge-driven and networked world, regions and cities have assumed heightened significance as the interconnected nodes of economic, social and cultural production, and as sites of new modes of economic and territorial governance and policy experimentation. This book series brings together incisive and critically engaged international and interdisciplinary research on this resurgence of regions and cities, and should be of interest to geographers, economists, sociologists, political scientists and cultural scholars, as well as to policy-makers involved in regional and urban development.

For more information on the Regional Studies Association visit www.regionalstudies.org

There is a **30% discount** available to RSA members on books in the *Regions and Cities* series, and other subject related Taylor and Francis books and e-books including Routledge titles. To order just e-mail alex.robinson@tandf.co.uk, or phone on +44 (0) 20 7017 6924 and declare your RSA membership. You can also visit www.routledge.com and use the discount code: **RSA0901**

81. Dynamics of Economic Spaces in the Global Knowledge-Based Economy
Theory and East Asian cases
Sam Ock Park

80. Urban Competitiveness
Theory and practice
Daniele Letri and Peter Kresl

79. Smart Specialisation
Opportunities and challenges for regional innovation policy
Dominique Foray

78. The Age of Intelligent Cities
Smart environments and innovation-for-all strategies
Nicos Komninos

Dynamics of Economic Spaces in the Global Knowledge-Based Economy

Theory and East Asian cases

Sam Ock Park

Routledge
Taylor & Francis Group

LONDON AND NEW YORK

First published 2015 by Routledge

2 Park Square, Milton Park, Abingdon, Oxfordshire OX14 4RN
52 Vanderbilt Avenue, New York, NY 10017

Routledge is an imprint of the Taylor & Francis Group, an informa business

First issued in paperback 2019

British Library Cataloguing in Publication Data
A catalogue record for this book is available from the British Library

Library of Congress Cataloging in Publication Data
A catalog record for this book has been requested

ISBN: 978-0-415-74018-0 (hbk)
ISBN: 978-0-367-86945-8 (pbk)

Typeset in Times New Roman
by Florence Production, Stoodleigh, Devon, UK

Contents

Figures

Tables

Preface

This book was supported by a research grant from the National Research Foundation of Korea (No. 2008-B00027). In Korea, this grant was offered to only a few selected and distinguished scholars in the field of Humanities and Social Sciences. The grant promotes five-year research and requires scholars to write a book in English. Before I received this grant, I mainly published articles in journals and edited books in the field of economic geography. Thus, this book could not have been published without this funded grant from the Ministry of Education.

Since the early 1980s, I have been interested in the dynamic structural changes of countries that have been undergoing industrialization. I established the International Geographical Union Commission on the Dynamics of Economic Spaces in 2000 and served as its chairperson for four years. In 2005, I ceased to be a participant in the Commission because I served academically as a Dean of the College of Social Sciences at Seoul National University. Despite my inactivity in the Commission, I have continued to investigate the dynamic economic spaces in Korea. Thus, this book is a continuation of my research on the dynamics of economic spaces and synthesizes the studies I conducted in the last five years.

This book addresses the dynamic changes in economic spaces in the context of global knowledge-based economy. Specifically, it synthesizes and conceptualizes dynamic changes in global economy given the global mega-trends of globalization, knowledge-based economy, information society, service world, climate change, and the aging population. The book focuses on East Asia, Korea in particular, and examines the processes and patterns of these global dynamics through case studies. These case studies investigate economic spaces at various spatial scales, as well as types of economic actors.

The integrated theoretical framework studied in this book provides an integrative perspective on spatial disparities in the global economy. To understand the dynamics of economic spaces in East Asia, the following factors are essential: an integral model of service innovation; the integration of path dependence and regional resilience; the interaction between firms and regions in the accumulation of intangible assets; and the roles of governments and global firms in the variations in regional, national, and global economy.

Sam Ock Park
Institute of Space & Economy, Seoul, Korea
March, 2014

Acknowledgments

I am grateful for permission to use articles originally published in the following media: *Journal of Korean Geographical Society* (Chapters 5 and 7) and *Urban Geography* (Chapter 6). I would also like to thank the *Journal of Economic Geography* and *Economic Geography* for the consent to use figures (Figures 2.2, 4.1, 4.2, and 4.3).

I would like to thank the following individuals for their considerable contribution in providing data, tables, and figures: Homin Yang, Dr. Dongsuk Huh, Dr. Jinhyung Lee, Dr. Dochai Chung, Dr. Younghoun Lim, and Yongrong Kim, who were research assistants at Seoul National University when they were graduate students. During my five-year research period, each of them assisted me for one or two years. I also thank Dr. Yangmi Koo and Homin Yang for conducting joint interviews with a dermatology service firm and a manufacturer of dermatology instruments. Furthermore, I thank Dr. Dongsuk Huh for formatting the draft of the book manuscript. Special thanks are given to the CEO of Leaders Dermatology Clinics; the CEO and manager of Lutronic; and a former CEO, executive director, and managing director of Samsung, for consenting to interviews.

I began my research for this book at Seoul National University, but I retired from this university under the age limit. I completed the study at Gachon University; therefore, I thank President Gil Ya Lee for allowing me to conduct research as a Chair Professor here.

I also thank the chairman of Sungji Culture Publishing Company, Mr. Hyung-Gyu Choi, who has provided an office space for the Institute of Space & Economy where I have conducted my research since I retired from Seoul National University.

Early versions of the chapters in this book were presented at the annual meetings of the Association of American Geographers in Las Vegas, Washington, DC, Seattle, New York, and Los Angeles; North American meetings of the Regional Science Association International in San Francisco, Denver, New York, and Miami; the meeting of the Pacific Regional Science Conference Organization in Gold Coast, Australia; the International Conference of IGU Commission on the Dynamics of Economic Spaces in Groningen, the Netherlands; international conferences in Shanghai, Beijing, Zhengzhow, Taipei, Macao, Singapore, and Torino; and colloquiums in the World Bank,

Georgia Institute of Technology, and Georgia State University. The participant feedback from these conferences was beneficial to this book.

I would also like to thank the editorial and production teams at Routledge— Lisa Thomson, Natalie Tomlinson and Robert Langham—and Amy Wheeler at Florence Production, who helped to publish this book. Last, but certainly not the least, I thank my lovely wife, Myunghoun Um, who always supports me with her patience and hearty prayers.

1 Introduction

Background and objectives of the book

Economic spaces are an expression of economic institutions in society as well as spatial processes and forms of economic practices. Economic spaces are analyzed in terms of the relationships and networks created among different economic agents, such as nation states, firms, institutions, organizations, local authorities, trade unions, and consumers. New spatial processes and forms of economic practices have evolved in the global society during the last two decades with the development of a knowledge-based economy in relation to the techno–economic paradigm shift. Economic spaces cannot be organized by only a single criterion of economic rationality. The processes of shaping economic spaces have become diverse over time and in regions. The changes in economic spaces have been well recognized during the last quarter of a century at various spatial scales through the emergence of the following: "new industrial spaces" (Scott, 1988) or "sticky places in a slippery space" (Markusen, 1996), shift of the economic gravity center (Park, 1997), development of spatial innovation systems (Oinas and Malecki, 1999), diverse clusters (e.g. temporary and virtual clusters) (Park, 2005; Torre, 2008; Bathelt and Glückler, 2011), and the global financial market (Clark and Wójcik, 2007). These changes are closely related to techno–economic paradigm shifts that have distinctive characteristics in production, business, and innovation systems. Spatial dynamics have been reinforced with the development of information and communication technology (ICT) and a knowledge-based economy in the twenty-first century. In the next twenty years, climate change and the progress of an aging society will surely affect the reshaping of economic spaces in the global society. This condition suggests that new theoretical frameworks for understanding new economic spaces are necessary.

Freeman and Perez (1988) categorized technological changes into incremental innovations, radical innovations, new technological systems, and techno–economic paradigms. Among these types of technological changes, techno–economic paradigms have the most significant and widest impact on the society and economy. New techno–economic paradigms evolve from a down-swing phase of the previous Kondratieff wave and include various new product and process innovations, which in turn form new industries (Freeman, 1987; Hayter, 1997). Moreover, changes in techno–economic paradigms result in corresponding changes in major industrial and infrastructure innovations, the source of productivity improvements, and business organizations. This model of techno-economic paradigms indicates that the most recent shift in the paradigms is related to the development of ICT.

Different spatial processes have occurred with the development of ICT and the Internet. Many high-technology start-ups and spin-offs are clustered in large metropolitan regions, even in newly industrialized or developed countries. Likewise, new knowledge-based industries and services have developed in these regions in recent years. Virtual or nonspatial clusters within the electronic network continue to evolve beyond spatial clustering in the Internet era. However, the effects of the ICT revolution on economic spaces are complex and take multiple forms.

A great paradox has been observed in the speculation on the spatial impact of ICT because of the existence of tacit knowledge that cannot be traded through the Internet and smart innovation space. On one hand, the rapid development of ICT in the last decade, particularly the rapid increase in the number of Internet users, has been considered an important impetus for reducing spatial disparities and promoting the even development of economic activities over space. On the other hand, many geographical studies have revealed that spatial proximity and the nodality of cities retain their importance in economic development, although communication has improved and the economy has become globalized with the development of ICT (Florida, 1995, 2002c; Gertler, 1995; Malecki, 2002; Zook, 2002; Rutten and Boekema, 2007; Karlsson, 2008). Along with the development of the Internet, the creation of knowledge for innovation and the flow of knowledge, information, and materials are critical for the dynamics of economic spaces. The Internet infrastructure, knowledge-intensive manpower, innovation clusters and networks, and the "cluster of wants" are not evenly distributed over space and thus become important factors in the reorganization of economic spaces (Park, 2004b).

The reason such a paradox exists in the spatial manifestation of the effect of ICT on economic spaces is closely related to the disparity that exists in physical space. The social, material, and environmental conditions of physical space are unevenly distributed. Linguistic, cultural, and institutional differences exist over physical space. Significant variations are also present in the characteristics of local labor markets, culture, and social relations in physical space. The disparities that exist in the physical space of the real world significantly affect the spatial manifestation of electronic space because electronic space is intrinsically embedded in physical space. Furthermore, differences in local cultures, institutions, and labor markets in physical space have a significant impact on innovations in the knowledge-based economy. Although physical and electronic spaces differ significantly, the two are complementary in the process of economic space. Therefore, the ICT infrastructure cannot be separated from the social, political, economic, and cultural context in which the technological infrastructure is embedded. The intrinsic nature of the embedding of electronic space in physical space causes the local characteristics to affect electronic space and results in the continuous importance of physical place and space even in the era of digital convergence.

The complexity resulting from the megatrends of the global knowledge-based information economy in economic spaces has caused the emergence of diverse processes of the change in economic spaces that are different from the previous ones. Various possibilities can result in new forms of industrial clusters, city regions, global networks, global organization of firms, and global systems of innovation. We are living in continuously reshaping economic spaces in which physical and electronic spaces are interlinked. The processes that produce new economic spaces are important in understanding the global economy and in clarifying the dynamics of economic spaces in the global knowledge-based economy. Considering the reshaping and dynamic spatial changes, this book focuses on the development of frameworks and theories that explain the dynamics of economic spaces with the aim of ameliorating spatial disparities in the global knowledge-based economy.

The major objectives and contributions of this book can be summarized in four aspects. First, the book attempts to develop an integrated theory to explain the dynamics of economic spaces in the global knowledge-based economy. New and diverse processes and forms of the organization of economic spaces exist in the global knowledge-based economy. Accordingly, complex economic spaces can be viewed as a global jigsaw puzzle of the organization of economic activities (Vertova, 2006). A considerable number of studies have dealt with the theories on the special forms of economic spaces, such as cultural and relational turns. In addition, contrasting approaches to the study of economic spaces between economics and economic geography have been regarded as "geographical economics" or "new economic geography" by economists with emphasis on space focusing on economic rationality. Although theoretical approaches on the organization of economic spaces in the field of economic geography have a long history, most of them deal with only a segment in terms of the spatial and temporal aspects of economic spaces and cannot fully explain the complex and dynamic realities of such spaces. The integrated theoretical framework contributes to the understanding of spatial disparities in the global economy and to the establishment of future policies for regional development.

Second, the book emphasizes the analysis of empirical studies that focus on East Asian countries, particularly Korea. As suggested by Peter Dicken (2006), both theories and empirical studies on economic spaces should avoid ethnocentrism that is characteristic of most economic geographical studies as it tends to be embedded in Western industrialized countries. Most spatial theories and case studies in the last century have focused on Western countries. Asian countries are currently experiencing profound changes in economic spaces and emerging diverse forms of networks, clusters, global relations, and city regions since the introduction of the Internet and digital convergence in the last two decades. Case studies in East Asian countries can complement Western-oriented studies and will surely contribute to understanding reshaping global economic spaces as a whole.

Third, the book considers the evolutionary processes in the dynamics of economic spaces at various spatial scales. Economic spaces evolve over time through dynamic processes, such as path creation, path dependency, restructuring, or stagnation with lock-in. These dynamic processes are not limited to the local area. As globalization progresses, the processes in economic spaces and the emergence of new forms of economic spaces extend beyond local and national boundaries over time. However, most network and cluster studies have focused on the local level within national boundaries at certain points in time. Although the agglomeration phenomenon is a local characteristic, the impact of global economy and its networks are embedded into the local agglomeration. This book contributes to the study of economic geography and regional economics by considering the dynamics at different spatial scales and an evolutionary perspective over time.

Fourth, the book analyzes both service and material production activities to understand the dynamics of economic spaces in the service world. Most theories on innovation, with regard to the dynamics of economic spaces, have focused on material production activities. In a knowledge-based economy, knowledge-intensive services serve an important function in the production of high-technology products and are important in reorganizing economic spaces. Diverse services are closely linked to each stage of manufacturing, from production to distribution as well as service activities. Global flows of capital, labor, technology, engineering, and even policy are very important to the changes in economic spaces. This book contributes to the understanding of dynamic and integrating global economies that consolidate services and manufacturing products.

In sum, the book aims to establish an integrated theory that explains the dynamic changes in economic spaces in a global knowledge-based economy. It also seeks to conduct empirical studies to confirm the theoretical framework of the dynamics of economic spaces. Moreover, the book intends to suggest policy implications for developing countries, particularly in Asian and African regions, with regard to regional development and innovation policies. The scope and contents of the analysis are different from those of existing studies and thus characterize the distinctive nature of the book.

Global megatrends and economic spaces

The four most influential global megatrends in economic spaces in the last two decades are globalization, knowledge-based economy, information society, and service economy. These four megatrends can be regarded as major forces or processes that shape and reshape economic spaces in a global knowledge-based economy. Since the beginning of the twenty-first century, climate change and aging society have emerged as other global forces that affect global economic spaces in addition to the four global megatrends. These megatrends and their interrelation with other megatrends in the global space economy are discussed individually in this section. The four global megatrends are examined first followed by the additional megatrends.

Globalization

Globalization has been defined differently over time, "with some connotations referring to progress, development and stability, and integration and co-operation and others referring to regression, colonialism, and destabilization" (Al-Rodhan and Stoudmann, 2006, p. 3). Some definitions emphasize economic aspects, whereas others emphasize social or cultural aspects (Wallerstein, 1974; Harvey, 1989; Giddens, 1990; Dicken, 1992; Ohmae, 1992; Robertson, 1992). For example, Giddens (1990) defined globalization as "the intensification of worldwide social relations which link distant localities in such a way that local happenings are shaped by events occurring many miles away and vice versa" (p. 64). Meanwhile, Wallerstein (1974) emphasized economic aspects by focusing on the capitalist world economy and global division of labor. Dicken (1992) focused on the interdependence and integration between national economies. Global economic organizations, such as the World Bank and OECD (2005), generally emphasize international economic integration. Al-Rodhan and Stoudmann (2006), basing on the comprehensive review of globalization definitions, proposed that "globalization is a process that encompasses the causes, course, and consequences of transnational and transcultural integration of human and non-human activities" (p. 5).

Despite its diverse definitions, globalization is not a static concept but a dynamic one, with spatial interdependence among economic, social, and cultural aspects from the geographical perspective. Globalization represents integration as well as networking or interdependence between national economies. According to Giddens's (1998) definition, which is a much broader concept compared with the definition he provided in 1990, globalization "is not only, or even primarily, about economic interdependence but about the transformation of time and space in our lives" (p. 31). Globalization in the capitalist economy cannot be viewed as totalizing and homogenizing in nature (Le Heron and Park, 1995). Globalization processes tend to have contradictory effects: homogenize and fragment within and between countries (Vellinga, 2000a). When globalization is viewed as a dynamic process over time and in the global economic space, the process by which new and various forms of organizations or firms emerge and interact in global economic spaces should be considered.

Diverse proximities should be considered to understand the globalization process in a global knowledge-based economy. Proximity is a driving force of actors' interaction and coordination in space. Proximity has four different types (Rychen and Zimmerman, 2008).

Torre and Rallet (2005) make the distinction between a geographical proximity that can be measured in terms of distance (length or time) in the geographical space and an "organized proximity" that results from the existence of common routines, rules, or even representations or beliefs that permit coordination. Thinking about the role of proximity in the innovation space, Boschma (2005) introduces the notion of "cognitive proximity" that facilitates communication and means "that people sharing the same knowledge base and expertise may learn from each other," while "social proximity," defined "in terms of socially embedded relations between agents at the micro level [. . .] involves trust based on friendship, kinship, and experience" (pp. 767–768).

Owing to diverse proximities, "[p]ractices that enable transnational arrangements in economic production include global business travelling, Internet thinking studios, transnational epistemic communities and international professional gatherings such as international trade fairs" (Bathelt and Schuldt, 2008, p. 855). Different types of clusters, including "temporary clusters" (Bathelt and Schuldt, 2008) and "virtual innovation clusters" (Park, 2004a), make economic spaces dynamic with interface between local and global networks. The diverse types of clusters and agglomerations in economic spaces indicate that the globalization process is not a homogenizing process but a dynamic one that reveals different patterns of economic activities through the influence of diverse types of proximities, cultures, national and regional policies, and governance systems in the global knowledge-based economy. Globalization and localization are closely interwoven and can be considered the two sides of the same coin. This global–local nexus is identified by the term "glocalization," which involves the local conditioning of global processes (Vellinga, 2000b).

Globalization has progressed in connection to other global megatrends. The development of communication technologies has contributed to the speed and ease of the progress of globalization, and the emergence of a knowledge-based economy has promoted the global network of knowledge in the process of knowledge creation and knowledge spillover. The "global buzz" created by information flows and different forms of interaction in trade fairs (Bathelt and Schuldt, 2008) can be regarded as an integration process between globalization and the knowledge-based economy. Globalization is also clearly related to climate change in terms of global warming, air pollution, carbon trade, global network of green NGOs, and so on.

Knowledge-based economy

Knowledge is the most strategic resource in the knowledge-based economy, which differs from the post-Fodist industrial economy (Best, 1990). Historically, knowledge is a crucial and well-recognized factor for advancing economic and social development. The differences in the wealth or level of economic development of countries can be ascribed not only to minimal capital but also to minimal knowledge (World Bank, 1998). The results of empirical studies by the OECD reveal that the overall economic performance of OECD countries is based on their stock of knowledge and their learning capabilities (OECD, 1996). Developing countries have less knowledge on technology than industrialized countries; knowledge gaps are thus created. Even within countries, knowledge gaps in acquiring, absorbing, and communicating knowledge exist among regions. However, the knowledge gaps between industrialized and developing countries may cease to widen because of the development of ICT despite the fact that knowledge is often much more costly to create in a developing country.

Despite the fact that the recognition of the importance of knowledge in both Western and Eastern societies is not new, three main reasons for emphasizing the shift toward a knowledge-based economy in the turn of the twenty-first century have been identified as follows (Park, 2002, p. 44):

First, new job creation is predominantly occurring in knowledge-intensive economic activities, which include both the knowledge industry and knowledge-based industry. Knowledge industries are those sectors whose output is knowledge, in forms such as patents, inventions, and new products, as well as services that are mainly knowledge. Knowledge-based industries are those sectors whose main product or service is dependent on technology or knowledge. Knowledge industries and knowledge-based industries are interdependent since the output from the former and input into the latter. Together they make up the knowledge-based economy.

Second, a significant part of the workforce in modern industrial countries comprises knowledge workers such as information system designers, managers, professionals, educators, scientists, skilled manufacturing teams, and the like. It is expected that the traditional 'job' will fade and knowledge entrepreneurs will replace traditional service and factory workers in the more flexible workplace of tomorrow (Halal, 1996). In the most of industrialised countries, the principal contribution to employment growth has been the advanced service sector which creates and uses knowledge products in exactly the way that manufacturing transforms raw materials into physical products (Berry et al., 1997). Concurrently, new technology has been adopted in manufacturing and, as a result, there has been a dramatic growth of high-tech industrial production involving substantial R&D inputs. These same trends are also evident in newly industrialised countries in recent years (Clark and Kim, 1995). In these places, too, knowledge industries and knowledge-based industries are driving forces in the knowledge-based economy.

Third, the rapid development of ICT has promoted the shift toward the knowledge-based economy. Many characteristics of the knowledge-based economy, such as the new dynamics of tacit and codified knowledge, the growing importance of networked knowledge, and the acceleration of process of interactive learning, are related with the increasing use of ICT

(Freeman and Soete, 1993). The rapid diffusion of ICT to developing countries in recent years has reduced the information gap between industrialised and developing countries, making the knowledge-based economy more important in the global society as a whole.

Knowledge is generated not only from a firm's internal R&D activities but also through university research and scientific advances. Accordingly, a high level of human capital, skilled labor force, and strong local presence of scientists and engineers are important factors in generating new knowledge. However, knowledge can be generated by both formal and informal learning modes. For example, knowledge can be accumulated through informal mechanisms, such as learning-by-doing and learning-by-interacting with customers and suppliers, and through the more formalized activities of research and development (R&D). Owing to the diversity of learning modes, the relationships are weak or even nonexistent when the knowledge production function that links knowledge inputs and innovative outputs is examined at the level of the firm (Audretsch, 1995). These weak relationships arise because many firms, particularly small firms, have considerable innovative output but minimal or even no R&D expenditure. Knowledge spillover from other firms that conduct R&D or from research institutions, such as universities, is the major source of knowledge inputs for innovative small firms (Feldman and Audretsch, 1999; Baptista, 1997; Cohen and Levinthal, 1989).

Three major mechanisms produce knowledge spillover (Park, 2002). First, firms can develop the capacity to adapt new technologies and innovations developed by other firms. Thus, firms can appropriate some of the returns accruing to investments in the innovative outputs produced by other firms or research institutions (Cohen and Levinthal, 1989). Second, interfirm networks and collaboration with public institutions and universities can provide synergy effects for participating firms. Firms can develop new ideas and knowledge through formal and informal interactions with customers and suppliers as well as workshops or forums provided by public institutions or universities. Third, knowledge workers may leave the firms or universities where knowledge has been created to establish a new firm. If a scientist or engineer places more value on the ideas than on the decision-making bureaucracy of the incumbent firm, he or she might decide to establish a new firm to appropriate the value of those ideas (Audretsch, 1995). In this mechanism of knowledge spillover, knowledge is exogenous to the firm and embodied in a knowledge worker.

The effects of knowledge spillover have a spatial dimension. Malmberg et al. (1996) suggested that the effects of knowledge spillover are spatially limited because of three elements. First, innovation processes are locally confined because of the nature of the trial-and-error process of problem solving, the need for repeated interaction between related firms, and the need to exchange knowledge through face-to-face contact. Second, barriers exist in the spatial diffusion of locally embedded knowledge because the ability to gain access to the local informal and formal networks of knowledge exchange and accumulation is mostly limited to insiders within organizations or circles. Third, the knowledge resources provided by outsiders and the initiatives established by incumbents to tap knowledge resources from outside can enhance the process of knowledge accumulation within the local milieu. However, the effects of knowledge spillover can progress beyond the local milieu as seen in temporary spatial proximities or temporary clusters, such as trade fairs (Bathelt and Schuldt, 2008; Bathelt and Glückler, 2011). The development of ICT and transportation systems promotes knowledge spillover from diverse formal planned and informal unplanned meetings, and from trade fair interactions in recent years.

A knowledge economy can be characterized by a learning economy and a network economy because no single company possesses all the types of knowledge and technology necessary for new product development. However, the perspective of knowledge economy has changed into a more complex one during the last two decades. According to Rutten and Boekema (2012), the changes in perspective with relation to knowledge creation and spillover can be identified as a shift from "Knowledge Economy 1.0" to "Knowledge Economy 2.0." The shift is summarized in Table 1.1. In the 1990s, territorial production systems, where intra-regional production networks capitalize on indigenous knowledge, were emphasized in regional knowledge economies. However, Rutten and Boekema (2012) argued that understanding the knowledge economy based on territorial production systems is no longer valid because "the nature of the economy itself has changed profoundly" and "conceptual understanding of knowledge and learning has become more sophisticated" (p. 984). "Knowledge Economy 2.0" can be regarded as a "creative economy" because it creates new knowledge and technology through the fusion of diverse technologies and complex formal and informal networks of diverse actors. Despite the shifting trend of the knowledge economy, a mix of "Knowledge Economy 1.0" and "Knowledge Economy 2.0" exists. The degree of such mix differs by country and region in the global economic space.

Information society

The information society has developed with the rapid development of ICT in the last three decades. The distribution, use, integration, and manipulation of information are significant economic activities in the creation of the information society. The Internet has been one of the most important contributors to the development of the information society. The Internet has contributed to the rapid decrease in the costs of information exchange and transactions. The global spatial economy has been fundamentally reorganized by the development of ICT and the Internet (Leinbach and Brunn, 2001). For example, the development of electronic commerce (EC), such as business-to-business EC, business-to-consumer EC, and consumer-to-consumer EC, has reshaped not only the global economy but also the regional one (Park, 2004b). As Kenney and Curry (2001) pointed out in the beginning of the twenty-first

Table 1.1 The shift of knowledge economy

	Knowledge economy 1.0 (1990s)	Knowledge economy 2.0 (21st century)
Major innovation performance	Manufacturing based	Service industry driven (Doloreux et al., 2010)
Locus of innovation	Vertically integrated firms and supply chains	Social and professional networks of individual
Value creation	Flexible production technologies (Best, 1990)	New knowledge (Malecki, 2010)
Globalization	Countries, firms	Also individuals: social and professional networks
Communication	Email, mobile phone, Internet	Integrated we-based devices: smart phone; iPad
Transformation of world economy	From developed and emerging economies	To emerging global economy
Knowledge	Codified versus tacit (Nonaka and Takeuchi, 1995)	Context-dependent (Tsoukas, 2009)
Process of learning	Formal, organized in firms (Cooke and Morgan, 1998)	Informal, social interaction of individual (Amin and Roberts, 2008)
Social capital for learning	Firms, inter-firm networks and societies (Storper, 1993)	Networks of individuals (Gertler, 2003)
Networks	Interfirm relations	Relation between individuals
Relation between space and learning	Territorial production systems: bounded territories	Wider networks: often global, spatial envelope

Source: Revised from Rutten and Boekema, 2012.

century, a new wave of EC has become prevalent in the industrialized countries in recent years because of the Internet acquiring a wireless form.

A great paradox in the spatial impact of ICT has been observed as some scholars have speculated. In the 1990s, many futurists predicted that the friction of distance would disappear and economic activities would disperse to distant places to compete with large metropolitan areas, resulting in the end of cities and geography (Negroponte, 1995; Cairncross, 1997; Harris, 1998). However, many geographical studies have revealed that the distance of spatial proximity and nodal cities retain their importance in local economic development despite the globalization of the economy with the development of ICT (Malecki and Oinas, 1999; Zook, 2002; Florida, 2002a, 2002b). Currently, the paradox coexists in the real world of economic space. Temporary proximity or temporary cluster is a good example of the coexistence of the paradox in the real world with the development of communication and transportation technologies. Business-to-business EC strengthens the local network on one hand and promotes long-distance networking and global sourcing on the other hand (Park, 2004b).

The coexistence of the paradox in the information society is related to Castells's space of flows and the intrinsic nature of ICT to overcome the distance. According to Castells (2000, p. 442), the space of flow is "the material organization of timesharing social practices that work through flows." He described the space of flows as the combination of three layers of material support: a circuit of electronic exchanges, its nodes and hubs, and the spatial organization of the dominant, managerial elite (Castells, 2000). The spatial manifestation of the three layers of the space of flows in the information society suggests that considerable flows are directional and grounded in physical places via material flows and social relations (Park, 2003). The development of ICT clearly enhances the exchange of information and knowledge. East Asian countries have experienced rapid growth in the last two decades with the rapid development of the information society in conjunction with the development of the Internet and ICT. The development of the Internet in China, for example, has significantly contributed to knowledge networks at the global level and has thus enabled rapid economic growth. The emergence of the information society in East Asian countries can be seen from the changes in the development of submarine cables from 1989 to 2005. In 1989, only one country from East Asia was included in the top ten countries in the world ranked by total bandwidth in service. However, in 2005, seven countries from East Asia were included in the global top ten ranked by total bandwidth and full capacity as installed (Malecki and Wei, 2009). Trade fairs, which contain both the space of flows and the intrinsic nature of ICT to overcome the distance, are a good example.

Indeed, the global economy has been reshaped in the information society. East Asian countries reap numerous benefits from the progress of the information society. However, considering the notion of the space of flows, spatial disparities continue to exist in the global space economy. Digital divide is one example of such disparities. Despite the presence of a trend of convergence, disparities still exist between industrialized and developing economies. In the long-term perspective, a trend of convergence might be observed in the global economic space; such trend could comprise the dynamics of economic space in the knowledge-based information society. The information society progresses together with the knowledge-based economy, as discussed in the previous section.

Service economy

The service economy is entitled so because of the increased importance of the service sector in industrialized economies on one hand and because of the relative importance of the service component in a product on the other hand. In most of the economically developed countries, more than 75 percent of jobs are from the service sector. Even in low-income countries, the service sector constitutes more than half of GDP. The importance of services in the economy continues to grow. Approximately 90 percent of new jobs are from the service sector in developed and newly industrialized countries; thus, this sector is among the top ten fastest-growing industrial groups between 1992 and 2003 (Bryson and Daniels, 2007).

However, the shift toward a service-dominated economy involves a shift or restructuring in employment rather than the demise of manufacturing or the complete displacement of direct production by service work. Bryson and Daniels (2007) argued that the shift results from restructuring and that the decline of manufacturing has been overemphasized in developed market economies as follows:

> [I]t is crucial to recognize that a complex restructuring of economic activity is occurring in which new types of economic activity such as computer services or information management are flourishing alongside the development of innovation in existing services, for example in insurance, banking and retailing . . . This restructuring reflects, first, the externalization of previously in-house services to independent providers and, second, the ongoing development of an extended division of labor. The latter arises from the growing complexity of production as well as service innovation that have been and are being developed by service providers in an effort to refine product differentiation in the marketplace.
> (Bryson and Daniels, 2007, p. 8)

In recent years, the traditional dichotomy between product and service has been replaced by a service–product continuum. Even in manufacturing firms, such as Samsung Electronics, the physical goods are a small portion of the added value of products. Service knowledge is interwoven at all levels of the production process: pre-production, during production, and post-production (Figure 1.1). The upper part of the figure indicates that the production processes are formally conducted within a manufacturing firm. However, nowadays, these processes are mostly separated from the manufacturing plant and conducted by separate affiliates or independent service firms. Thus, a dramatic increase in service sector is observed. In particular, numerous new start-ups have been generated in knowledge-intensive services. Service knowledge has been integrated into all the production processes.

Another important phenomenon that represents the service economy is the global sourcing of the elements of the service sector. A significant enhancement in the internationalization of service activities has been observed recently (OECD, 2005; Daniels et al., 2005). The term "global sourcing" was developed to describe two processes: a company establishes a foreign affiliate to provide a service and "a firm may outsource the service to a third-party supplier which can be locally owned or managed or be a foreign affiliate of another transnational corporation" (Bryson and Daniels, 2007, p. 12). The development of ICT has significantly contributed to global sourcing and reflects the close

Figure 1.1 The production process: production to consumption

Source: Revised from Bryson et al., 2004, p. 52.

relationship between service economy and information society. Global outsourcing of services can be regarded as a new international division of service labor beyond the new international division of manufacturing labor.

The recent globalization of R&D activities and the advanced services provided by multinational enterprises (MNEs) to explore local knowledge suggest that the international division of labor is unclear and complex. As indicated in Chapter 8, Samsung Electronics has aggressively invested in R&D activities in China in addition to those in the USA and EU in recent years; this phenomenon indicates that the international division of labor in the service sector is unclear. Such complex organization of service activities in the global economic space is closely related to the development of ICT and transportation services. Globalization, knowledge economy, information society, and service economy are not independent of one another. These concepts are interrelated and complementary; they comprise the global knowledge-based economy.

Additional global megatrends in the twenty-first century

In addition to the four global megatrends observed in the last two decades, climate change and an aging society with population aging have also emerged as global megatrends in the twenty-first century. The forces of climate change and an aging society are not as serious as those of the four megatrends; however, their significance continues to increase in the dynamics of economic spaces.

Climate change

Human-induced alterations of the natural world cause global warming and affect climate change. Laurence Smith (2011) identified "climate change" as one of the four forces that shape civilization's Northern Hemisphere in his book *The World in 2050*. He introduced several studies on the measurement of the global warming trend induced by greenhouse gases. According to Smith, "it is observed fact that human industrial activity is changing the chemical composition of the atmosphere such that its overall temperature must, on average, heat up" (Smith, 2011, p. 21). Based on the results of several scientific measurements and observations, he concluded that the global average temperature, particularly after the 1970s, has exhibited an upward trend along with the steady measured growth of greenhouse gas concentration in the atmosphere. The trend of average global warming and changes in climate are "consistent with greenhouse gas forcing but inconsistent with other known causes, like urban heat islands, changing solar brightness, volcanic eruptions, and astronomic cycles" (Smith, 2011, p. 23). With the climate change warning, many private industries have shifted toward environment-friendly industrial activities. By 2008, many MNEs have joined the US Climate Action Partnership. However, in late 2009, the rush of firms to join the US Climate Action Partnership slowed down following the failure of the climate treaty conference in Copenhagen (Smith, 2011).

The primary interest in the field of economic geography has been the location of economic activities that focus on space and place rather than the economy–environment relations of economic activities. However, a growing engagement of economic geography with issues on environment and climate change has been observed in the beginning of the twenty-first century (Angel, 2000; 2006; Bridge, 2002; Gibbs, 2002). The issues on environment and resources with regard to climate change are now part of the contested dynamics of industrial change for firms and industries as described by Angel (2006, p. 130) as follows:

> Innovation and learning, subcontracting relations, and supply chains are being examined from the perspective of environmental performance and resource use in a way that was far from common even a decade ago. Concepts such as design-for-the environment, ISO 14000 certification, life-cycle analysis, resource use score-cards, environmental footprints, are now common place tools of business practice among large firms. At the same time, the relation between environmental quality, resource use and economic change is now of central concern, not just to environmental regulatory agencies, but also to institutions responsible for economic development, ranging from Ministries of Industry to multi-lateral development agencies, such as the Asian Development Bank and the World Bank.

In addition to the general concern regarding climate change, firms and industries are currently concerned about environmental issues because their activities are being scrutinized by a wide array of actors around the world. Angel (2006) identified the trend of firms' efforts to improve environmental performance as a "greening industry." Firms attempt to manage not just from the viewpoints of cost, productivity, and quality but also with respect to improving environmental performance (Angel, 2006). New environmental product and process development, the transfer of environmental technology, and environmental knowledge spillover will surely reshape economic spaces in the future. The emergence of new industries, such as new or alternative energy development industries and environmental finance, will be the significant forces for the dynamics of economic spaces. With regard to the issue of climate change, the development of new energy systems to replace fossil fuel energy in the future may enforce the reshaping of global economic spaces. Rifkin (2011) strongly argued that in the future, the fusion of new communication and energy systems will lead to the third industrial revolution, which will be discussed in detail in Chapter 9.

Aging society

Since the beginning of the twenty-first century, population aging has been regarded as an ongoing serious issue in newly industrialized economies as well as in Western industrialized economies and Japan. For example, Korea entered the "aging society" in 2000 with 7.2 percent of its population comprising individuals over 65 years old (aged people). The percentage increased to more than 10 percent in 2010. Korea is expected to enter the "aged society" in 2018 (14.3 percent) and the "super aged society" in 2026 (20.8 percent)[1] (Park et al., 2007). Korea is regarded as having the most rapidly aging population.

Japan has the highest percentage of old population (65 years old and over) in the world; it entered into the super aged society before 2010. Korea has experienced the most rapid increase in population aging and a sharp increase in life expectance, as seen in Table 1.2. China is now in the aging society, whereas India and Indonesia have not yet reached the aging society. Although China has exhibited a slower trend of population aging compared with Korea, it has shown a more rapid trend compared with European countries. Considering the population size and increase in life expectancy in China, population aging is now a serious issue in East Asia.

Population aging is related to increasing life expectancy and declining birth rates. Rapid population aging generates serious problems because the ratio of economically productive population decreases and the government expenditure for aged people increases because of pension and medical fees. Population aging is currently widespread across the world; however, Europe and Asia are experiencing a more serious situation. Problems related to the exhaustion of pension funds, increasing medical care expenditure, decreasing productivity, labor shortage, and renovation and reorganization of urban facilities require careful attention and appropriate policies. The MacArthur Foundation (2008) recommends smart solutions for aging societies, such as promoting productivity, improving healthcare and support, and promoting lifelong learning in an aging society.

Table 1.2 Changes in demographic structure, 1980–2011 (percent, years)

Country	65 years old and over (% of total population)				Life expectancy (years)			
	1980	*1990*	*2000*	*2011*	*1980*	*1990*	*2000*	*2011*
China	5.2	5.9	7.0	8.4	67.1	69.5	71.3	73.5
France	13.9	14.0	16.1	17.1	74.3	76.9	79.2	82.2
Germany	15.5	15.5	16.4	20.7	72.9	75.3	78.2	80.8
India	3.6	3.8	4.2	5.0	55.4	58.4	61.6	65.5
Indonesia	3.6	3.8	4.6	5.6	57.7	62.1	65.6	69.3
Italy	13.1	14.9	18.3	21.0	74.0	77.1	79.9	82.7
Japan	9.1	12.1	17.4	23.3	76.1	78.9	81.2	82.7
South Korea	3.8	5.1	7.2	11.4	65.9	71.4	75.9	81.1
Russian Federation	10.2	10.2	12.4	12.8	67.0	68.9	65.3	69.0
Spain	11.0	13.6	16.8	17.6	75.4	77.0	79.4	82.4
United Kingdom	15.0	15.7	15.8	16.2	73.2	75.7	77.9	81.1
United States	11.3	12.5	12.4	13.2	73.7	75.3	76.7	78.7

Source: Organisation for Economic Co-operation and Development (OECD), each year.

An aging society promotes the emergence of new services and industries with the increase in the number of aged people. Such increase requires the development of elderly-friendly industries. Clusters for high-tech medical products, industrial restructuring for the integration of ICT and traditional industries for the elderly, and new transportation systems for the elderly will become significant issues in many industrialized economies sooner or later. Labor retraining and lifelong education systems will be strengthened in most of these countries because of the shortage of productive labor in industrialized economies in the future. The restructuring of industries, innovation of new products, and restructuring of urban spaces will contribute to the dynamics of global economic spaces.

Interrelations and evolution of concepts regarding global megatrends

The changes in economic spaces during the last two decades are closely related to four global megatrends: globalization, knowledge-based economy, information society, and service world (*Regional Studies*, 2008; Bryson et al., 2004; Park, 2008). They are not independent or separate from one another; instead, they are interrelated. Globalization and information society are related to dispersion and distance networks, whereas knowledge-based economy and service world are more related to agglomeration and localized networks. Owing to the contrasting spatial trends that govern economic spaces, the forces and processes that organize economic activities in space are dynamic. Accordingly, uneven development in the global economy persists. Global forces are unlikely to eliminate or even substantially reduce spatial disparities.

Space remains important, and increasing differentiations among localities, territories, regional areas, or continents characterize the dynamics of the global knowledge-based economy. Two additional global megatrends will render the global economic space more complex and dynamic in the next two decades. Climate change will result in significant changes in landscapes through the integration of new technology with energy systems and the development of environmental technology (Rifkin, 2011). The aging society will strengthen service activities and the knowledge-based economy (Park et al., 2007).

Most of the geographic studies in the 1990s focused on one of the four megatrends and did not integrate them. For example, globalization as well as regional and national policies were the most prominent topics for academic research in the early 1990s, whereas studies on information society and knowledge-based economy were extremely popular during the 1990s (Vellinga, 2000a; Le Heron and Park, 1995). However, since the late 1990s when the ratio of Internet users increased sharply even in industrializing countries, research on the integration of more than two megatrends has become more prominent than research on single megatrends (Dunning, 2000; Bryson et al., 2004; Le Heron and Harrington, 2005). Along with geographical studies on global megatrends, important concepts emerged to improve the understanding of global changes. The concurrent interrelationship of these concepts with more than two megatrends results in integrative views.

The relationships between the megatrends and emerging concepts are shown in Figure 1.2. Competition/cooperation, innovation systems focusing on territorial innovation systems, and networking/cluster/agglomeration are the major concepts that link the megatrends and the organization of economic space. Networking has been the most important concept in organizing economic spaces with the progress of the four global megatrends during the last two decades. The four megatrends are related to networking/cluster/ agglomeration. Innovation systems are related to the knowledge-based economy, information society, and service world. In the 1990s, innovation systems were mainly related to regional innovation systems in geographical studies (Cooke et al., 1998; *Papers in Regional Science*, 2012). Competition among firms has become critical with the progress of globalization and the knowledge-based economy. During the 1990s, cooperation among firms was regarded as important; however, competition among firms was significantly emphasized. Competition and cooperation were emphasized even in the concept of industrial district (Park, 1996). Knowledge-based economy was linked with all three concepts and was the most important megatrend in the 1990s.

The addition of two global megatrends has resulted in the emergence of more diverse concepts for the organization of economic space. The three concepts mentioned previously continued to be important, but their content changed significantly. Cooperation has become more important than competition because of the complex processes of innovation and new technology

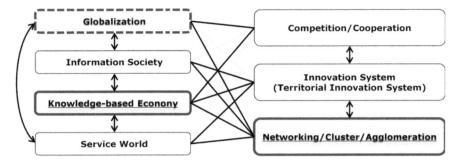

Figure 1.2a Global megatrends and evolution of concepts in the last two decades

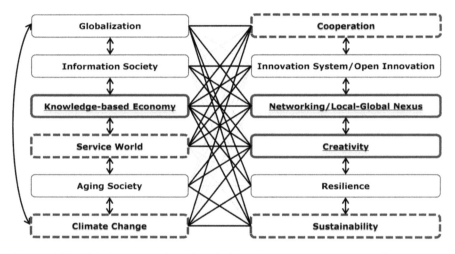

Figure 1.2b Global megatrends and evolution of concepts in the twenty-first century

development by the fusion of diverse technologies. Open innovation has emerged as an important concept in the development of innovation systems. In networking, local–global nexus has become important in addition to the cluster/agglomeration concept (Park, 2005). The global economy has confronted an increasing social, economic, and environmental uncertainty with complex effects and networks of global megatrends. Accordingly, new concepts have been introduced to understand the dynamics of economic spaces. Three new concepts have emerged: creativity, resilience, and sustainability. Creativity emerged as an important concept for knowledge-based economy, information society, service world, and climate change. Creative cities and creative economy have been emphasized in most industrialized countries (Cooke and Lazzeretti, 2008). Resilience and sustainability emerged with global economic crisis and natural hazard.

Nevertheless, knowledge-based economy continues to be the most important megatrend. Networking and creativity are currently the most important concepts for the organization of economic spaces as seen in Figures 1.2a and 1.2b. Considering the emergence of complex and diverse concepts, an integrated theoretical framework is required to understand the dynamics of economic spaces.

Emergence of East Asia in the global economy

The emergence of East Asian economies with regard to the global megatrends during the last two decades has been most striking. In particular, the rapid rise of Korea in the global economy has been most significant. The four global megatrends are clearly manifested in East Asia. Rapid globalization was realized from the rapid growth of international trade during the last two decades, particularly since the beginning of the new century. From 1990 to 2000, the volume of international trade increased by 75 percent. However, from 2000 to 2012, the volume increased by 180 percent (Figure 1.3). Another striking change is the emergence of East Asian countries, particularly China and Korea. In 1990, only Japan and Hong Kong were included in the top ten countries in the world in terms of export. In 2012, China, Japan, Hong Kong, and Korea were included in the said list, with China ranking first in the world

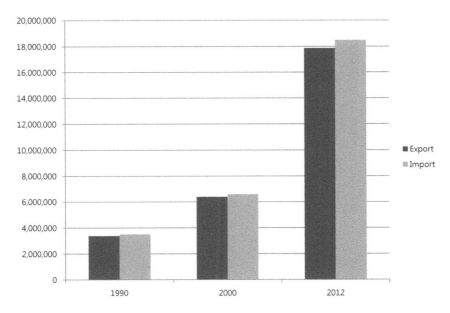

Figure 1.3 Changes in world trade (millions of dollars), 1990–2012

Source: IMF, Direction of Trade Statistics (DOTS), each year.

Table 1.3 Changes in world trade, 1990–2012 (millions of dollars, percent)

Rank*	1990			2000			2012		
	Country	Export	Import	Country	Export	Import	Country	Export	Import
0	World	3,383,215 (100.0)	3,517,426 (100.0)	World	6,388,302 (100.0)	6,593,789 (100.0)	World	17,873,246 (100.0)	18,494,997 (100.0)
1	Germany	409,286 (12.1)	346,471 (9.9)	United States	772,280 (12.1)	1,238,292 (18.8)	United States	2,114,370 (11.8)	1,482,387 (8.0)
2	United States	393,106 (11.6)	517,020 (14.7)	Germany	548,962 (8.6)	500,285 (7.6)	China, PR: mainland	1,510,797 (8.5)	2,215,145 (12.0)
3	Japan	288,000 (8.5)	235,361 (6.7)	Japan	478,542 (7.5)	379,624 (5.8)	Germany	1,128,916 (6.3)	1,378,118 (7.5)
4	France	216,466 (6.4)	234,439 (6.7)	France	323,528 (5.1)	331,840 (5.0)	Japan	783,187 (4.4)	857,808 (4.6)
5	United Kingdom	185,154 (5.5)	223,055 (6.3)	United Kingdom	282,873 (4.4)	334,974 (5.1)	France	674,836 (3.8)	576,677 (3.1)
6	Italy	170,495 (5.0)	181,773 (5.2)	Canada	275,184 (4.3)	262,830 (4.0)	United Kingdom	658,670 (3.7)	456,344 (2.5)
7	Netherlands	130,717 (3.9)	123,383 (3.5)	China, PR: mainland	249,223 (3.9)	225,175 (3.4)	Netherlands	650,224 (3.6)	605,677 (3.3)
8	Canada	126,448 (3.7)	131,643 (3.7)	Italy	236,668 (3.7)	235,283 (3.6)	China, PR: Hong Kong	639,630 (3.6)	85,232 (0.5)
9	Belgium–Luxembourg	117,477 (3.5)	119,415 (3.4)	Netherlands	229,757 (3.6)	215,720 (3.3)	South Korea	499,231 (2.8)	571,379 (3.1)
10	China, PR: Hong Kong	82,400 (2.4)	82,498 (2.3)	China, PR: Hong Kong	202,508 (3.2)	213,337 (3.2)	Italy	466,461 (2.6)	496,940 (2.7)
	Total (China, Japan, South Korea)	500,978 (14.8)	446,073 (12.7)	Total (China, Japan, South Korea)	1,102,965 (17.3)	978,618 (14.8)	Total (China, Japan, South Korea)	3,432,846 (19.2)	3,729,564 (20.2)

Source: International Monetary Fund (IMF), Direction of Trade Statistics (DOTS), each year.
* Sorted by export volumes

total trade (Table 1.3). China, Japan, and Korea share almost 20 percent of world total trade; this condition reveals the emergence of East Asian countries in the world economy.

Korea is one of the leading countries of information society. The percentage of Internet users in Korea is 84.2 percent, which is the second highest percentage in the world following UK, among countries with a population of more than 50 million (Table 1.4). The percentage of Internet users in China is less than half of its population. However, the percentage has increased sharply in the last decade. The increase in the percentage of Internet users in China has produced a significant change in the diffusion of knowledge and technology in the last decade. The converging trend of mobile-cellular subscriptions in Asia and the Pacific region reveals a leapfrogging trend of information society in developing countries (Table 1.5).

The service economy has rapidly progressed in Korea during the last four decades. The service sector shares more than 70 percent of the total value added in most Western countries. The share of the service sector in Korea is similar to that in the UK (Table 1.6). The share of China's service sector is less than half of the total value added but is increasing rapidly. Korea is a leading country for knowledge-based industries. The share of knowledge-based industries in Korea is higher than that in advanced Western countries, such as the US, the UK, Germany, and France (Table 1.7). However, the share of business services as a percentage of the total value added in Western countries is considerably higher than that in East Asian countries (Table 1.8). Korea exhibits the highest share of business services among Asian counties that have a population of more than 50 million. Considering that business services are mostly knowledge-intensive advanced services, East Asian countries lag behind Western countries. However, the relatively rapid increase in the business service sector in China is striking.

Table 1.4 Changes in percentage of individuals using the Internet, 2000–2012

Country	2000	2011	2012
China	1.78	38.30	42.30
France	14.31	79.58	83.00
Germany	30.22	83.00	84.00
India	0.53	10.07	12.58
Indonesia	0.93	12.28	15.36
Italy	23.11	56.80	58.00
Japan	29.99	79.05	79.05
South Korea	44.70	83.80	84.10
Russian Federation	1.98	49.00	53.27
Spain	13.62	67.60	72.00
United Kingdom	26.82	86.84	87.02
United States	43.08	77.86	81.03

Source: International Telecommunications Union (ITU), World Telecommunication/ICT Indicators database, each year.

Table 1.5 Changes in key ICT indicators, 2005–2013 (per 100 inhabitants)

Region	Mobile-cellular subscriptions			Active mobile-broadband subscriptions			Fixed (wired)-broadband subscriptions		
	2005	2012*	2013*	2005	2012*	2013*	2005	2012*	2013*
World	33.9	91.2	96.2	N/A	22.1	29.5	3.0	9.0	10.0
Africa	12.4	59.8	63.5	N/A	7.1	10.9	0.0	0.3	0.3
Arab states	26.8	101.6	105.1	N/A	14.3	18.9	0.3	2.6	3.3
Asia and Pacific	22.6	83.1	88.7	N/A	15.8	22.4	2.2	6.9	7.6
CIS	59.7	158.9	169.8	N/A	36.0	46.0	0.6	11.3	13.5
Europe	91.7	123.3	126.5	N/A	50.5	67.5	10.9	25.8	27.0
The Americas	52.1	105.3	109.4	N/A	39.8	48.0	7.5	16.0	17.1

Source: ITU, world telecommunication/ICT indicators database, each year.
Note:
* Estimate
N/A: Not available
Regions in this table are based on the ITU BDT regions; see: www.itu.int/ITU-D/ict/definitions/regions/index.html

Table 1.6 Changes in service sector value added, 1980–2010 (percent of total value added)

Country	1980	1990	2000	2010
World	55.8	60.7	66.7	69.9
China	21.6	31.5	39.0	43.2
France	63.3	68.7	74.2	79.2*
Germany	56.5	61.2	68.2	71.2
India	40.3	44.5	50.8	54.4
Indonesia	34.3	41.5	38.5	37.8
Italy	55.9	64.5	69.0	72.8
Japan	57.9	60.4	67.4	71.4
South Korea	57.2	64.4	71.7	77.7
Russian Federation	N/A	35.0	55.6	60.6
Spain	56.2	60.8	66.3	71.2
United Kingdom	57.2	64.4	71.7	77.7
United States	63.6	70.1	75.4	79.0

Source: World Bank, World Development Indicators, each year.
Note:
* Value (2009)
N/A: Not available

The above examination of East Asia indicates that among countries with more than 50 million population, the emergence of the Korean economy is the most striking. Korea has changed from one of the poorest countries in the world with less than $100 per capita of gross national product (GNP) in 1960 to one of the top ten countries in the international trade. Korea is the only country in the last six decades that has changed from one that receives aid to one that

Table 1.7 Changes in value added of knowledge-based industries (percent of total value added)

Country	2000	2009 or latest available year
France	50.6	50.0
Germany	49.6	50.5
Italy	41.2	42.0
Japan	41.8	44.5
Netherlands	46.5	51.1
South Korea	45.1	52.7
Spain	39.6	42.9
United Kingdom*	44.7	47.4
United States*	48.5	52.0

Source: OECD, STAN database for structural analysis, each year.
Note:
Knowledge-based industries (including C64 Post and telecommunications; C65T67 Financial intermediation; C72 Computer and related activities; C73 Research and development; C74 Other business activities; C75 Public admin. and defense; C80 Education; C85 Health and social work; C92 Recreational, cultural and sporting activities; C93 Other service activities; High and medium-high technology manufactures)
* UK (excluded C92&93), USA (excluded C73&93)

Table 1.8 Changes in value added of business services (percent of total value added)

Country	2000	2011 or latest available year
China	8.3	10.7
France	27.5	30.1
Germany	26.2	27.4
India	N/A	16.8
Indonesia	8.3	7.2
Italy	24.4	27.8
Japan	15.9	16.9
South Korea	19.3	19.3
Russian Federation	4.6	15.9
Spain	16.9	19.2
United Kingdom	24.7	29.8
United States	31.7	33.5

Source: OECD, each year.
N/A: Not available

provides aid. Owing to the emergence of Korea in the last two decades, the case studies in this book are from Korea with examples in East Asia.

Organization of the book

This book is composed of nine chapters. Chapter 1 provides an introduction to the book and sets the global megatrends as the major forces of change in the global knowledge-based economy. Chapter 2 introduces the theoretical framework of the dynamics of economic spaces. Based on this theoretical framework, the integrated model of service innovation, the model of path dependence, regional resilience, and regional development are examined in Chapters 3 and 4 with empirical case studies. Chapter 5 deals with innovation and spatial inequality in East Asia. The empirical case studies are then extended to case studies at firm, cluster, and international levels. The conceptual model of the accumulation of intangible assets is examined with case studies in Chapter 6. Corporate firm restructuring and industrial clusters are analyzed in Chapters 7 and 8. Chapter 9 provides policy implications and future perspectives for the dynamics of economic spaces. Each of these chapters is outlined below.

Chapter 1 presents a discussion of the changes in the global megatrends in the last two decades and their effects on global economic spaces. Until the early 1990s, globalization, knowledge-based economy, information society, and service world were regarded as important global megatrends that changed global economic spaces. In 2000, climate change and aging society were added to the four global megatrends. The global society has confronted a severe economic crisis and spatial restructuring because of the complex interrelations of the megatrends in the global economy. Complex and diverse forms of economic spaces require integrated aspects to understand global economic spaces. As the background of the study, the effects of the changes in global megatrends in the last two decades are discussed in relation to regional resilience and intangible assets to understand the global economic crisis, environmental issues, and continuing spatial disparity in the global society. The chapter contributes to the understanding of the effects of the global megatrends on reshaping the global economy in a broad context and presents the need for a new integrated theory and case studies, which are the objectives of the book.

Chapter 2 presents the theoretical model of the dynamics of economic spaces. During the last two decades, diverse spatial processes and various forms of economic practices evolved in the global society because of the progress of global megatrends. Economic spaces are dynamic and cannot be organized by a single criterion of economic rationality. Most theories deal with only a segment in terms of the major actors, processes, mediators, and spatial and temporal aspects of economic spaces, and thus cannot fully explain the complex and dynamic realities of economic spaces. Therefore, an integrated theoretical framework of the dynamics of economic spaces in the global knowledge-based economy is developed in this chapter. The integrated theory considers global megatrends, innovation systems, the roles of various economic actors, the various spatial forces that affect changes in economic spaces, and the mediators of the changes of economic spaces. The major forms of dynamic economic spaces that result from dynamic processes are discussed with diverse examples from Asian and Western countries. Thus, the chapter contributes to setting the theoretical frameworks in understanding the dynamic global economic spaces and spatial disparity in the global economy.

Chapter 3 introduces the development of the integral model of service innovation in a broad context and presents the case study. In a knowledge-based economy, distinguishing the boundary between innovations of goods and those of services is difficult. By considering the characteristics of services and the definition of service innovation, eight propositions of the integral model of service innovation are obtained. These propositions include: (1) sources of information for innovation, (2) collaboration with suppliers and customers for innovation, (3) collaboration with competitors and public institutions, (4) importance of the concept of service encapsulation, (5) development of an innovation chain, (6) path-dependent evolution, (7) innovation systems, and (8) spatial dimensions of service innovation. Overall, the case study supports the eight propositions of the proposed integral model of service innovation. Evidently, the boundary between manufacturing and services has become indistinguishable because of the concept of two-direction innovation chains. Such characteristics of the integral model are associated with the intensification of "relational economy" of Bathelt and Glückler (2011) in the knowledge-based economy. This chapter contributes to the understanding of the dynamics of economic spaces in the context of the integral aspects of services and manufacturing products.

Chapter 4 discusses a conceptual framework for path dependence, regional resilience, and regional development by examining regional resilience with regard to path dependence in the face of major economic challenges in the global economy. In the evolutionary context, regional resilience is the ability of regional actors and institutions to adapt to change over time. The chapter focuses on how regional resilience is related to the evolutionary concept of path dependence. Regional resilience and path dependence are dynamic processes and evolutionary. Innovation network and restructuring governance are important in building successful regional resilience in the evolutionary process of path dependence. The paths and responses of the four Korean industrial clusters to external shocks support the conceptual framework of path dependence evolution and regional resilience. The four cases show diverse paths and regional resilience, such as reinforcement of paths, regional economic restructuring, and dynamic processes. Innovation strategy significantly contributes to high resilience. The chapter contributes to the explanation of the spatial forces in the dynamics of economic spaces with the new theoretical framework and concepts.

Chapter 5 aims to analyze spatial economic inequalities in East Asia under the framework of the dynamics of economic spaces in relation to the four global megatrends—namely, globalization, knowledge-based economy, information society, and service world. The variables related to the four megatrends clearly explain the variations in international inequalities in East Asia as well as interregional inequalities within a nation. However, the individual effects of the variables on spatial inequalities differ significantly depending on the spatial scale of analysis and national characteristics. Overall, a convergence trend exists in the international per capita GNI in East Asian nations, whereas both divergent and convergent trends are evident at the regional scale within a nation. Two global oil crises in the 1970s and the East Asian financial crisis in the late 1990s resulted in the discontinuity of the general convergence trend, and led to the increase in international and interregional inequalities in economic activities. Although the effect of the global crisis differs in each country, this situation suggests that the economies of peripheral countries and regions are more vulnerable during a global economic crisis. The chapter supports the significance of the global megatrends in reshaping economic spaces at various spatial scales.

Chapter 6 explores the conceptual framework of the accumulation of intangible assets based on the interaction between a corporate and an urban system through case studies. Global economic spaces have been significantly reshaped in the last two decades by the spatial reorganization of manufacturing production and services along with the increasing importance of intangible assets. The findings suggest that the intangible assets of a firm are critical in ensuring competitiveness within a knowledge-based information society. In the process of intangible asset accumulation and interactions with urban systems, firms differentiate their strategies from those of cities based on the level of the development of a country and the status within the urban system. Intangible assets are also important in maintaining the competitive advantages of cities and regions. The accumulation of local intangibles is the result of the evolutionary development of the relationships between corporate and urban systems. The chapter contributes to the understanding of the dynamics of economic spaces in terms of the firm–region relationship with regard to intangible assets.

Chapter 7 provides an analysis of the evolution process of the Gumi electronics industrial cluster to understand the changes in the role of diverse economic actors in the evolution of industrial agglomeration in Korea. Gumi was a typical satellite platform type of a new industrial district until the mid-1990s. However, in the last two decades, Gumi has evolved into an electronics industrial cluster with considerable local interfirm linkages and innovation activities of small and medium enterprises (SMEs). Recognizing government industrial policies is critical in understanding the process of the Gumi electronics cluster evolution. In the early stage, the national state was the developer and locator of business activities within the confines of the Gumi industrial park. In recent years, Gumi City and Gyungsangbuk Province promoted the innovative activities of SMEs through the support of cooperative networks between universities and SMEs. The increasing importance of SMEs and local governments, aside from the large branch plants and the central government, has become the basis of the evolution of the industrial cluster in Gumi. The chapter confirms the theoretical importance of the changes in the role of economic actors in the dynamics of economic spaces with the evolution of a cluster over time.

Chapter 8 examines Samsung, particularly Samsung Electronics (SEC), as a case study in terms of corporate evolution and restructuring, brand development, innovation and firm strategy, and global networks. The case of SEC reveals that global manufacturing firms are closely related to the activities of product and process innovation, marketing, branding, diverse services, and the society in the global space economy. SEC has shifted from subcontracting manufacturing products to being an innovation flagship for the production of world-class products. SEC has also changed from conducting innovation to integrating innovation, marketing, and culture. In its evolution, SEC has exhibited the processes of path dependence, restructuring, and new path creation. The processes of path dependence, restructuring, and new path creation are not completely separate but rather overlapping in a continuous complex process. Production and process innovations were previously regarded as critical for the competitiveness of firms. However, design innovation, brand marketing, and network with society are currently regarded as important for competitiveness and reflect the need for complex processes and strategies. The chapter confirms the importance of evolutionary aspects and global networks in the theoretical framework of the dynamics of economic spaces.

Chapter 9 provides a discussion of the future perspectives in reshaping global economic spaces by considering the integrated model of the dynamics of economic spaces and focusing on climate change in the global society. In conjunction with the continuous progress of the four global megatrends, spatial restructuring, resilience, and spatial reorganization are expected in the new creative economy under climate change and the aging society. Moreover, the chapter examines the development of intelligent energy systems combined with communication and energy systems as well as the effect on economic spaces. Global environmental issues and regional problems that arise from the new global trends are examined to reconsider the regional policy appropriate for the changes in global megatrends in the next two decades. New policy implications for regional development are provided in consideration of climate change and the aging society. The chapter highlights the significance of the theoretical framework of the dynamics of economic spaces and provides new policy implications for the future.

Note

1 The general terminology of an aging society can be classified into three: "aging society," "aged society," and "super aged society." "Aging society" represents a population 7 percent, which comprises individuals more than 65 years old (aged people). "Aged society" represents a population 14 percent, which comprises individuals above 65 years old, and "super aged society" represents a population 20 percent, which comprises individuals above 65 years old.

References

Al-Rodhan, N. R. F. & Stoudmann, G. (2006). Definitions of globalization: a comparative overview and a proposed definition. *Program on the Geopolitical Implications of Globalization and Transnational Security*, Geneva Center for Security Policy (GCSP).

Amin, A. & Roberts, J. (2008). Knowing in action: beyond communities of practice. *Research Policy*, 37(2), 353–369.

Angel, D. P. (2000). Environmental innovation and regulation. In G. Clark, M. Gertler & M. Feldman (Eds.), *Handbook of Economic Geography* (pp. 607–622). Oxford: Oxford University Press.

Angel, D. P. (2006). Towards an environmental economic geography. In S. Bagchi-Sen & H. Lawton Smith (Eds.), *Economic Geography: Past, Present and Future* (pp. 126–135). London and New York: Routledge.

Audretsch, D. B. (1995). *Innovation and Industry Evolution*. Cambridge, MA: MIT Press.

Baptista, R. (1997). *An empirical study of innovation, entry and diffusion in industrial clusters*. Ph.D. dissertation, London Business School, University of London.

Bathelt, H. & Glückler, J. (2011). *The Relational Economy: Geographies of Knowing and Learning*. Oxford: Oxford University Press.

Bathelt, H. & Schuldt, N. (2008). Between luminaires and meat grinders: international trade fairs as temporary clusters. *Regional Studies*, 42(6), 853–868.

Berry, B. J. R., Conkling, E. C. & Ray, D. M. (1997). *The Global Economy in Transition* (2nd edn). Upper Saddle River, NJ: Prentice Hall.

Best, M. (1990). *The New Competition: Institutions of Industrial Restructuring*. Cambridge, MA: Harvard University Press.

Boschma, R. (2005). Proximity and innovation: a critical assessment. *Regional Studies*, 39(1), 61–74.

Bridge, G. (2002). Grounding globalization: the prospects and perils of linking economic processes of globalization to environmental outcomes. *Economic Geography*, 78(3), 361–386.

Bryson, J. R. & Daniels, P. W. (Eds.). (2007). *The Handbook of Service Industries*. Cheltenham and Northampton, MA: Edward Elgar.

Bryson, J. R., Daniels, P. W. & Warf, B. (2004). *Service Worlds: People, Organizations, Technologies*. London and New York: Routledge.

Cairncross, F. (1997). *The Death of Distance: How the Communication Revolution Will Change Our Lives*. Boston, MA: Harvard Business School Press.

Castells, M. (2000). *The Rise of the Network Society: The Information Age: Economy, Society and Culture* (2nd edn). Oxford and Malden: Blackwell.

Clark, G. L. & Kim, W. B. (Eds.). (1995). *Asian NIEs & the Global Economy*. London and Baltimore, MD: The Johns Hopkins University Press.

Clark, G. L. & Wójcik, D. (2007). *The Geography of Finance: Corporate Governance in the Global Marketplace*. Oxford: Oxford University Press.

Cohen, W. M. & Levinthal, D. A. (1989). Innovation and learning: the two faces of R&D. *The Economic Journal*, 99 (September), 569–596.

Cooke, P. & Lazzeretti, L. (Eds.). (2008). *Creative Cities, Cultural Clusters and Local Economic Development*. Cheltenham and Northampton, MA: Edward Elgar.

Cooke, P. & Morgan, K. (1998). *The Associational Economy: Firms, Regions and Innovation*. Oxford: Oxford University Press.

Cooke, P., Uranga, M. G. & Etxebarria, G. (1998). Regional systems of innovation: an evolutionary perspective. *Environment and Planning A*, 30(9), 1563–1584.

Daniels, P. W., Ho, K. C., and Hutton, T. A. (2005). *Service Industries and Asia-Pacific Cities*. London: Routledge.

Dicken, P. (1992). *Global Shift: The Internationalization of Economic Activity* (2nd edn). London: Guildford Press.

Dicken, P. (2006). Foreword. In S. Bagchi-Sen & H. Lawton Smith (Eds.), *Economic Geography: Past, Present and Future* (pp. xiii–xv). New York: Routledge.

Dunning, J. H. (Ed.). (2000). *Regions, Globalization, and the Knowledge-Based Economy*. Oxford: Oxford University Press.

Feldman, M. P. & Audretsch, D. B. (1999). Innovation in cities: science based diversity, specialization and localized competition. *European Economic Review*, 43(2), 409–429.

Florida, R. (1995). Towards the learning region. *Futures*, 27(5), 527–536.

Florida, R. (2002a). Bohemia and economic geography. *Journal of Economic Geography*, 2(1), 55–72.

Florida, R. (2002b). The economic geography of talent. *Annals of Association of American Geographers*, 92(4), 743–755.

Florida, R. (2002c). *The Rise of the Creative Class*. New York: Basic Books.

Freeman, C. (1987). *Technical Policy and Economic Performance: Lessons from Japan*. London: Pinter.

Freeman, C. & Perez, C. (1988). Structural crises of adjustment, business cycles and investment behavior. In G. Dosi, R. Freeman, R. R. Nelson, R. Silverberg & L. Soete (Eds.), *Technical Change and Economic Theory* (pp. 38–66). London: Pinter.

Freeman, C. & Soete, L. (1993). *Information Technology and Employment*. Maastricht: Universitaire Pers Maastricht.

Gertler, M. S. (1995). "Being there": proximity, organization, and culture in the development and adoption of advanced manufacturing technologies. *Economic Geography*, 71(1), 1–26.

Gertler. M. S. (2003). Tacit knowledge and the economic geography of context, or the undefinable tacitness of being (there). *Journal of Economic Geography*, 3(1), 75–100.

Gibbs, D. (2002). *Local Economic Development and the Environment*. London: Routledge.

Giddens, A. (1990). *The Consequences of Modernity*. Cambridge: Polity Press.

Giddens, A. (1998). *The Third Way, the Renewal of Democracy*. Cambridge: Polity Press.

Halal, W. E. (1996). The rise of the knowledge entrepreneur. *The Futurist*, 30(6), 13–16.

Harris, R. (1998). The Internet as a GPT: factor market implications. In E. Helpman (Ed.), *General Purpose Technologies and Economic Growth* (pp. 140–165). Cambridge, MA: The MIT Press.

Harvey, D. (1989). *The Conditions of Postmodernity*. Oxford: Blackwell.

Hayter, R. (1997). *The Dynamics of Industrial Location*. Chichester, New York, Weinheim, Brisbane, Singapore and Toronto: Wiley.

Karlsson, C. (Ed.). (2008). *The Handbook of Research on Cluster Theory*. Cheltenham: Edward Elgar.

Kenney, M. & Curry, J. (2001). Beyond transaction costs: e-commerce and the power of the Internet database. In T. R. Leinbach & S. D. Brunn (Eds.), *Worlds of E-Commerce* (pp. 45–66). Chichester and New York: John Wiley & Sons.

Le Heron, R. & Harrington, J. W. (Eds.) (2005). *New Economic Spaces: New Economic Geographies*. Aldershot: Ashgate.

Le Heron, R. & Park, S. O. (Eds.). (1995). *The Asian Pacific Rim and Globalization*. Aldershot: Avebury.

Leinbach, T. R. & Brunn, S. D. (Eds.). (2001). *Worlds of E-Commerce*. Chichester and New York: John Wiley & Sons.

MacArthur Foundation. (2008). The MacArthur Foundation Research Network on An Aging Society. Retrieved from www.agingsocietynetwork.org/ (accessed July 22, 2013).

Malecki, E. J. (2002). The economic geography of Internet's infrastructure. *Economic Geography*, 78(4), 399–424.

Malecki, E. J. (2010). Global knowledge and creativity: new challenges for firms and regions. *Regional Studies*, 44, 1033–1052.

Malecki, E. J. & Oinas, P. (Eds.). (1999). *Making Connections: Technological Learning and Regional Economic Change*. Aldershot: Ashgate.

Malecki, E. J. & Wei, H. (2009). A wired world: the evolving geography of submarine cables and the shift to Asia. *Annals of the Association of American Geographers*, 99(2), 360–382.

Malmberg, A., Solvell, O. & Zander, I. (1996). Spatial clustering, local accumulation of knowledge and firm competitiveness. *Geografiska Annaler*, 78B(2), 85–97.

Markusen, A. (1996). Sticky places in slippery space: a typology of industrial districts. *Economic Geography*, 72(3), 293–313.

Negroponte, N. (1995). *Being Digital*. New York: Knopf.

Nonaka, I. & Takeuchi, H. (1995). *The Knowledge-Creating Company: How Japanese Companies Create the Dynamics of Innovation*. Oxford: Oxford University Press.

OECD. (1996). *Employment and Growth in the Knowledge-Based Economy*. Paris: OECD.

OECD. (2005). *OECD Handbook of Economic Globalization Indicators*. Paris: OECD.

Ohmae, K. (1992). *The Borderless World: Power and Strategy in the Global Marketplace*. London: HarperCollins.

Oinas, P. & Malecki, E. J. (1999). Spatial innovation systems. In E. J. Malecki & P. Oinas (Eds.), *Making Connections: Technological Learning and Regional Economic Change* (pp. 7–34). Aldershot: Ashigate.

Papers in Regional Science. (2012). Special issue on regional innovation system. *Papers in Regional Science*.

Park, S. O. (1996). Network and embeddedness in the dynamic types of new industrial districts. *Progress in Human Geography*, 20(4), 476–493.

Park, S. O. (1997). Rethinking the Pacific Rim. *Tijdschrift voor economische en sociale geografie (Journal of Economic and Social Geography)*, 88(5), 425–438.

Park, S. O. (2002). Paths of sustainable industrialization in the knowledge-based economy. In R. Hayter & R. Le Heron (Eds.), *Knowledge, Industry and Environment* (pp. 31–48). Aldershot: Ashgate.

Park, S. O. (2003). Economic spaces in the Pacific Rim: a paradigm shift and new dynamics. *Papers in Regional Science*, 82(2), 223–247.

Park, S. O. (2004a). Knowledge, networks and regional development in the periphery in the internet era. *Progress in Human Geography*, 28(3), 283–286.

Park, S. O. (2004b). The impact of business to business electronic commerce on the dynamics of metropolitan spaces. *Urban Geography*, 25(4), 289–314.

Park, S. O. (2005). Network, embeddedness, and cluster processes of new economic spaces in Korea. In R. Le Heron & J. W. Harrington (Eds.), *New Economic Spaces: New Economic Geographies* (pp. 6–14). Aldershot: Ashgate.

Park, S. O. (2008). A history of Korea's industrial structural transformation and spatial development. Paper presented at the World Bank Workshop, Tokyo, March 29. (Published in 2009 *World Bank Report*. Washington, DC: World Bank Publications.)

Park, S. O., Park, S. C., Choi, S. J., Lee, J. J., Han, G. H., Lee, M. S., Kwak, C. S., Song, G. U. & Jeong, E. J. (Eds.). (2007). *Long-lived Persons and Areas of Longevity in Korea: Changes and Responses*. Seoul: Seoul National University Press (in Korean with English summary).

Regional Studies. (2008). Special issue: Clusters in the global knowledge-based economy: knowledge gatekeepers and temporary proximity. *Regional Studies*, 42(6), 767–904.

Rifkin, J. (2011). *The Third Industrial Revolution: How Lateral Power is Transforming Energy, the Economy, and the World*. New York: Palgrave Macmillan.

Robertson, R. (1992). *Globalization: Social Theory and Global Culture*. London: Sage.

Rutten, R. & Boekema, F. (2012). From learning region to learning in a socio-spatial context. *Regional Studies*, 46(8), 981–992.

Rutten, R. & Boekema, F. (Eds.). (2007). *The Learning Region: Foundations, State of the Art, Future*. London: Routledge.

Rychen, F. & Zimmermann, J. B. (2008). Clusters in the global knowledge-based economy: knowledge gatekeepers and temporary proximity. *Regional Studies*, 42(6), 767–776.

Scott, A. J. (1988). *New Industrial Spaces: Flexible Production Organization and Regional Development in North America and Western Europe*. London: Pion.

Smith, L. C. (2011). *The World in 2050*. New York: Plume.

Storper, M. (1993). Regional worlds of production: learning and innovation in the technology districts of France, Italy, and the USA. *Regional Studies*, 27(5), 433–455.

Torre, A. (2008). On the role played by temporary geographical proximity in knowledge transmission. *Regional Studies*, 42(6), 869–889.

Torre, A. & Rallet, A. (2005). Proximity and localization. *Regional Studies*, 39(1), 47–59.

Tsoukas, H. (2009). A dialogical approach to the creation of new knowledge in organizations. *Organization Science*, 20(6), 941–957.

Vellinga, M. (Ed.). (2000a). *The Dialectics of Globalization: Regional Response to World Economic Processes: Asia, Europe, and Latin America in Comparative Perspective*. Boulder, CO and Oxford: Westview.

Vellinga, M. (2000b). The dialectics of globalization: internationalization, regionalization, and subregional response. In M. Vellinga (Ed.), *The Dialectics of Globalization: Regional Response to World Economic Processes: Asia, Europe, and Latin America in Comparative Perspective* (pp. 3–16). Boulder, CO and Oxford: Westview.

Vertova, G. (Ed.). (2006). *The Changing Economic Geography of Globalization: Reinventing Space*. London and New York: Routledge.

Wallerstein, I. (1974). *The Modern World System: Capitalist Agriculture and the Origins of the European World-Economy in the Sixteenth Century*. New York: Academic Press.

World Bank. (1998). *Knowledge for Development, World Development Report, 1998/1999*. Washington, DC: World Bank.

Zook, M. A. (2002). Hubs, nods and by-passed places: a typology of e-commerce regions in the United States. *Tijdschrift voor Economische en Sociale Geografie*, 93(5), 509–521.

Website references

International Monetary Fund (IMF), Direction of Trade Statistics (DOTS): http://elibrary-data.imf.org/finddatareports.aspx?d=33061&e=170921

International Telecommunications Union (ITU), World Telecommunication/ICT Indicators database: www.itu.int/en/ITU-D/Statistics/Pages/publications/default.aspx

OECD, STAN Database for Structural Analysis: www.oecd.org/industry/ind/stan structuralanalysisdatabase.htm

Organisation for Economic Co-operation and Development (OECD): www.oecd.org/

World Bank, World Development Indicators: http://data.worldbank.org/data-catalog/world-development-indicators

2 Dynamics of economic spaces
A theoretical framework

Introduction

During the last two decades, diverse spatial processes and various forms of economic practices have evolved in the global society because of the progress of global megatrends. Economic spaces are dynamic and cannot be organized by a single criterion of economic rationality. Most theories deal with only a segment in terms of the major actors, processes, mediators, and spatial and temporal aspects of the economic spaces and thus cannot fully explain the complex and dynamic realities of economic spaces. Therefore, an integrated theoretical framework of the dynamics of economic spaces in the global knowledge-based economy is developed in this chapter. The integrated theoretical framework considers the global megatrends, innovation systems, roles of various economic actors, various spatial forces that affect changes in economic spaces, and mediators of the changes of economic spaces. The major forms of dynamic economic spaces that result from dynamic processes are discussed with diverse examples from the East Asian countries. Thus, this chapter contributes to setting the theoretical frameworks in understanding the dynamic global economic spaces and spatial disparity in the global economy.

Uneven development persists in the global economy. Global forces are unlikely to eliminate or even substantially reduce spatial disparities. Space continues to be important, and an increasing differentiation among localities, territories, regional areas, or continents characterizes the global knowledge-based economy. The changes in economic spaces are related to the four global megatrends of the global knowledge-based economy—namely, globalization, knowledge-based economy, information society, and service world (*Regional Studies*, 2008; Bryson et al., 2004; Park, 2008). These trends are not independent or separate from one another. Instead, they are interrelated. Globalization and information society are related to dispersion and distance networks, whereas knowledge-based economy and the service world are related to agglomeration and localized networks. The forces and processes that organize economic activities in space are dynamic in reality because of the contrasting spatial trends that govern economic spaces.

To promote regional development and reduce spatial disparities that exist at different spatial scales, we need to understand the major dynamic features of economic spaces, the major processes and forces that govern the changes in economic spaces, and the roles of major actors and mediators in the changes in economic spaces.

Considering the necessity and the recent research trends, the main purpose of this chapter is to establish an integrated theory that explains the dynamic changes in economic spaces in the global knowledge-based economy. With this primary purpose, this study attempts to analyze the following issues on the dynamics of economic spaces. The scope and contents of the analysis are different from those in existing studies and thus reveal the distinctive nature of this research.

First, the study analyzes the governance of the major actors of economic spaces. Most studies on economic spaces in the global society focused on the role of firms, particularly transnational corporations (TNCs). However, multiple actors govern economic spaces in the global knowledge-based economy. The major actors are the state, the firm (both TNCs and SMEs), labor, the community, and consumers. The role of the major actors and their inter-actions in the economic spaces are analyzed in this study. Second, analyzing the spatial differences of innovation and the impact of innovation systems on the changes in economic spaces is essential. Open innovation, knowledge base, the processes of knowledge creation, knowledge spillover, and diffusion are examined. Third, the mediators of economic spaces are analyzed. Institution, culture, ethnicity, and gender are regarded as major mediators that connect the social processes to the dynamic features of economic spaces. Furthermore, mediators are viewed as having a significant impact on the creation, spillover, and diffusion of knowledge and technology in and among networked spaces. Fourth, analyzing the contrasting spatial forces or pro-cesses and the major forms of economic spaces that appear in the global knowledge-based economy is important. The focus of such analysis in this study is on the relationships between the contrasting processes and the formation of diverse economic spaces.

The dynamics of economic spaces under the influence of the global megatrends are the result of the interactions and integrations of major actors, mediators, contrasting spatial processes, innovation systems, and dynamic forms. The interaction and integration under the influence of the global megatrends are the basic principles of the theoretical framework as shown in Figure 2.1. The major actors in the economic spaces do not only interact among themselves but also interact with innovation systems and the major forms of economic spaces. The actors also affect the contrasting spatial processes. The contrasting spatial processes have a direct impact on innovation systems and the formation of major forms of economic spaces. Culture, social institutions, ethnicity, and gender mediate the mechanisms that underlie the effects of contrasting spatial processes on the formation of economic spaces and generate

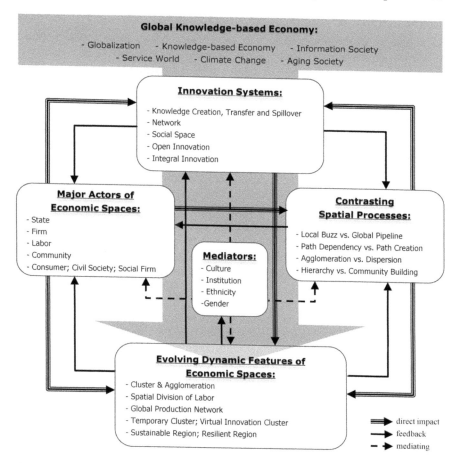

Figure 2.1 A theoretical framework of the dynamics of economic spaces

an impact on the evolution of diverse innovation systems. Innovation systems likewise have a significant impact on shaping the dynamic economic spaces. Moreover, the major forms of dynamic economic spaces generate feedback effects on the major actors and contrasting spatial forces.

Such interactions of actors, mediators, spatial forces, innovation systems, and dynamic forms comprise the primary concept of the theoretical framework of the dynamics of economic spaces. The following sections discuss the role of economic actors, contrasting spatial forces, diverse mediators in the organization of economic spaces, innovation systems, and resulting major features of economic spaces based on this basic theoretical framework. The analyses of the theoretical aspects and case studies with regard to the theoretical framework are presented from Chapter 3 of this book.

Roles of major actors in economic spaces

Changes in economic spaces should be viewed as trans-local dynamic processes of growth and change, where multiple actors operate in a variety of geographical spaces. Yeung (2005) urged the study of the complex strategic couplings of economic actors, particularly large business firms, operating in specific regions in East Asia with their lead firm counterparts orchestrating production networks on a global basis. However, in the research on the dynamics of economic spaces, the role of other actors and the interactions among them are critical beyond the production networks and large business firms. The major actors involved in organizing and reorganizing economic spaces include nation states, TNCs, labor, the community, and consumers.

Despite the advancement of globalization, the nation state continues to shape the economic activity in the global economy profoundly through such mechanisms as the promulgation of basic laws and property rights, provision of basic infrastructure and education, and the establishment of a range of policies for regional development and financial incentives. Governance and regulation in the global economy become complex with the interaction of various institutions and the combination of diverse spaces and spatial scales. International regulatory bodies, such as the World Trade Organization (WTO) and international institutions that establish technical standards such as the international quality management standard, ISO 9000, or the international environment standard ISO 1400, are significant in influencing the organization of industrial activities (Nadvi, 2008; Coe et al., 2008a). However, nation states remain the key actor in the organization of economic spaces in the globalized knowledge-based economy (Hudson, 2004). International institutions exist only because they are sanctioned by nation states. The propensity for nation states to enter into preferential trading agreements (PTAs) with other states has increased dramatically in the last two decades (Dicken, 2007). This condition reveals the importance of the role of nation states in the dynamics of economic spaces.

Diverse types of nation states exist in relation to their different forms of governance and power relations; these types are neoliberal, welfare, developmental, transitional, weak and dependent, and failed states (Coe et al., 2007). The influence of nation states on the organization of economic spaces may differ according to the types of nation states. For example, the Chinese government has a strong power over the control of the entry of automobile industries and a unique bargaining power, whereas countries in Eastern Europe have adopted neoliberal market policies and reduced their individual bargaining power (Liu and Dicken, 2006). Despite the differences in the type of states and the significant ongoing processes of rescaling and hollowing out, nation states remain critical actors in the shaping of political–economic activities worldwide.

The role of TNCs is important for regional economic growth in the globalization era, with the integration of ideas from the intangible assets, the organization of innovation, and regional innovation systems of these corporations (Kramer and Revilla Diez, 2012). Indeed, TNCs have the capability to organize their own diverse economic activities in different parts of the world. The role of TNCs is important for the organization of industrial space, particularly in the period of global economic recession or crisis, in the changes of economic spaces. TNCs organize transnational economic activities through intra-firm relations among corporate and regional headquarters, research and development (R&D) facilities, and various transnational operating units of production and services. TNCs have increasingly invested in overseas R&D in recent years for asset-exploiting and/or asset-seeking foreign R&D (Dunning and Narula, 1995; Verspagen and Schoenmakers, 2004). TNCs also organize their transnational economic activities through intra-firm relations, such as international subcontracting, joint ventures and strategic alliances, and franchising and cooperative agreements, as seen in the case of Samsung Electronics in Chapter 8.

TNCs tend to utilize their global networks to enhance their competitive advantage by tapping into geographically dispersed knowledge in regional innovation systems (Revilla Diez and Berger, 2005; Boutellier et al., 2008). In particular, TNCs utilize regional embeddedness, such as dynamic local buzz in regional innovation systems, to establish new combinations of knowledge required for innovation (Kramer and Revilla Diez, 2012). The roles of knowledge spillover and externalities are important in establishing the location of the R&D activities of TNCs. The findings in Cantwell and Piscitello's research (2005) on the European region indicated below confirm the importance of knowledge spillover and externalities in the selection of the location of R&D activities of TNCs.

> Specifically, the relative attractiveness of regions in Europe for the technological efforts of foreign owned MNCs depends upon: (1) the presence of industry-specific spillovers and specialization externalities; (2) the breadth of local technological activities in the region, i.e. the opportunity to enjoy diversity externalities and to capture inter-industry spillover; and (3) the presence of external sources of knowledge and science-technology spillovers.
>
> (p. 11)

However, different factors attract the R&D activities of TNCs in the case of developing economies. The location of economic activities is the result of the negotiating and bargaining processes between firms and nation states or regional governments. Firms and states or regional governments continuously engage in negotiating and bargaining processes to decide on the location of investment projects (Hayter, 1997; Dawley, 2007; Dicken 2007). In recent years, the role of regional headquarters (RHQs) has also become important in shaping global economic spaces. RHQs are generally established "to respond to local imperatives that cannot be effectively handled by distant head offices" (Edgington and Hayter, 2013, p. 651).

Labor, consumers, the community, and civil society organizations (CSOs) are also major actors involved in organizing and changing economic spaces. Traditionally, labor is regarded as a factor similar to raw materials for location decision as in Weber's location theory (1929) and is assumed to be an intrinsic part of the production process. However, labor is currently regarded "as an active constituent of the global economy, rather than the passive victim of restructuring processes" (Cumbers et al., 2008, p. 369). Labor union or organized labor can have a significant effect on the location decision of firms, including both TNCs and SME (Hayter, 1997; Smith et al., 2002; Cumbers et al., 2008). Workers act alone or in coalition with other groups in society in space by moving among places and connecting across places (Coe et al., 2007). However, labor is highly segmented within and between places by skill, gender, age, and ethnicity (Coe et al., 2008a). Accordingly, the ability to act varies socially and spatially. Creative class and brain circulation even in the international level are important for innovation and cluster formation (Saxenian, 2006). Labor in developing countries exhibits minimal mobility. Despite labor being much less mobile than capital, "we need to recognize that workers have the agency to strive to improve their relative position and, at the same time, to contribute towards reshaping economic geographies" (Coe et al., 2008a, p. 285).

Demand location, final consumption, and community have been neglected in the reshaping of economic geography. However, consumption geography and the role of consumers and the community in the shaping of economic spaces are gaining interest recently (Coe et al., 2008a; Mansvelt, 2012). Knowledge flows between producers and consumers are significantly enhanced by the development of ICTs, particularly the development of social network services (SNS). Even the processes of co-production and innovation in the interaction between the manufacturer and service provider have been observed, as indicated in Chapter 3 of this book. The community has also become important in reshaping economic spaces, with its increased bargaining power for the location of economic activities. Negotiating for the location of the aversion facilities of dangerous facilities, such as atomic plants or radioactive waste-disposal facilities, is difficult even in developing countries.

Most global production network studies focus on the silent civil society organization. Labor and consumers are often regarded as relatively powerless compared with TNCs. However, a considerable growth in the number of CSOs, many of which are transnational in their scope (Kaldor, 2003; Coe et al., 2008a), has been observed during the last two decades. Although et al CSOs exhibit significant diversity and their effects have significant differences, CSOs experience increasing influence in the global dynamics of economic spaces (Coe et al., 2008a).

The major actors mentioned above are not independent of one another. They are interlinked and interact with one another. For example, TNCs organize economic spaces in the face of intense market competition, opposition of the civil society, and political barriers. The effective globalization of TNCs is difficult because extensive global operations require TNCs to consider spatial differences in the physical, political, economic, social, and cultural realms. Therefore, the interrelationship among the major actors of economic spaces should be considered. Although many studies have been conducted on the role of individual actors, particularly TNCs, the forms of integration of the inter-action among the actors are not well documented. Nevertheless, the roles of nation states and TNCs are critical in the shaping of economic spaces. Moreover, the role of labor, consumers, and the civil society continue to gain influence in the organization of economic spaces in the knowledge-based information society.

Contrasting spatial processes in the organization of economic spaces

Several contrasting spatial processes exist for the organization of economic activities in space. These contrasting forces are related to dispersion from globalization and information society on one hand and to concentration from trends in the development of the knowledge-based economy and advanced services on the other. In addition, the contrasting spatial processes in the organization of economic activities are related to the diverse actors, which may exhibit conflicts in their behavior and strategies. In this chapter, four major spatial processes are examined as processes that shape dynamic economic spaces. These four spatial processes are network (local buzz) versus global pipeline, path dependence versus path creation, centripetal versus centrifugal forces, and hierarchical versus community building.

Networking is one of the most important processes for knowledge creation in economic spaces. The transfer of tacit knowledge is often regarded as confined to the local milieu, whereas codified knowledge may circulate around the globe almost frictionlessly. In this view, the learning processes occur among actors embedded in a community by being there (local buzz). The term "buzz" utilized by Bathelt et al. (2004) and Storper and Venables (2004)

> consists of specific and continuously updated information, intended and unintended learning processes in both organized and accidental meetings, the application of shared interpretive schemes, common understandings of new knowledge and technologies, as well as shared cultural traditions within a particular technology field.
>
> (Bathelt and Glückler, 2011, p. 132)

The exchange of tacit knowledge is the key role of local buzz. The process of local buzz is prominent in cultural industries. Currid and Williams (2010) identified five aspects of local buzz from case studies of cultural industries in Los Angeles and New York City as follows:

The research has produced five important results. (i) Social milieus have nonrandom spatial clustering tendencies. (ii) These clustering tendencies may reinforce themselves as each social event further brands particular locations as sites of cultural activity. (iii) Even enclaves demonstrate homogenous spatial patterns across all cultural industries. (iv) The recursive nature of branding particular locations as cultural hubs may partially explain why some places within a city are important consumption sites. (v) Part and parcel of the type of dataset we employed, we find that the media also tends to cluster and consequently plays a critical role in cultivating social agglomerations and has unintended consequences for the development of place and place branding.

(p. 441)

However, other studies suggest that knowledge can be attained and created by investing in building channels of communication called pipelines in selected providers located outside the local milieu (Bathelt et al., 2004; Rychen and Zimmermann, 2008). Firms, therefore, develop global pipelines not only to exchange products or services but also to benefit from outside sources of novel ideas and knowledge inputs. The term "pipeline" used by Owen-Smith and Powell (2002, 2004) refers to trans-local interaction and linkages at the global level. Knowledge flows and interaction in trans-local pipelines, unlike in the local buzz, are targeted toward certain goals and planned in advance; they "do not result from the spontaneous meeting of actors, which have a mutual understanding and share the same interpretative schemes" (Bathelt and Glücker, 2011). This global knowledge network suggests that the exchange of tacit knowledge with practices embedded at the local scale and the emphasis on place-based sticky knowledge are controversial because of the existence of multiple geographies of tacit knowledge (Faulconbridge, 2006). Many examples of the globally networked tacit knowledge management in TNCs have been provided in studies, such as those by Bartlett and Ghoshal (1998), Bunnell and Coe (2001), Amin and Cohendet (2004), and Faulconbridge (2006). Accordingly, a high level of local buzz and global pipelines coexists and provides firms located in clusters with a string of particular advantages that are unavailable to outsiders. The coexistence of both local and global knowledge flows results in innovation dynamics of clusters and the generation of dynamics of knowledge creation within a cluster. However, the spatial network of knowledge becomes more complex and flexible beyond the local buzz and global pipeline dichotomy. Trippl et al. (2009) suggested that knowledge linkages have differentiated typologies beyond the local buzz and global pipeline dichotomy, as shown in Table 2.1 They argued that knowledge spillover and informal networks are extremely important at all spatial scales beyond the local buzz and global pipeline dichotomy, and that informal knowledge flows are complemented by formalized R&D collaborations at both local and national scales.

Table 2.1 Types of linkages to external sources of knowledge and partners

	Static (knowledge transfer)	*Dynamic (collective learning)*
Formal/traded relation	Market relations • Contract research • Consulting • Licenses • Buying intermediate goods	Formal networks • R&D collaborations • Shared use of R&D facilities
Informal/untraded relation	Spillovers • Recruiting specialists • Monitoring competitors • Participating in fairs, conferences • Reading scientific literature, patent specifications	Informal networks • Informal contacts

Source: Adapted from Trippl et al., 2009, p. 448.

The network or relational approach gives rise to new research issues but does not lend itself to casual explanations and schemas (Sunley, 2008). Recent evolutionary approaches may provide valuable insights into understanding dynamic economic spaces. Path dependence and "lock-in" are useful for understanding the evolution of the economic landscape and regional development because the concepts are place-dependent processes. A path-dependent process or system is "one whose outcome evolves as a consequence of the process's or system's own history" (Martin and Sunley, 2006, p. 399). Martin and Sunley (2006) identified three major aspects of path dependence—namely, technological lock-in, dynamic increasing returns, and institutional hysteresis (Table 2.2). They found many unresolved issues associated with path dependence, such as insufficient discussion of path creation and problems in the meaning and nature of "lock-in."

However, the concept of path dependence overemphasizes lock-in and neglects the process of new path creation. The issue of new regional path creation is regarded as being equally important in recent studies on the evolutionary approaches in economic geography (Martin and Sunley, 2006). New path creation for regional development and economic landscapes has many possibilities. For example, considering that industrial restructuring is "a process of deliberate or planned structural reconfiguration in response to the changing market conditions" (Clark, 1993, p. 5), it is related to new path creation and the processes of reshaping economic spaces. Accordingly, traditional canonical path-dependent theory has been reinterpreted by suggesting an alternative path-dependent model (Martin, 2010). Considering the importance of regional resilience in understanding the changes in economic spaces, particularly under an economic crisis, a recession, or a natural disaster, Chapter 4 of this book extends Marin's alternative path-dependent model by

Table 2.2 Three aspects of path dependence

Perspective	Main arguments
As technological 'lock-in	The tendency for particular technological fields, themselves the outcome of temporally remote events, to become locked on to a trajectory, even though alternative (and possibly more efficient) technologies are available.
As dynamic increasing returns	The argument that the development of many phenomena is driven by a process of increasing returns, in which various externalities and learning mechanisms operate to produce positive feedback effects, thereby reinforcing existing development paths.
As institutional hysteresis	The tendency for formal and informal institutions, social arrangements and cultural forms to be a self-reproducing over time, in part through the very systems of socioeconomic action they engender and serve to support and stabilize.

Source: Adapted from Martin and Sunley, 2006, p. 400.

incorporating the notion of regional resilience. Path dependence and new path creation coexist simultaneously in the evolution of economic spaces; such coexistence helps in the understanding of the dynamics of economic spaces under complex global megatrends.

The agglomeration economies of economic activities have long been one of the core themes of economic geography. Marshall's (1890) notion of industrial district can be regarded as a traditional agglomeration theory. Marshall (1920) suggested that agglomeration in industrial districts with close geographical proximity could result in increasing returns from a trinity of agglomeration economies—namely, local pool of skilled labor, local supplier linkages, and local knowledge spillover. Marshall's agglomeration theory was recently revived by Paul Krugman (1991) under the title of new economic geography or geographical economics. New economic geography from economics reveals the concentration of economic activities because of the existence of increasing returns and imperfect competition (Fujita and Krugman, 2004; Krugman and Venables, 1995). Firms wish to locate close to the largest possible market, and workers want to have access to a large number of goods; hence, geographical concentration is observed. Given that spatial proximity for face-to-face contact is important to the effective sharing of tacit knowledge, concentration reinforces the importance of innovative clusters and regions (Polenske, 2007). Such concentration can be regarded as a centripetal force.

However, the agglomeration of economic activities may result in diminishing returns. Such diminishing returns result in industry dispersion. Firms that produce standardized products, wherein innovation is not the key issue in the production process, may not wish to agglomerate in large cities because of the high labor and land costs. The third stage of the product life cycle, standardization, exhibits decentralization or filtering down from the core regions to the peripheral regions (Erickson, 1976; Park and Wheeler, 1983; Rees, 1979). Firms need to serve peripheral markets, a condition that results in geographical dispersion. The dispersion trend can be regarded as a centrifugal force. In addition to the dispersion of standardized products and back offices in selected low-cost areas, brain circulation among global innovation centers and industrial clusters in China and India is related to the centrifugal forces in space. Several economic geographers have recently suggested that increasing returns or diminishing returns is related to the evolution of the industry life-cycle (Maskell and Malmberg, 2007; Potter and Watts, 2011). In particular, Potter and Watts (2011) suggested the importance of time in agglomeration or dispersion economies as identified in the agglomeration life-cycle model shown in Figure 2.2. The four lines of the agglomeration life-cycle model describe the relationship among returns, agglomeration economies, and dispersion economies during the four different stages of industry life-cycles—namely, embryonic, growth, maturity, and decline (Potter and Watts, 2011, p. 421). The agglomeration life-cycle model can be applied to a firm, an industry, and a region.[1] Accordingly, the contrasting agglomeration and dispersion economies coexist in the economic spaces with the coexistence of different stages of the industry life-cycle in the real world.

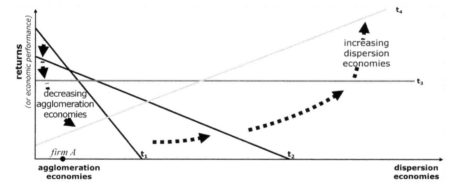

time	industry life cycle	agglomeration economies	dispersion economies	agglomeration life cycle
t_1	embryonic stage	*increasing returns*	*diminishing returns*	embryonic agglomeration
t_2	growth stage	*increasing returns*	*diminishing returns*	growth agglomeration
t_3	mature stage	*constant returns*	*constant returns*	mature agglomeration
t_4	decline stage	*diminishing returns*	*increasing returns*	decline agglomeration

Figure 2.2 The agglomeration life-cycle model

Source: Adapted from Potter and Watts, 2011, p. 420.

In the Marshallian industrial district, horizontal interactions and collaboration in a community are important (Marshall, 1890, 1920). Horizontal interaction in a community was also a major process of regional industrial development in Italian industrial districts in the 1980s (Bellandi, 1989; Becattini, 1990; Park, 1996). Horizontal cooperation and collaboration are also important for innovation in most high-tech clusters. Global trends also exist in the horizontal relationship among regions beyond the national boundaries in the era of globalization and information society. In a temporary cluster (which will be examined in the latter section of this chapter), horizontal networks and interactions among the participants of trade fairs or international conferences are important for the exchange of knowledge and technology for innovation (Bathelt and Glückler, 2011). The development of ICT and SNS, such as Facebook and Twitter, in recent years contributed to the mobilization of horizontal networks in global spaces. Rifkin (2011) argues that the development of communication technology has a critical impact on democratization in northern Africa and that the fusion of communication and energy systems in the future will considerably enhance the horizontal interactions in our community.

However, the global hierarchical structuring of urban systems is also a strong phenomenon. For example, while financial activities are overwhelmingly concentrated in world financial centers such as New York, London, and Tokyo, diverse and newly developed financial products from major financial centers are beginning to serve major high-tech clusters across countries (Clark and Wójick, 2007). Advanced services, such as corporate or financial services, are distributed hierarchically in global, national, and regional centers (Wheeler, 1986; Bryson and Daniels, 2007). Hierarchical structures in commodity chains and innovation stages are common in global economic spaces. Therefore, the forces of hierarchy of control and horizontal interaction for community building coexist in economic spaces and result in dynamic interplay.

The above-mentioned four contrasting processes are not independent of one another. They are interrelated and affect the changes in global economic spaces. They are the result of the interactions of diverse economic actors and mediators, and they result in diverse spatial economic patterns, such as clusters, innovation systems, spatial division of labor, and temporary clusters, in the real world. They are the processes that shape the dynamics of economic spaces, and they differentiate regional innovations.

Social and cultural forces as mediators in organizing economic spaces

Social and cultural forces can be regarded as mediators in the processes of changing economic spaces beyond the spatial proximity. Social, cognitive, and spatial proximity are significant for knowledge flows and innovation (Huber, 2012). Actors and firms benefit from the same language and attitude, but the similarity in terms of technical language is very important for knowledge flows

(Huber, 2012). Culture is embodied in material artifacts and social worlds, and is dynamic rather than static. Economic and innovation processes are always shaped by cultural forces (Coe et al., 2007). The economic cultures of firms are highly differentiated and often reflect the influence of where the firms come from. Owing to cultural diversity, the economic behavior of firms and their spatial organization are considerably diverse even though firms, regions, and nations have commonalities in their business practices. However, the task of identifying the economic culture is complicated and difficult. Institutional proximity beyond the spatial proximity or corporate culture is also important in the process of organizing economic spaces. The shared norms, conventions, values, expectations, and routines arising from commonly experienced frameworks of institutions can be regarded as institutional proximity and are the basis for a social system (Bathelt, 2003; Gertler, 2007). The institutional systems of industrial regulation continue to exert some influence on firms' day-to-day practices in the workplace and their innovation activities.

Most studies on the spatial organization of economic activities and innovation are silent about the roles of gender and ethnicity in the dynamics of economic spaces. In the global knowledge-based economy, however, the impact of gender and ethnicity on the organization of economic spaces is growing (Coe et al., 2007; Polenske, 2007). Global female migrants have been a core issue in the debates on economic globalization. Feminist scholars have examined global female migrants, particularly racialized low-income women workers, "as recruited into migration systems organized by the ongoing devaluation and feminization of global social reproduction and care work" (Silvey, 2012, p. 420). In contrast to the feminist approaches, the liberal development view suggests the importance of migrant women and the role they play in promoting economic growth in their home countries (World Bank, 2008). A third approach also exists. This approach focuses on "how gender and other forms of social difference are relationally produced with economic change" (Silvey, 2012, p. 421). A recent study has suggested that intra-firm learning and innovation processes are fundamentally gendered and gender relations exert some impact on the mechanism by which information is diffused among firms in a region (Gray and James, 2007). Ethnic identity intersects with economic practice, and economic space is integral to the intersection. New ethnic clusters have emerged, and flows of ethnic migration at the global scale accompanying flows of capital, technology, knowledge, and brain power exist. The Silicon Valley ethnic network in Taiwan's Hsinchu Science Park in the late twentieth century and the recent Zhongguancun cluster in China are good examples of ethnic networks for regional development and innovation (Saxenian, 2006).

In sum, cultural and social processes are integral to how economic processes work. The mediating roles of cultural and social forces in organizing dynamic economic spaces are not specifically analyzed in this study but are considered in the analysis of the dynamics of economic spaces. The role of mediators is tacitly considered in the interpretation of the dynamics of innovation and economic spaces.

Innovation systems and spatial dynamics

Since Hägerstrand's research (1953) on the process of innovation diffusion, innovation and its implications on changes in economic landscapes have interested geographers. Innovation is an important factor in analyzing the changes in the patterns of production and economic landscapes. Owing to the development of ICT in recent years, the explosion in knowledge production has resulted in the significant widening of knowledge distribution in global economic spaces (Gertler and Levitte, 2005; Howells and Bessant, 2012). However, the creation and diffusion of knowledge differ depending on the knowledge bases.

In the knowledge-based economy, innovation is fundamental for economic performance at the level of both firms and regions. Innovation reflects cumulative processes of interaction, where different organizations, firms, and individuals combine efforts to create, diffuse, and use knowledge (Lundvall et al., 2007). In-house R&D activities remain extremely important for knowledge creation and innovation. However, formal and informal interactions among R&D, production, and marketing are crucial for innovation. Inter-personal relations and interorganizational networks are also important for knowledge creation and transfer.

Historically, countries differed in the manner by which they organized the development, introduction, and improvement of new products and processes within their national economies (Freeman, 1995). In the era of the knowledge-based economy, however, differences in national innovation systems are regarded as a major source of differences in terms of national growth. National innovation systems (NISs) are systems that promote innovation by transferring, storing, and creating knowledge and technology through interaction among diverse economic actors within a nation. The main idea of NISs is that differences among nations in terms of technological change and innovation are related to the interaction between diverse private and public actors that combine to create, develop, and diffuse new technologies and innovations (Freeman, 1988). As a result of these interactive aspects of innovation in the knowledge-based economy, the production of goods and services has become more knowledge intensive but not necessarily more R&D intensive (OECD, 1999). Accordingly, in the knowledge-based economy, differences in economic development and growth by country are related to the differences in NISs, which can provide firms with favorable institutions and valuable conditions for innovation that are unavailable to competitors located in other countries even under the open market conditions of the globalization era (Lundvall and Maskell, 2000; Park, 2003).

Regional innovation systems (RISs) are important in the processes of innovation because innovation and industrial activities are actually being practiced in the workplaces of the applicable regions. By contrast, NISs can provide broad directions of national industrial development. The regional differences in economic development and growth among nations are closely related to the differences in RISs; such relationship is analogous to the relationship between national development and NISs. For example, Saxenian's study (1996), which identified the major source of the regional advantages of Silicon Valley over Route 128, contributed to the consideration of RISs as an important policy issue in regional development in many industrializing and advanced countries. Knowledge can be central to innovation systems, and knowledge transfer is a key factor for regional innovation performance. For successful regional innovation performance, several factors, such as "the strength of science base and knowledge transfer system, the institutional setting, the financial system, education and training, the availability and mobility of skilled labor (human capital), and public policy measures designed to promote innovation and growth" (Asheim et al., 2011, p. 880), are inter-related and mediate the relationship between regional economic performance and innovation.

Given the fact that innovation and economic performance are related to the systemic interaction of organizations or actors, differences by nations and regions persist over time and space as follows:

> This is the case even in the era of increasing trade, capital mobility and globalization, because some type of knowledge and intellectual capital are less mobile than other resources and because the complexity of transferring knowledge from its basic form, into new product and process innovations, and the diffusion of innovations, is a complex, dynamic process that is difficult to replicate and transfer across borders. As a result, even in the face of globalization, localities and regions may grow in importance as the increasing role of intellectual capital leads to the creation of what Markusen (1996) has termed 'sticky places in slippery space'.
>
> (Asheim et al., 2011, p. 883)

The development of ICT has significantly contributed to the wide diffusion of codified knowledge in the global economic space. However, face-to-face contact is important to transfer tacit knowledge, but limitation exists for knowledge transfer across space. The different characteristics of knowledge bases should be considered in addition to knowledge type. These three types of knowledge bases have different characteristics—namely, analytical, synthetic, and symbolic (Asheim and Gertler, 2005; Asheim and Hansen, 2009, Gertler, 2008). Table 2.3 describes the different types of knowledge base and its characteristics. Face-to-face interaction for different industries differs because of the differences in the knowledge base of different activities (Tether et al., 2012). Different patterns of industrial development exist by industry types and regions because of the existence of different knowledge bases.

Table 2.3 Differentiated knowledge bases and their characteristics

	Analytical (science based)	Synthetic (engineering based)	Symbolic (arts based)
Rationale for knowledge creation	Developing new knowledge about natural systems by applying scientific laws; *know why*	Applying or combining existing knowledge in new ways; *know how*	Creating meaning, desire, aesthetic qualities, affect, intangibles, symbols, images; *know who*
Development and use of knowledge	Scientific knowledge, models, deductive	Problem solving, custom production, inductive	Creative process
Actors involved	Collaboration within and between research units	Interactive learning with customers and suppliers	Experimentation in studios, project teams
Knowledge types	Strong codified knowledge content, highly abstract, universal	Partially codified knowledge, strong tacit component, more context specific	Importance of interpretation, creativity, cultural knowledge, sign values; implies strong context specificity
Importance of spatial proximity	Meaning relatively constant between places	Meaning varies substantially between places	Meaning highly variable between place, class and gender
Locus of new knowledge production	R&D departments and collaborations, including with the 'science base'	Interactive learning, especially with clients, but also in the community of practice	'Studio' projects, and learning through interaction with the professional/artistic community, and wider cultural interactions
Means of sharing and diffusing knowledge	Patents, publications and the Internet, but also scientific conferences	Attending to 'field problems' (von Hippel, 1988), mainly through face-to-face interactions	Hard to share or diffuse. Developed in practice over time and 'possessed' by key individuals
Outcome	Drug development	Mechanical engineering	Cultural production, design, brands

Source: Adapted from Asheim et al., 2011, p. 898; Tether et al., 2012, p. 976.

Considering the growing complexity and diversity of knowledge creation and innovation process, firms need to acquire new knowledge from external sources to supplement their internal core knowledge base. Thus, firms collaborate with external firms through cooperation and joint investment for R&D activities with universities or research institutes to acquire and integrate external knowledge. The RIS model highlights the beneficial effects of local interaction with knowledge flows within a geographically bounded region (Jaffe et al., 1993). However, recent studies on the channels of knowledge spillover challenge the argument of geographical dimension of knowledge flows (Brenner et al., 2013). Successful regions like Silicon Valley show that actors cooperate in knowledge exchange and R&D by formal and informal basis, not only with co-located actors but also with external actors (Park, 1996; Ter Wal, 2013). The trend of acquiring and integrating external knowledge is regarded as a shift toward globally "distributed knowledge network" and "open innovation" (Chesbrough, 2003). With the increasing importance of open innovation, firms tend to organize innovation in interaction with outside organizations, especially in less urbanized areas (Teirlinck and Spithoven, 2008). Spatial innovation systems may extend beyond the national boundary like cross-border learning regions because of open innovation. Manpower, information, and capital can flow easily beyond the national boundary in the globalization era, which promotes active collaborations and interactions among regions in a global society.

The processes of knowledge creation and transfer—namely, NISs and RISs—can be regarded as processes of learning and competence building. Interactions among the major actors in economic spaces, relations with processes of contrasting forces, and cultural and social processes are related with the innovation systems. For example, Crescenzi et al. (2007) argued the existence of "territorial dynamics of innovation" in the USA and the EU because "there are different contemporary institutions, rules and incentives governing the creation and geographical mobility and combination of such inputs to innovation" (p. 674). The differences in territorial dynamics are related with diverse factors as follows:

> The analysis shows that the higher mobility of capital, population, and knowledge in the economically and culturally integrated US market facilitates the combinations of factors that respond rapidly to shifts of the technological frontier, and allows full exploitation of local innovation activities and (informational) synergies. By contrast, imperfect market integration in the European Union and institutional and cultural barriers across the continent produce a spatial configuration both less dynamic and less coherent at the local level.
>
> (Crescenzi et al., 2007, p. 675)

These actors or organizations, contrasting spatial forces, mediators, and innovation systems are not separate from each other, but are interlinked to manifest dynamics of economic spaces in the global economy. The outcomes of the interactions and integration of the factors and processes are diverse features of economic spaces. Major features of the dynamics of economic spaces are examined in the next section.

Major features of the dynamics of economic spaces

Uneven development may intrinsically exist or persist in the global knowledge-based economy, even in the globalized information society (Asheim et al., 2011). However, this development is not fixed, but dynamic over time. In the advances of global megatrends examined in Chapter 1, new forms of economic spaces evolved through the interaction of diverse economic actors, mediators, innovation systems, and contrasting spatial forces. Five major dynamic features of economic spaces are discussed in this study as a result of interactions and integration of the role of major actors, contrasting forces, mediators, and innovation systems. These features include the dynamics of cluster/agglomerations, the evolution of spatial division of labor, dynamic, the development of temporary clusters, and sustainable development and resilience. However, the dynamic features of economic spaces examined in this section are not the complete set of features of economic spaces, but an example of evolving dynamics. Moreover, these features are not independent, but are interrelated, which cause economic spaces to become dynamic and complex.

Clusters/agglomerations

Industrial clusters are "geographic concentrations of interconnected companies, specialized suppliers, service providers, firms in related industries, and associated institutions" in particular fields that compete but also cooperate (Porter, 1998, p. 197). The term "cluster" was first introduced by Michael Porter (1990), but the underlying concept was obtained from the agglomeration economies and industrial district introduced by Alfred Marshall (1890). Therefore, network, interaction, and geographical proximity are key dimensions of cluster concept. Clusters have been at the center of numerous regional development studies and industrial strategies in economic geography, regional economics, urban studies and related disciplines in both Western and Eastern countries in the last two decades (Rychen and Zimmermann, 2008; Morrison, 2008; Boschma and Kloosterman, 2005; Karlsson, 2008). Clusters have been a key strategy for promoting industrial development and competitiveness in most countries.

In addition to the cluster of industrial production, other clusters such as those in the software industry, venture capital, advanced financial services, producer services, and others can be clearly identified in the global space economy. Even in industrialized and newly industrialized countries, the clustering of the advanced services are prominent, as seen in Bangalore, Beijing, Seoul, Hong Kong, and Singapore (Park, 2005; Yeh, 2005). Despite the ability of the

Internet to transcend space, dot-com companies also agglomerate in a few major metropolitan areas (Zook, 2005). In Korea, more than three-quarters of B2C e-market places, B2B e-commerce sites, and Internet domains are clustered in the capital region (Park, 2004). The supply of skilled labor, the organization of labor, government-support programs, and regional innovation capacity can be regarded as factors that account for geographic clustering (Zook, 2005). The process of knowledge generation is another factor. Proximity does not matter in transferring codified knowledge in the Internet era because the codified knowledge can be transferred through the Internet globally at a low cost. However, the transfer of tacit knowledge usually takes place at a local level where firms share the same values, background and understanding of technical and commercial problems (Maskell and Malmberg, 1999). Geographical and cultural proximity provides the access to local relational networks for the transfer of tacit knowledge (Park, 2003).

Despite the impact of geographic proximity on knowledge spillovers, nongeographical proximities such as "organized proximity" and "cognitive proximity" may affect distant knowledge spillover (Torre and Rallet, 2005; Boschma, 2005). The co-location of actors in geographic proximity can contribute to its efficiency, but it is not a sufficient condition for coordination to enhance competitiveness (Rychen and Zimmermann, 2008). For example, firms develop global networks to benefit from outside noble ideas, and knowledge inputs and growth impulse, and to exchange products and services (Maskell et al., 2006). The importance of nongeographic proximity beyond the local advantages of geographical proximity has resulted in a new concept of cluster such as a temporary cluster, which will be discussed later.

In recent years, considering the dynamics of the existence and structure of clusters over time, economic geographers have been interested in cluster life-cycle and cluster evolution (Boschma and Fornahl, 2011). The cluster life-cycle model portrays four main phases—namely, birth or emergence, growth, maturity and decline, and even death, which used to be measured by the number of firms, employment, innovativeness, market share, and others (Press, 2006). According to a recently proposed cluster life-cycle model by Menzel and Fornahl (2010), firms enter and exit the cluster, firms interact within the cluster, and interorganizational networks within and outside the cluster are established and dissolved along the life cycle. However, the life-cycle approach is being criticized because it is too deterministic. Clusters change over time and can be understood as products of a path-dependent process (Martin and Sunley, 2006). Clusters evolve because "they emerge, grow, may change in complex and orientation, may undergo reinvention and transformation, and may eventually decline and even disappear" (Martin and Sunley, 2011, p. 1300). Martin and Sunley (2011) proposed a modified cluster adaptive cycle model along the evolutionary approach based on an adaptive cycle model taken from ecology literature. They consider clusters as complex adaptive systems and suggest six possible alternative evolutionary trajectories, as shown in Table 2.4. The modified adaptive cycle model of cluster evolution is useful

Table 2.4 Some alternative cluster evolutionary trajectories under the adaptive cycle model

Evolutionary trajectory	Phases of evolution and typical characteristics	Possible mechanisms
1 Cluster full adaptive cycle	Emergence, growth, maturation, decline and eventual replacement by a new cluster. Follows the archetypal adaptive cycle. The replacement cluster is likely to draw upon resources and capabilities inherited from the old cluster.	Resilience rises and then falls as the cluster passes through phases of the cycle. The cluster atrophies because of either internal rigidities or exhaustion of increasing returns effects, or it is unable to withstand major external competitive shock. But sufficient resources, inherited capabilities and competencies are left to provide a basis for the emergence of a new cluster based on related or cognate specialism.
2 Constant cluster mutation	Emergence, growth, and constant structural and technological change. The cluster continually adapts and evolves, possibly by the successive development of new branches of related activity. This is particularly likely where basic technology has a generic or general-purpose characteristics.	Cluster firms are able to innovate more or less continuously and the cluster constantly mutates or widens in terms of industrial specialization and technological regime. There are high rates of spin-offs from existing firms and spin-outs from local research institutes or universities. Cluster has a high degree of resilience.
3 Cluster stabilization	Emergence, growth and maturation, followed by stabilization, though possibly in a much reduced and restricted form. The cluster might remain in this state for an extended period of time	Though the cluster possibly experiences a phase of decline in scale, the remaining firms survive by upgrading products and/or focusing on niche or prestige market segments. The cluster retains a modest degree of resilience, but it remains potentially vulnerable to (further) decline.
4 Cluster reorientation	Upon reaching or nearing maturation, or upon the onset of early cluster decline, firms reorientate their industrial and technological specialisms, and new cluster emerges.	The cluster in effect branches into a new form without going through a long period of decline. The more innovative lead firms may play a key role in this process—for example, by reacting to market saturation or a rise of major competitors, or a technological breakthrough may activate reorientation.
5 Cluster failure	The emergent cluster fails to take off and grow. Any remaining firms do not constitute a functioning cluster.	The cluster fails to achieve sufficient critical mass, externalities or market share. Innovation may also falter. New firm formation is low and/or the firm failure rate is high, which deters new entrants.
6 Cluster disappearance	Emergence, growth, maturation, decline and elimination. No conversion into or replacement by a new cluster. Classic life-cycle trajectory.	The cluster experiences the same eventual atrophy and decline as in the full adaptive cycle pattern (see point 1 above), but inherited resources and competences are not sufficient or ill-suited to form the basis of new cluster formation.

Source: Adapted from Martin and Sunley, 2011, p. 1313.

in understanding the evolution of clusters over time. The cluster coevolves with the industry and other clusters in both local and global context.

Another aspect that should be considered in the cluster is the ability of industries with "related variety" to enhance economic knowledge spillover and innovation. Clusters used to assume that firms in specialized regions benefit from local externalities because of the input procurement from specialized input suppliers, a local pool of labor skills, and local knowledge spillover. This concept was obtained from Marshall's localization economies in industrial districts (Marshall, 1890). However, in contrast to the localization economies, Jacobs (1969) emphasizes that spatial externalities come from the knowledge learned by a firm from other local firms in a range of other diverse sectors, which is called "Jacobs' externalities." The debates whether localization economies and Jacobs' externalities are a matter of urban and regional growth were inconclusive (Boschma et al., 2012). However, Frenken et al. (2007) explored the relatedness effect with disentangling two variety effects—namely, related and unrelated variety, and concluded the importance of related variety. The effects of related variety are explained by Boschma et al. (2012) as follows:

> The related variety effect includes externalities that may come from a diversity of related industries in a region. The notion of regional related variety tries to capture a delicate balance between cognitive proximity and distance across sectors in a region that is needed for knowledge to spillover effectively between sectors. Thus, the more variety across related sectors in a region, the higher the number of technologically related sectors, and the more learning opportunities there are for local industries. This will result in more inter-sectoral knowledge spillovers, which enhance regional performance. This stands in contrast to localization economies in which regional specialization produces too much cognitive proximity between local firms (lock-in), while Jacobs' externalities *per se* may involve too much cognitive distance between local firms active in different industries.
>
> (p. 243)

Along the same line of logic, Cainelli and Iacobucci (2012) found that "a higher level of vertical related variety in a local system significantly reduces the need for firms to integrate activities along the production chain" (p. 271). However, the cluster effect is different across space based on the characteristics of firms and clusters. For example, significant differences between the North-west regions in Italy exist, which are characterized by the presence of large firms and large urban areas, and regions of Third Italy, which is characterized by the presence of small firms organized in industrial district. In the Northwest regions "specialization and variety do not significantly influence the degree of vertical integration," whereas in Third Italy "both specialization and vertically related variety are significant for firms' decision to control activities along the production chain" (Cainelli and Iacobucci, 2012, p. 271).

Several studies were conducted on the factors and types of clusters. In addition to localized learning through spatial proximity, organizational proximity, and untraded dependencies, the evolution of creative class has also been emphasized in recent studies (Clark et al., 2000; Coe et al., 2007; Florida, 2002; Gertler, 2007; Storper and Salais, 1997). Major cluster examples in Asian countries show different characteristics in terms of cluster life cycle and the development of local systems. Differences exist in terms of culture, national innovation systems, and importance of the role of diverse actors (Crescenzi et al., 2007; Crescenzi et al., 2012; Lee and Rodrigues-Pose, 2013). However, most of the recent clusters and agglomerations have increasing networks beyond the local boundary within a nation and at the international level over time. Clusters are not a static concept. They are dynamic over time, which results in the dynamics of economic spaces in the globalized knowledge-based economy as changes of the networks of industrial districts over time (Park, 1996).

Spatial division of labor

Massey (1995) describes how a contemporary capitalist economy develops a spatial structure that assigns distinct roles or functions to particular places. Spatial division of labor (SDL) has two types—namely, the sectoral division of labor by regional specialization in particular industries and all related skills, and the intrasectoral division of labor by a firm's specialization of functions, tasks, and occupations by location (Massey, 1984). Historically, sectoral division of labor was prominent during the nineteenth century in Europe; North America was largely organized by regionally focused firms, which created regions specialized in particular industries with a vertical concentration of all the necessary occupations, control, and production skills related to particular industries (Marshall, 1890; Hayter, 1997). In addition to the sectoral division of labor, intrasectoral functional division of labor, which is called the new SDL, has been promoted along the growth of multiregional and multinational corporations since the twentieth century.

An intrasectoral functional division of labor occurs when firms choose to locate different tasks and occupations within an individual industry in different places. Different functions within individual industries such as management, marketing, R&D activity, and manufacturing processes require different locations because of industrial development. New international division of labor has also increased with the decentralization of production activities from core to peripheral and semi-peripheral countries (Frobel et al., 1980). Locational hierarchies of the 100 largest manufacturing companies in the USA also represent the clear SDL in the urban systems (Hayter, 1997). Product life cycles can be one reason for the functional division of labor because standardized production can be dispersed to low-cost locations (Vernon, 1966; Park and Wheeler, 1983). Firms can also strategically separate the well-paid managerial or R&D manpower from low-paid production occupations to limit the bargaining power of low-paid production workers (Clark, 1981).

Most newly industrialized countries have experienced considerable new SDL in recent years. However, SDL is not a static concept, but evolves over time with the processes of path dependent and new path creation. For example, new SDL in Korea, which spatially separated the locations of headquarters in Seoul with the locations of plants outside Seoul, has occurred since the 1970s with the evolution of large conglomerates during the heavy and chemical industrialization phase in the 1970s (Park, 1993). In the 1980s, another type of new SDL occurred with the spatial concentration of high-tech industries and R&D activities in the capital region beyond the spatial separation between headquarters and manufacturing plants, whereas the noncapital region specialized in nonhigh-tech industries. Intensified SDL existed because the R&D activities in Seoul were more oriented toward basic and applied research activities, whereas the production research activities relatively dispersed to the peripheral areas (Park, 1995). This finding reflects that more complex and basic research activities within the R&D activities that require high-quality manpower tend to concentrate in a few major metropolitan areas. In the twenty-first century, new SDL with concentration on knowledge-based advanced services tend to be concentrated in the capital region while production activities dispersed to noncapital regions. A relative dispersion of headquarters and high-tech industries to the noncapital region was observed since the 1990s, whereas the concentration of producer services such as design, legal and financial services, management consulting and others were in Seoul (Park and Koo, 2010).

Spatial division of labor in the Internet era may be intensified in advanced services and in Internet-related activities. The development of ICT affects the promotion of the concentration of ICT-related advanced services in Seoul. Internet domains are highly concentrated in Seoul, and transactions of business-to-business e-commerce tend to concentrate in Seoul (Park, 2004). The case of Korea clearly shows that the new SDL continuously evolves over time and results in the dynamics of economic spaces. This tendency toward spatial separation within the same function has intensified the existing functional spatial division of labor. However, the spatial division of labor may not coalesce, and, thus, may remain problematic in some industries as production becomes more flexible (Hayter, 1997). This finding indicates that regional disparities may not be reduced in the Internet era as the economic space becomes more complex.

Global production networks

Economic activities are geographically networked in the global knowledge-based economy. In producing tangible products such as computers, various activities are linked in a network/chain-like fashion. Each stage adds value to the process of production of goods or services. The network/chain is not limited to the manufacturing processes because several inputs to the network/chain, and most of the final commodities produced take the form of intangible services. Every production network/chain is delineated by a particular sequence of value-adding activities, a distinct geographical configuration, different combinations of mode of governance, which cross various institutional contexts (Coe et al., 2007)— that is, production networks or commodity chains are inherently geographical-organizational features of the contemporary global economy that dynamically organize global economic spaces.

The approach to the networks/chains in the global economy has three interlinked strands from a multidisciplinary field. These approaches are global commodity chain (GCC), global value chain (GVC), and (GPN). The major developers of the frameworks and key contents are well summarized by Coe et al. (2008b) in Table 2.5.

Table 2.5 Initiation and major concerns of GCC, GVC and GPN

	GCC	*GVC*	*GPN*
Initiation	Stemming from a relatively structuralist world systems perspective (Gereffi and Korzeniewicz, 1994).	Developed by researchers at the Institute of Development Studies in Sussex and later expanded into a wider research network (see: www.global valuechains.org/).	Developed by researchers in Manchester and their collaborators (Henderson et al., 2002; Dicken and Henderson, 2003; Coe et al., 2004).
Concern	'Understanding how global industries are organized. It consists of identifying the full set of actors (i.e. firms) that are involved in the production and distribution of a particular good or service and mapping the kinds of relationships that exist among them' (Bair, 2005, p. 157).	Investigating the governance structures in different global industries, but in addition attempts are made to delineate the varying governance structures both within, and between, different sectors in terms of varying knowledge characteristics (Dolan and Humphrey, 2004; Gereffi et al., 2005).	Combining insights gained from GCC/GVC analysis with ideas derived from the actor-network theory (ANT) and varieties of capitalism/business systems literatures, and aim to reveal the multi-actor and multi-scalar characteristics of transnational production systems through intersecting notions of power, value and embeddedness. In particular, attempts are made to connect with understandings of subnational regional development and clustering dynamics.

Source: Adapted from Coe et al., 2008b, p. 269.

The three approaches have similarities and differences (Coe et al., 2008b). These approaches are grounded in a network/chain approach and "acknowledge that governance structures and their related power asymmetries within a chain/network have a major impact on firm level upgrading prospects and the related regional development opportunities of the places they interconnect" (p. 268). Differences exist in relative emphasis of framework regarding subnational regional institutions and dynamics, the role of nonfirm actors, and the relative importance of territorial development impacts. Chains can be understood as sequential activities from production sourcing to distribution and consumption, whereas networks are related to open-ended relations. Therefore, limitations exist in the studies on chains. A central problem is the inherent assumption of the linearity of value-adding activities. The linear structures of a commodity chain that are enmeshed within complex networks of relationships involve a wide range of institutional actors, such as labor unions and NGOs, and corporate actors such as financiers and logistic providers (Coe et al., 2007). GPN has been considered in the framework of the dynamics of economic spaces in this book because the open-ended network approach has more advantages in understanding the complexity of production systems in the global knowledge-based economy. Furthermore, GPN is considered as one of the major features of the dynamics of economic spaces because GPN is related to the regional development and dynamics of clusters.

The GPN framework has several advantages in understanding the dynamics of economic spaces, which include major economic actors, flexibility in terms of geographical scale, recognition of the influence of social-spatial context, distinguishing territorial and network embeddedness, the presence of a more "nuanced articulation of power relationships, identification of the points of value created within the network, and the possibility of potential points of intervention and resistance within the network (Henderson et al., 2002; Dicken, 2004; Coe et al., 2008a). Despite the advantages of the GPN approach in understanding the economic spaces, it is suggested as an integrative perspective that combines the insights from political and cultural economies (Coe et al., 2008a).

GPN is also a dynamic evolutionary process, wherein the three principal elements of value, power, and embeddedness change in the global economy. The dynamics can be the result of the role of economic actors in contrast to the spatial processes and innovation systems identified in Figure 2.1. Value is created by firms and other diverse actors in the production network. Regions enhance regional value and production through appropriate strategies and innovation systems, whereas focal firms endeavor to increase their value-added activities through technological innovations, supply chain management, and reduction of costs in the GPN. Power is derived from structural conditions, such as markets and political institutions, which is mobilized by actors who participate in the GPN (Murphey, 2012). Embeddedness has three dimensions—namely, spatial, network, and societal institutions (Hess, 2004). Embeddedness is closely related to the dynamics of economic spaces. The dynamics of value, power, and embeddedness may result in different types of GPN and regional development in the global economic space.

Temporary clusters

New forms of dynamic economic spaces are evolving in the global knowledge-based economy. Spatial proximity is essential for knowledge creation, but it does not always indicate the co-location of innovation and research activities. The need for spatial proximity in certain stages of the process of production and R&D affects the evolution of new forms of economic spaces. Short- or medium-term visits are often sufficient for the partners to exchange the information and knowledge needed for cooperation (Torre, 2008). More flexibilities of firm location exist, and the spatial strategy of the firm may differ by the size of firms because of the advantage of temporary geographical proximity (Torre, 2008, p. 886).

• The combination of permanent geographical proximity and organized proximity is an essential factor of the success of clusters that 'work'; indeed, in these successful clusters internal knowledge diffusion rests on both types of proximity.
• Face-to-face interactions are only required during certain stages of the innovative process; for such face-to-face interactions to occur, permanent co-location is not required; only temporary co-location, through meetings between individuals, is necessary; and these meetings are possible thanks to individuals' mobility and spatial events (such as fairs and trade shows). This is what is called temporary geographical proximity.
• Small firms are more tied to their territories than are large firms; their lack of financial or human resources forces them to locate close enough to the organizations with which they need to exchange knowledge. They benefit less easily from the advantages of temporary geographical proximity because of the high transport costs and because of their insufficient human resources.

Such temporary meetings in the knowledge-based information society are possible with the increased mobility of qualified manpower and special events, such as trade shows and conferences. The issue of temporary geographical proximity contributes to understanding the organization of economic spaces in terms of temporary cluster with global buzz, establishing a global pipeline, and developing a new industry project and virtual innovation cluster.

Trade fairs and conferences can be regarded as temporary clusters. Bathelt and Glückler (2011) suggest that trade fairs can be characterized as a temporary cluster that "develop unique information and communication ecology, referred to as global buzz" (p. 190). Diverse formal planned and informal unplanned meetings and different forms of interactions result in "global buzz" (Bathelt and Schuldt, 2008). Trade fairs provide numerous formal and informal networks between customers and suppliers, and enable firms to acquire information systematically about world market trends and the state-of-the-art in production and innovation (Bathelt and Glückler, 2011). Such trade fairs support the economic processes of interactive learning and knowledge creation for the actors who participated in the events.

Trade shows are viewed as relational spaces, wherein numerous and diverse actors interact and learn spontaneously in those places and temporarily take the role of clusters. Rinallo and Golfetto (2011) suggest that the "geographical scale of the process of exchanging and acquiring knowledge in temporary cluster is socially and politically constructed at several levels—from the merely local to the truly global" (p. 453). International trade fairs in recent years play an important role in the global economic space because they provide diverse opportunities with new business partners worldwide and establish "global pipelines" after the fairs, in addition to deepening the existing networks (Bathelt and Schuldt, 2008; Bathelt and Glückler, 2011).

Temporary geographical proximity can be identified in the initial development of new industries such as industries for the elderly in Korea (Koo and Park, 2012). The continuation of the temporary meeting for the elderly project may lead to the development of clusters for industries for the elderly. Temporary clusters can provide an initial seedbed for preparing the development of new industry and later promote a permanent cluster for the new industry.

Virtual space or cyber space in the Internet era represents another dimension of communication and social space. The flows of information and knowledge in the virtual space take place along the networks of the Internet. Some places help coordinate a smooth interaction in the network by becoming communication hubs, whereas other places can be nodes of the networks (Castells, 2000). Virtual innovative clusters in cyberspace can be organized through virtual networks of skilled workers in addition to the actual meetings. In this case, hubs and nodes are not necessary conditions for the formation of a virtual innovation cluster. Actual face-to-face contacts easily take place in the hubs and nodes of economic spaces, which accompany the transfer of tacit knowledge and knowledge conversion processes among high-quality manpower such as engineers and information or managerial elites. In peripheral areas, the daily networking of qualified workers through face-to-face contacts is not easy. However, a clustering of information and knowledge can be conducted in a given location by combining online and offline meetings. Research groups can be organized through the Internet, and periodic face-to-face meetings of the researchers can be set up for the transfer of tacit knowledge into peripheral areas. An innovation cluster can be formed by combining online and offline networks even if there is no actual clustering of innovation manpower (Park, 2004). In this case, the off-line network is a temporary geographical proximity and can be regarded as a temporary cluster.

In Korea, where the Internet infrastructure is well developed, virtual innovation clusters for the development of a new product from local traditional resources and culture in peripheral areas are evolving (Park, 2005). The virtual innovation cluster may evolve as a new form of dynamic economic spaces by combining a temporary cluster and virtual cluster in the global knowledge-based economy.

Sustainable development

One of the important challenges confronted in industrial society is devising ecologically and environmentally sustainable forms of production system because of the growing concerns about serious damage brought about by industrial growth to the environment and health. The Report of Rome Club on "Limit to Growth" is the turning point of concerns and debates about environmental constraints on growth. However, the growing concerns about the sustainability of current industrial development patterns have spread globally, especially since the Rio Earth Summit in 1992 (UNIDO, 1996). Diverse environmental problems since the 1980s, such as global carbon pollution, ozone depletion, loss of species, forests, and fertile soils, and climate change, have suggested that environmental damage has become more global and more serious than expected (Schmidheiny and Zorraquin, 1996; Curtis and Oven, 2012; O'Brien, 2012). The importance of sustainable development policies has been well recognized even in developing countries in recent years because the rapid industrialization and economic growth in the developing countries since 1990s, especially in India and China, has led to severe environmental degradation and pollution (UNIDO, 1996; Zhang et al., 1999; Angel and Rock, 2000). Sustainable development has been regarded as urgent concerns in industrializing and industrialized countries because of environmental issues and climate change.

Doryan (1993) identified the four dimensions of sustainability that underlie a competitive view of development, such as productivity increases, environmental conditions, socio-political stability, and enhancement of human resources:

- Productivity sustainability is defined by market, macroeconomic and financial dynamism, infrastructure development, industrial efficiency, and globalization of the domestic economy.
- Environmental sustainability is defined by pollution indicators, rules and procedures to control waste, institution building to manage natural resources, and behavior of citizens toward the environment.
- Socio-political sustainability is defined by indication of institutions that allow freedom of expression, human rights, and confidence toward the judiciary system and the government.
- Finally, "humanware", or human resources sustainability, is defined by educational and training opportunities and by openness of the population and the labor force toward technology and managerial changes and science and technology infrastructure.

(p. 453)

The above dimensions of sustainability are quite comprehensive, but they are defined mainly for measuring the competitive sustainability and performance of countries in South America. Productivity sustainability in this case can be regarded as economic sustainability, and socio-political and human resources sustainability can be considered as social sustainability. Accordingly, these four dimensions can be reduced to three dimensions at the conceptual level—namely, economic, social, and environmental or ecological (Park, 2002). Considering that current industrial production systems cause negative environmental and social impacts, an environmental point of view has been emphasized for the improvement of the industrial systems in recent studies (Erkman, 1997; Wallner, 1999; Truffer and Cohen, 2012). Cleaner production and eco-efficiency are considered priorities for sustainable development. Ecological dimension has been given clear priority even if sustainability has economic, social, and ecological dimensions (Wallner, 1999). Hudson (1995, p. 39) also considers sustainability in terms of "social sustainability of the level and distribution of employment and of income, and of the ecological sustainability of the level and composition of output." Even if ecological sustainability is more emphasized in some of recent studies, industry cannot be viable without economic sustainability or profitability. Therefore, the three dimensions of economic, social, and ecological sustainability should be considered in sustainable industrialization paths (Park, 2002).

In the past, the natural environment was conventionally discussed as something separate from development, and continuous economic growth was a priority for industrial development. However, the environment and development has been seen as two sides of the same coin since the 1990s. Ecological sustainability has become an important issue because of the increasing evidence of environmental problems and damage since the early 1980s. At present, the protection of natural environments from the waste, outputs, and effects of economic production is becoming a commodity with a tradable value. The rise of markets for trading emission credits and certifying environmental protection are examples of the commodification of environmental degradation (Coe et al., 2007).

Studies on environmental economic geography in recent years have focused on the greening of industry and the political ecology of industrial change. The application of the concept of industrial ecology to industrial systems, such as eco-industrial parks and systemic dematerialization, was also been suggested in recent years (Park, 2002). The emphasis of sustainable industrialization will leave a profound effect on the dynamics of economic spaces in Asian countries in the future. The greening of industry and the innovation of environmental technology and performance have changed the global production networks in recent years.

In the USA, sustainable development is applied to local and regional development strategies. A set of policy approaches related to sustainable development is collectively referred as "smart growth" (Krueger and Gibbs, 2008). Smart growth, like the Local Agenda 21, has built-on tripartite concerns for community integrity, environmental protection, economic development, and regulatory reforms that enable the market to promote these concerns (Environmental Protection Agency, 2006). However, Krueger and Gibbs (2008) argue that the goal of smart growth may contradict its mechanisms for delivery because it is "a paradigm shift from more state-based regulatory mechanisms to market-based mechanism, primarily incentives" (p. 1272). Krueger and Gibbs (2008) referred to a comment of an anonymous reviewer as:

> Europeans are 'dark green,' concerned about energy shortages, land scarcity, and environmental and climate change while Americans are 'light green', they recycle, but they buy the Eddie Bauer edition of their sports utility vehicle (SUV) and live in a 5000 square foot home on a one acre suburban lot.
>
> (p. 1272)

They believe that smart growth only provides an alternative for the consumption of open space and does not address the large issue of consumption.

In recent years, new research topics are developed in the environmental economic geography, in addition to environmental problems with regard to climate change. Environmental finance service industry emerged with regard to the climate change. For example, carbon financial service industry has emerged and argued that the development of new carbon markets is suitable for established financial centers such as London and New York because of social connectivity and proximity (Knox-Hayes, 2009). The development of a new alternative energy system with regard to climate change, such as solar energy and wind power, has been reshaping energy supply systems; thus, the integration of the energy system with the communication system may result in more horizontal network of economic spaces (Rifkin, 2011). Most regional development policies and strategies in advanced countries advocate three dimensions of sustainability such as smart growth in the USA, but in reality, they tend to promote market-based mechanisms, which may contradict the Local Agenda 21. They identify environmental problems and issues with regard to climate change, but the development plans and policies tend to give a priority to market mechanisms. Accordingly, climate change presents significant challenges for issues on human health, adaptation and resilience, sustainability, and environmental justice (Curtis and Oven, 2012). Diverse scales beyond local level should be considered in sustainable development strategies.

These major features of the dynamics of economic spaces cannot be regarded as the entire set of changes in the global knowledge-based economy. Only important features are discussed. These features should be understood in terms of dynamic evolutionary aspects because economic space is not static but continuously evolves over time. The major features of the economic spaces are integral results of interactions of major actors, contrasting forces, mediators, and innovation systems under the global megatrends, as suggested in the theoretical framework identified in Figure 2.1.

The key elements of the theoretical framework in Figure 2.1 are integration, evolution, and network in economic spaces. The theoretical framework, integral model of service innovation, path dependence and regional resilience, and the accumulation process of intangible assets are investigated in Chapters 3, 4, and 5, respectively. Case studies of multinational firms, the evolution of the industrial cluster, and spatial inequalities with regard to the global megatrends are then analyzed in relation to the theoretical framework of dynamics of economic spaces. Future perspectives in the dynamic economic spaces and policy implications are discussed in the last chapter.

Note

1 For more information, see Potter and Watts, 2011.

References

Amin, A. & Cohendet, P. (2004). *Architectures of Knowledge: Firms, Capabilities, and Communities*. Oxford: Oxford University Press.
Angel, D. P. & Rock, M. T. (Eds.). (2000). *Asia's Clean Revolution: Industry, Growth and the Environment*. Sheffield: Greenleaf Publishing.
Asheim, B. T. & Gertler, M. (2005). The geography of innovation: regional innovation systems. In J. Fagerberg, D. C. Mowery & R. R. Nelson (Eds.), *The Oxford Handbook of Innovation* (pp. 291–317). Oxford: Oxford University Press.
Asheim, B. T. & Hansen, H. K. (2009). Knowledge bases, talents, and contexts: on the usefulness of the creative class approach in Sweden. *Economic Geography*, 85(4), 425–442.
Asheim, B. T., Boschma, R. & Cooke, P. (2011). Constructing regional advantage: platform policies based on related variety and differentiated knowledge bases. *Regional Studies*, 45(7), 893–904.
Asheim, B. T., Lawton Smith, H. & Oughton, C. (2011). Regional innovation systems: theory, empirics and policy. *Regional Studies*, 45(7), 875–891.
Bair, J. (2005). Global capitalism and commodity chains: looking back, going forward. *Competition and Change*, 9(2), 153–180.
Bartlett, C. A. & Ghoshal, S. (1998). Beyond strategic planning to organization learning: lifeblood of the individualized corporation. *Strategy & Leadership*, 26(1), 34–39.
Bathelt, H. (2003). Geographies of production: growth regimes in spatial perspective (I)—innovation, institutions and social systems. *Progress in Human Geography*, 27(6), 763–778.
Bathelt, H. & Glückler, J. (2011). *The Relational Economy: Geographies of Knowing and Learning*. Oxford: Oxford University Press.
Bathelt, H. & Schuldt, N. (2008). Between luminaires and meat grinders: international trade fairs as temporary clusters. *Regional Studies*, 42(6), 853–868.
Bathelt, H., Malmberg, A. & Maskell, P. (2004). Clusters and knowledge: local buzz, global pipelines and the process of knowledge creation. *Progress in Human Geography*, 28(1), 31–56.

Becattini, G. (1990). The Marshallian industrial district as a socio-economic notion. In F. Pyke, G. Becattini & W. Sengenberger (Eds.), *Industrial Districts and Inter-firm Co-operation in Italy* (pp. 37–51). Geneva: International Institute for Labour Studies.

Bellandi, M. (1989). The industrial district in Marshall. In E. Goodman & J. Bamford (Eds.), *Small Firms and Industrial Districts in Italy* (pp. 136–152). London and New York: Routledge.

Boschma, R. (2005). Proximity and innovation: a critical assessment. *Regional Studies*, 39(1), 61–74.

Boschma, R. & Kloosterman, R. C. (Eds.). (2005). *Learning from Clusters: A Critical Assessment from an Economic-Geographical Perspective.* Dordrecht: Springer.

Boschma, R. A. & Fornahl, D. (2011). Cluster evolution and a roadmap for future research. *Regional Studies*, 45(10), 1295–1298.

Boschma, R. A., Minondo, A. & Navarro, M. (2012). Related variety and regional growth in Spain. *Papers in Regional Science*, 91(2), 241–256.

Boutellier, R., Gassmann, O. & von Zedtwitz, M. (Eds.). (2008). *Managing Global Innovation: Uncovering the Secrets of Future Competitiveness.* Heidelberg: Springer-Verlag.

Brenner, T., Cantner, U. & Graf, H. (2013). Introduction: structure and dynamics of innovation networks. *Regional Studies*, 47(5), 647–650.

Bryson, J. R. & Daniels, P. W. (Eds.). (2007). *The Handbook of Service Industries.* Cheltenham and Northampton, MA: Edward Elgar.

Bryson, J. R., Daniels, P. W. & Warf, B. (2004). *Service Worlds: People, Organizations, Technologies.* London and New York: Routledge.

Bunnell, T. G. & Coe, N. M. (2001). Spaces and scales of innovation. *Progress in Human Geography*, 25(4), 569–589.

Cainelli, G. & Iacobucci, D. (2012). Agglomeration, related variety, and vertical integration. *Economic Geography*, 88(3), 255–277.

Cantwell, J. & Piscitello, L. (2005). Recent location of foreign-owned research and development activities by large multinational corporations in the European regions: the role of spillovers and externalities. *Regional Studies*, 39(1), 1–16.

Castells, M. (2000). *The Rise of the Network Society: The Information Age: Economy, Society and Culture* (2nd edn). Oxford and Malden, MA: Blackwell.

Chesbrough, H. (2003). *Open Innovation: The New Imperative for Creating and Profiting from Technology.* Boston, MA: Harvard Business School Press.

Clark, G. L. (1981). The employment relation and the spatial division of labor: a hypothesis. *Annals of the Association of American Geographers*, 71(3), 412–424.

Clark, G. L. (1993). Costs and prices, competitive strategies and regions. *Environment and Planning A*, 25(1), 5–26.

Clark, G. L. & Wójcik, D. (2007). *The Geography of Finance: Corporate Governance in the Global Marketplace.* Oxford: Oxford University Press.

Clark, G. L., Feldman, M. P. & Gertler, M. S. (2000). *The Oxford Handbook of Economic Geography.* Oxford: Oxford University Press.

Coe, N. M., Hess, M., Yeung, H. W.-C., Dicken, P. & Henderson, J. (2004). "Globalizing" regional development: a global production networks perspective. *Transactions of the Institute of British Geographers*, 29, 468–484.

Coe, N. M., Dicken, P. & Hess, M. (2008a). Global production networks: realizing the potential. *Journal of Economic Geography*, 8(3), 271–295.

Coe, N. M., Dicken, P. & Hess, M. (2008b). Global production networks: debates and challenges. *Journal of Economic Geography*, 8(3), 267–269.

Coe, N. M., Kelly, P. & Yeung, H. W.-C. (2007). *Economic Geography: A Contemporary Introduction*. Oxford, Malden, MA and Carlton, Victoria, Australia: Blackwell.

Crescenzi, R., Rodriguez-Pose, A. & Storper, M. (2007). The territorial dynamics of innovation: a Europe–United States comparative analysis. *Journal of Economic Geography*, 7(6), 673–709.

Crescenzi, R., Rodriguez-Pose, A. & Storper, M. (2012). The territorial dynamics of innovation in China and India. *Journal of Economic Geography*, 12(5), 1055–1086.

Cumbers, A., Nativel, C. & Routledge, P. (2008). Labour agency and union positionalities in global protection networks. *Journal of Economic Geography*, 8(3), 369–387.

Currid, E. & Williams, S. (2010). The geography of buzz: art, culture and the social milieu in Los Angeles and New York. *Journal of Economic Geography*, 10(3), 423–452.

Curtis, S. E. & Oven, K. J. (2012). Geographies of health and climate change. *Progress in Human Geography*, 36(5), 654–666.

Dawley, S. (2007). Fluctuating rounds of inward investment in peripheral regions: semiconductors in the North East of England. *Economic Geography*, 83(1), 51–73.

Dicken, P. (2004). Classics in human geography revisited. *Progress in Human Geography*, 28(4), 507–515.

Dicken, P. (2007). *Global Shift: Mapping the Changing Contours of the World Economy* (5th edn). New York: The Guilford Press.

Dicken, P. & Henderson, J. (2003). Making the connections: global production networks in Europe and East Asia. ESRC Research Project R000238535.

Dolan, C. & Humphrey, J. (2004). Changing governance patterns in the trade of fresh vegetables between Africa and the United Kingdom. *Environment and Planning A*, 36(3), 491–509.

Doryan, E. A. (1993). An institutional perspective of competitiveness and industrial restructuring policies in developing countries. *Journal of Economic Issues*, 27(2), 451–458.

Dunning, J. H. & Narula, R. (1995). The R&D activities of foreign firms in the United States. *International Studies of Management and Organization*, 25(1–2), 39–73.

Edgington, D. W. & Hayter, R. (2013). "Glocalization" and regional headquarters: Japanese electronics firms in the ASEAN region. *Annals of the Association of American Geographers*, 103(3), 647–668.

Erickson, R. (1976). The filtering down process: industrial location in a non-metropolitan area. *The Professional Geographer*, 28(3), 254–260.

Environmental Protection Agency. (2006). *This is Smart Growth*. Washington, DC: Office of Smart Growth (available at: www.smartgrowth.org/pdf/this_is_smart_growth.pdf).

Erkman, S. (1997). Industrial ecology: a historical view. *Journal of Cleaner Production*, 5(1–2), 1–10.

Faulconbridge, J. R. (2006). Stretching tacit knowledge beyond a local fix? Global spaces of learning in advertising professional service firms. *Journal of Economic Geography*, 6(4), 517–540.

Florida, R. (2002). *The Rise of the Creative Class*. New York: Basic Books.

Freeman, C. (1988). Japan: a new national innovation system?. In G. Dosi, C. Freeman, R. R. Nelson, G. Silverberg & L. Soete (Eds.), *Technological Change and Economy Theory* (pp. 330–348). London: Pinter.

Freeman, C. (1995). The "national systems of innovation" in historical perspective. *Cambridge Journal of Economics*, 19(1), 5–24.

Frenken, K., van Oort, F. G. & Verburg, T. (2007). Related variety, unrelated variety and regional economic growth. *Regional Studies*, 41(5), 685–697.

Frobel, F., Heinrichs, J. & Kreye, O. (1980). *The New International Division of Labor*. Cambridge: Cambridge University Press.

Fujita, M. & Krugman, P. (2004). The new economic geography: past, present and future. *Papers in Regional Science*, 83(1), 139–164.

Gereffi, G., Humphrey, J. & Sturgeon, T. (2005). The governance of global value chains. *Review of International Political Economy*, 12(1), 78–104.

Gertler, M. S. (2008). Buzz without being there? Communities of practice in context. In A. Amin & J. Roberts (Eds.), *Community, Economic Creativity and Organization* (pp. 203–226). Oxford: Oxford University Press.

Gertler, M. S. (2007). Tacit knowledge in production systems: how important in geography. In K. R. Polenske (Ed.), *The Economic Geography of Innovation* (pp. 87–111). Cambridge: Cambridge University Press.

Gertler, M. S. & Levitte, Y. M. (2005). Local nodes in global networks: the geography of knowledge flows in biotechnology innovation. *Industry and Innovation*, 12(4), 487–507.

Gray, M. & James, A. (2007). Theorizing the gendered institutional bases of innovative regional economies. In K. R. Polenske (Ed.), *The Economic Geography of Innovation* (pp. 129–156). Cambridge: Cambridge University Press.

Hägerstrand, T. (1953). On Monte Carlo simulations of diffusion. In W. L. Garrison & D. F. Marble (Eds.), *Quantitative Geography, Part I: Economic and Cultural Topics*. Evanston: Northwestern University, Northwestern Studies in Geography, No. 13.

Hayter, R. (1997). *The Dynamics of Industrial Location*. Chichester, New York, Weinheim, Brisbane, Singapore and Toronto: Wiley.

Henderson, J., Dicken, P., Hess, M., Coe, N. M. & Yeung, H. W.-C. (2002). Global production networks and the analysis of economic development. *Review of International Political Economy*, 9(3), 436–464.

Hess, M. (2004). Spatial relationships? Towards a reconceptualization of embeddedness. *Progress in Human Geography*, 28(2), 165–186.

Howells, J. & Bessant, J. (2012). Introduction: innovation and economic geography: a review and analysis. *Journal of Economic Geography*, 12(5), 929–942.

Huber, F. (2012). Do clusters really matter for innovation practices in Information Technology? Questioning the significance of technological knowledge spillovers. *Journal of Economic Geography*, 12(1), 107–126.

Hudson, R. (1995). Toward sustainable industrial production: but in what sense sustainable? In M. Taylor (Ed.), *Environmental Change: Industry, Power and Policy* (pp. 37–56). Avebury: Aldershot.

Hudson, R. (2004). Conceptualizing economies and their geographies: spaces, flows and circuits. *Progress in Human Geography*, 28(4), 447–471.

Jacobs, J. (1969). *The Economy of Cities*. New York: Random House.

Jaffe, A. B., Trajtenberg, M. & Henderson, R. (1993). Geographic localization of knowledge spillovers as evidenced by patent citations. *The Quarterly Journal of Economics*, 108(3), 577–598.

Kaldor, M. (2003). The idea of global civil society. *International Affairs*, 79(3), 583–593.

Karlsson, C. (Ed.). (2008). *The Handbook of Research on Cluster Theory*. Cheltenham: Edward Elgar.

Knox-Hayes, J. (2009). The developing carbon financial service industry: expertise, adaptation and complementarity in London and New York. *Journal of Economic Geography*, 9(6), 749–777.

Koo, Y. & Park, S. O. (2012). Structural and spatial characteristics of personal actor networks: the case of industries for the elderly in Korea. *Papers in Regional Science*, 91(1), 43–65.

Kramer, J.-P. & Revilla Diez, J. (2012). Catching the local buzz by embedding? Empirical insights on the regional embeddedness of multinational enterprises in Germany and the UK. *Regional Studies*, 46(10), 1303–1317.

Krueger, R. & Gibbs, D. (2008). "Third wave" sustainability? Smart growth and regional development in the USA. *Regional Studies*, 42(9), 1263–1274.

Krugman, P. (1991). *Geography and Trade*. Cambridge, MA: MIT Press.

Krugman, P. & Venables, A. (1995). Globalisation and the inequality of nations. *Quarterly Journal of Economics*, 110(4), 857–880.

Lee, N. & Rodriguez-Pose, A. (2013). Innovation and spatial inequality in Europe and USA. *Journal of Economic Geography*, 13(1), 1–22.

Liu, W. & Dicken, P. (2006). Transnational corporations and "obligated embeddedness": foreign direct investment in China's automobile industry. *Environment and Planning A*, 38(7), 1229–1247.

Lundvall, B. & Maskell, P. (2000). Nation states and economic development: from national systems of production to national systems of knowledge creation and learning. In G. L. Clark, M. P. Feldman & M. S. Gertler (Eds.), *The Oxford Handbook of Economic Geography* (pp. 353–372). Oxford: Oxford University Press.

Lundvall, B., Johnson, B., Anderson, E. S. & Dalum, B. (2007). National systems of production, innovation, and competence building, In K. R. Polenske (Ed.), *The Economic Geography of Innovation* (pp. 213–240). Cambridge: Cambridge University Press.

Mansvelt, J. (2012). Consumption, ageing and identity: New Zealander's narratives of gifting, ridding and passing on. *New Zealand Geographer*, 68(3), 187–200.

Markusen, A. (1996). Sticky places in slippery space: a typology of industrial districts. *Economic Geography*, 72(3), 293–313.

Marshall, A. (1890). *The Principles of Economics*. London: Macmillan.

Marshall, A. (1920). *The Principles of Economics* (8th edn). London: Macmillan.

Martin, R. (2010). The Roepke lecture in economic geography—rethinking regional path dependence: beyond lock-in to evolution. *Economic Geography*, 86(1), 1–27.

Martin, R. & Sunley, P. (2006). Path dependence and regional economic evolution. *Journal of Economic Geography*, 6(4), 395–437.

Martin, R. & Sunley, P. (2011). Conceptualizing cluster evolution: beyond the life cycle model?. *Regional Studies*, 45(10), 1299–1318.

Maskell, P. & Malmberg, A. (1999). Localized learning and industrial competitiveness. *Cambridge Journal of Economics*, 23(2), 167–185.

Maskell, P. & Malmberg, A. (2007). Myopia, knowledge development and cluster evolution. *Journal of Economic Geography*, 7(5), 603–618.

Maskell, P., Bathelt, H. & Malmberg, A. (2006). Building global knowledge pipelines: the role of temporary clusters. *European Planning Studies*, 14(8), 997–1013.

Massey, D. (1984). *Spatial Divisions of Labor: Social Structures and the Geography of Production*. New York: Methuen.

Massey, D. (1995). *Spatial Divisions of Labour* (2nd edn). London: Macmillan.

Menzel, M. & Fornahl, D. (2010). Cluster life cycles: dimensions and rationales of cluster evolution. *Industrial and Corporate Change*, 19(1), 205–238.

Morrison, A. (2008). Gatekeepers of knowledge within industrial districts: who they are, how they interact. *Regional Studies*, 42(6), 817–835.

Murphy, J. T. (2012). Global production networks, relational proximity, and the sociospatial dynamics of market internationalization in Bolivia's wood products sector. *Annals of the Association of American Geographers*, 102(1), 208–233.

Nadvi, K. (2008). Global standards, global governance and the organization of global value chains. *Journal of Economic Geography*, 8(3), 323–343.

O'Brien, K. (2012). Global environmental change II: from adaptation to deliberate transformation. *Progress in Human Geography*, 36(5), 667–676.

Organisation for Economic Co-operation and Development (OECD) (1999). *Managing National Innovation Systems*. Paris: OECD.

Owen-Smith, J. & Powell, W. W. (2002). Standing on shifting terrain. *Science Studies*, 15(1), 3–28.

Owen-Smith, J. & Powell, W. W. (2004). Knowledge networks as channels and conduits: the effects of spillovers in the Boston biotechnology community. *Organization Science*, 15 (1), 5–21.

Park, S. O. (1993). Industrial restructuring and the spatial division of labor: the case of the Seoul metropolitan region, the republic of Korea. *Environment and Planning A*, 25(1), 81–93.

Park, S. O. (1995). Seoul, Korea: city and suburbs. In G. L. Clark & W. B. Kim (Eds.), *Asian NIEs & the Global Economy, Industrial Restructuring & Corporate Strategy in the 1990s* (pp. 143–167). Baltimore, MD and London: The Johns Hopkins University Press.

Park, S. O. (1996). Network and embeddedness in the dynamic types of new industrial districts. *Progress in Human Geography*, 20(4), 476–493.

Park, S. O. (2002). Paths of sustainable industrialization in the knowledge-based economy. In R. Hayter & R. Le Heron (Eds.), *Knowledge, Industry and Environment* (pp. 31–48). Aldershot: Ashgate.

Park, S. O. (2003). Economic spaces in the Pacific Rim: a paradigm shift and new dynamics. *Papers in Regional Science*, 82(2), 223–247.

Park, S. O. (2004). The impact of business to business electronic commerce on the dynamics of metropolitan spaces. *Urban Geography*, 25(4), 289–314.

Park, S. O. (2005). Network, embeddedness, and cluster processes of new economic spaces in Korea. In R. Le Heron & J. W. Harrington (Eds.), *New Economic Spaces: New Economic Geographies* (pp. 6–14). Aldershot: Ashgate.

Park, S. O. (2008). A history of Korea's industrial structural transformation and spatial development. Paper presented at the World Bank Workshop, Tokyo, March 29. (Published in 2009 *World Bank Report*. Washington, DC: World Bank Publications.)

Park, S. O. & Koo, Y. (2010). Evolution of new spatial division of labor and spatial dynamics in Korea. *Regional Science Policy & Practice*, 2(1), 21–38.

Park, S. O. & Wheeler, J. O. (1983). The filtering down process in Georgia: the third stage in the product life cycle. *The Professional Geographer*, 35(1), 18–31.

Polenske, K. R. (Ed.). (2007). *The Economic Geography of Innovation*. Cambridge: Cambridge University Press.

Porter, M. E. (1990). *The Competitive Advantage of Nations*. New York: The Free Press.

Porter, M. E. (1998). Clusters and the new economics of competition. *Harvard Business Review*, 76(6), 77–90.

Potter, A. & Watts, H. D. (2011). Evolutionary agglomeration theory: increasing returns, diminishing returns, and industry life cycle. *Journal of Economic Geography*, 11(3), 417–456.

Press, K. (2006). *A Life-Cycle for Clusters? The Dynamics of Agglomeration, Change and Adaptation*. Heidelberg: Physica-Verlag.

Rees, J. (1979). Technological change and regional shifts in American manufacturing. *The Professional Geographer*, 31(1), 45–54.

Regional Studies. (2008). Special issue: Clusters in the global knowledge-based economy: knowledge gatekeepers and temporary proximity. *Regional Studies*, 42(6), 767–904.

Revilla Diez, J. & Berger, M. (2005). The role of multinational corporations in metropolitan innovation systems: empirical evidence from Europe and Southeast Asia. *Environment and Planning A*, 3, 1813–1835.

Rifkin, J. (2011). *The Third Industrial Revolution: How Lateral Power is Transforming Energy, the Economy, and the World*. New York: Palgrave Macmillan.

Rinallo, D. & Golfetto, F. (2011). Exploring the knowledge strategies of temporary cluster organizers: a longitudinal study on the EU fabric industry trade shows (1986–2006). *Economic Geography*, 87(4), 453–476.

Rychen, F. & Zimmermann, J. B. (2008). Clusters in the global knowledge-based economy: knowledge gatekeepers and temporary proximity. *Regional Studies*, 42(6), 767–776.

Saxenian, A. (1996). *Regional Advantage: Culture and Competition in Silicon Valley and Route 128* (2nd edn). Cambridge, MA: Harvard University Press.

Saxenian, A. (2006). *The New Argonauts: Regional Advantage in a Global Economy*. Cambridge, MA: Harvard University Press.

Schmidheiny, S. & Zorraquin, F. J. L. (1996). *Financing Change: The Financial Community, Eco-efficiency, and Sustainable Development*. Cambridge, MA: MIT Press.

Silvey, R. (2012). Gender, difference, and contestation: economic geography through the lens of transnational migration. In T. J. Barnes, J. Peck & E. Sheppard (Eds.), *The Wiley-Blackwell Companion to Economic Geography* (pp. 420–430). Chichester: John Wiley.

Smith, A., Rainni, A., Dunford, M., Hardy, J., Hudson, R. & Sadler, D. (2002). Networks of value, commodities and regions: reworking division of labor in macro regional economies. *Progress in Human Geography*, 26(1), 41–64.

Storper, M. & Salais, R. (1997). *Worlds of Production: The Action Frameworks of the Economy*. Cambridge, MA: Harvard University Press.

Storper, M. & Venables, A. J. (2004). Buzz: face to face contact and the urban economy. *Journal of Economic Geography*, 4(4), 351–370.

Sunley, P. (2008). Relational economic geography: a partial understanding or a new paradigm?. *Economic Geography*, 84(1), 1–26.

Teirlinck, P. & Spithoven, A. (2008). The spatial organization of innovation: open innovation, external knowledge relations and urban structure. *Regional Studies*, 42(5), 689–704.

Ter Wal, A. L. J. (2013). The dynamics of the inventor network in German biotechnology: geographic proximity versus triadic closure. *Journal of Economic Geography*, 13, 1–32.

Tether, B., Li, Q. C. & Mina, A. (2012). Knowledge-bases, places, spatial configurations and the performance of knowledge-intensive professional service firms. *Journal of Economic Geography*, 12(5), 969–1001.

Torre, A. (2008). On the role played by temporary geographical proximity in knowledge transmission. *Regional Studies*, 42(6), 869–889.

Torre, A. & Rallet, A. (2005). Proximity and localization. *Regional Studies*, 39(1), 47–59.

Trippl, M., Tödtling, F. & Lengauer, L. (2009). Knowledge sourcing beyond buzz and pipelines: evidence from the Vienna Software Cluster. *Economic Geography*, 85(4), 443–462.

Truffer, B. & Coenen, L. (2012). Environmental innovation and sustainability transitions in regional studies. *Regional Studies*, 46(1), 1–21.

United Nations Industrial Development Organization (UNIDO). (1996). *Industrial Development*. Oxford: Oxford University Press.

Vernon, R. (1966). International investment and international trade in the product cycle. *Quarterly Journal of Economics*, 80(2), 190–207.

Verspagen, B. & Schoenmakers, W. (2004). The spatial dimension of patenting by multinational firms in Europe. *Journal of Economic Geography*, 4(1), 23–42.

Von Hippel, E. (1988). *The Sources of Innovation*. Oxford: Oxford University Press.

Wallner, H. P. (1999). Towards sustainable development of industry: networking, complexity and eco-clusters. *Journal of Cleaner Production*, 7(1), 49–58.

Weber, A. (1929). *Theory of Location of Industries (Über den Standort der Industrien (1909))* (C. J. Friedrich, trans.). Chicago: University of Chicago Press.

Wheeler, J. O. (1986). Corporate spatial links with financial institutions: the role of the metropolitan hierarchy. *Annals of the Association of American Geographers*, 76(2), 262–274.

World Bank. (2008). *World Development Report 2008: Agriculture for Development*. Washington, DC: World Bank Publications.

Yeh, A. G. O. (2005). Producer services and industrial linkages in the Hong Kong–Pearl River Delta region. In P. W. Daniels, K. C. Ho & T. A. Hutton (Eds.), *Service Industries and Asia-Pacific Cities: New Development Trajectories* (pp. 150–172). London and New York: Routledge.

Yeung, H. W.-C. (2005). Rethinking relational economic geography. *Transactions of the Institute of British Geographers*, 30(1), 37–51.

Zhang, W., Vertinsky, I., Ursacki, T. & Nemetz, P. (1999). Can China be a clean tiger? Growth strategies and environmental realities. *Pacific Affairs*, 72(1), 23–33.

Zook, M. A. (2005). *The Geography of the Internet Industry*. Oxford: Blackwell Publishing.

3 Integral model of service innovation

Introduction

Traditional innovation studies mainly focus on innovation processes in manufacturing industries, whereas those in service industries have been relatively neglected (Howells, 2007). Innovation theory was mostly developed based on the analysis of technological innovations in manufacturing industries before the twenty-first century (Gallouj and Weinstein, 1997). However, innovations in service industries in recent years have become increasingly important because services significantly contribute to the national economic growth and comprise a large proportion of the gross national product in advanced economies. In a knowledge-based information society, innovation processes for services and manufacturing are difficult to differentiate because innovation emerges from the close interaction between the two industries (Bryson and Daniels, 2007; Daniels and Bryson, 2002; Miles, 2007; Howells, 2010).

The integral model of innovation, which combines manufacturing and services, has been emphasized by several scholars since the beginning of the twenty-first century, such as Daniels and Bryson (2002), Howells (2004, 2007), Illeris (2007), and Baltacioglu et al. (2007), with increasing importance on service innovation at the national and regional economic levels, and on their integral characteristics. However, the development of an integral model is not an easy task for three reasons. First, new service products and processes are naturally unclear and intangible, which result in the difficulty of measuring their effect on productivity and on the economy. Second, service sectors display significant differences in their pattern of innovation behavior within and among sectors (Tether, 2003). Third, services and manufacturing are difficult to differentiate in terms of the products and processes involved in implementing firm activities. The majority of innovations have been dependent on the combination of material and nonmaterial innovations since the late 1990s (Miles, 2007).

With the increasing dominant role of services in the global economy, along with the progress of a knowledge-based information society, globalization, and the integrative aspects of service and manufacturing industries, the development of an integral model of service innovation is necessary to understand the dynamics of economic spaces and changes in the global economy. This study aims to develop an integral model of innovation for service industries and to examine their specific cases. This research is considered as a preliminary study with the initial development of a conceptual integral model of innovation. A specific case study is performed on Leaders Dermatology Clinic, which is composed of a network of dermatology clinics. Leaders Dermatology Clinic was chosen for several reasons. First, medical services in Korea have significantly increased and expanded internationally in recent years, which suggests that a clinic is an appropriate example for understanding dynamic changes in space. Second, dermatology clinics are presently one of the leading medical services in service innovation with technological advancements in terms of equipment and treatments. Third, dermatological clinics are among the leading medical services with growing international networks, particularly in East Asian countries. Last, Leaders Dermatology Clinic exhibits a good example of organizational and service product innovations in terms of managing services and cooperation.

A conceptual integral model of service innovation is developed and described in the succeeding section of this chapter. The third section analyzes the case of Leaders Dermatology Clinic based on information gathered from in-depth interviews and on the geography of services in terms of the spatial distribution of customers in each branch of the service network. The spatial evolution of services and the differences with new services are also examined. A conclusion is drawn in the last section on whether the conceptual integral model is appropriate for the case of service industries.

Service innovation: a conceptual integral model of innovation

Major characteristics of services and service innovation

To develop a model of service innovation, we must first understand the meaning of services. In the traditional definition, services are completely distinguished from goods because services are activities that do not produce or permanently modify material goods. This traditional definition is not scientific. A more rigorous and academic definition was formulated by Hill (1977), which states that:

> a service may be defined as a change in the condition of a person, or of a good belonging to some economic unit, which is brought about as the result of the activity on some other economic unit, with the prior agreement of the former person or economic unit.
>
> (p. 308)

Hill's definition was widely accepted before the beginning of the twenty-first century, and consequently influenced the United Nations 1993 System of

National Account, wherein the criterion of immateriality was abandoned (Illeris, 2007). By the beginning of the twenty-first century, Hill's definition was reconsidered by several authors such as Gadrey (2000) and de Brandt and Dibiaggio (2002). Gadrey argued that Hill's definition referred only to the process and not the output, and emphasized the narrowness of Hill's central element on "the change of condition" because numerous services do not provide such effects. Gadrey (2000) alternatively defined the production of services as follows:

> when an organization A which owns or controls a technical or human capacity sells (or offers without payment in the case of non-market services) to an economic agent B the right to use that capacity for a certain period in order to produce useful effects on an agent C or on goods that he owns or for which he is responsible.
>
> (p. 384)

The definitions of Hill and Gadrey were examined and supported by scientific arguments. However, both definitions are complex and difficult to use, and neglect important groups of services that serve society as a whole, such as pure public services (Illeris, 1997). The complexity and specific exclusion of services in the definition facilitate the understanding of the characteristics of services and the development of a conceptual model of service innovation compared with a rigid definition.

Illeris (2007, pp. 25–26) identified six major characteristics of services. First, services are difficult to distinguish despite the possibility of distinguishing the effects, which reveals the inadequacy of measuring the product itself and the difficulty of applying the basic concept of gross domestic product and productivity. Second, numerous services connect producers and users, which suggests that producers and users must be present at the same place and time with face-to-face interaction; hence, the necessity of proximity. Third, service activities are often labor-intensive with limited possibilities for scale economies, standardization, and increases in productivity. The quality of services depends on the professional and social qualifications of personnel, which suggests the absolute absence of identical services. Fourth, the uniqueness of a service is dependent on the characteristic of co-production, which suggests that the service provider and the user engage in the relationship under a state of uncertainty. Therefore, both parties require mutual trust to reduce the uncertainty. Fifth, the effect of a service is often irreversible. Last, services have relatively high-income elasticity because the final consumption of services does not satisfy the majority of basic human needs.

The six characteristics of services mentioned by Illeris can be applied to medical services. However, medical services have a diverse degree of sophistication, and a number of these services only possess a few of the aforementioned characteristics. These characteristics have been summarized into the following major characteristics to facilitate its application in the model of service innovation: (1) "intangibility," which is related to the first and third characteristics, (2) "co-production" and "interactivity" between the service provider and the users, which are related to the second and fourth characteristics, and (3) "irreversibility" of the effect of services, which is related to the characteristic of difficulty in storing. "Relatively high income elasticity" is applicable only to high-quality services, and is not a major characteristic applicable to all services.

The three summarized characteristics are important in understanding service innovation. "Intangibility" indicates that the quality of services is diverse among similar types of services, and quality can be continuously improved through service innovation by accumulating knowledge and developing technology. A hierarchy of services exists from low to high levels in terms of quality and sophistication of services. These characteristics allow numerous possibilities for service innovation to move toward higher service quality.

"Co-production and interactivity" represent service innovations as a result of various networks involving diverse economic actors in addition to the relationship between producers and customers/client/users. Service will not be created without co-production or the interactive quality of service production. Service providers should improve the quality of service to satisfy the demand of users, which requires constant networking with providers of information, knowledge, technology, equipment, and others. Aside from establishing a network with service providers, tangible and intangible networks with competitors, community members, government officials, and others, in addition to that of customers, are important (see Figure 6.1). In the process of co-production, a number of service providers, such as in finance, consultancy, training, the government, and manufacturing producers of equipment or products, become connected by a network. Service providers tend to collaborate with competitors to reduce uncertainties.

In the "irreversibility" of service effect, service providers, such as those in medical services, continuously test and demonstrate new services to avoid problems and reduce uncertainties. Demonstrations and tests are important to anticipate problems, and to improve services and service innovation. Service providers can enhance the capacity and quality of services during the demonstration and testing of new services by observing the effects of learning. Considering the characteristics of services, service producers successfully develop new services over time and service innovation becomes more important.

The characteristics of intangibility and complex networking contribute to the difficulty in defining service innovation. Several definitions have been suggested after the first discussion on the concept of service innovation by Miles (1993). Howells (2007, p. 36) considered a basic typology of service and innovation based on a 2 × 2 matrix (technological and nontechnological dimension vs. manufacturing and service dimension) and identified service innovation as "disembodied, non-tangible innovations." In actual situations, however, innovations rarely reside entirely in a cell with a 2 × 2 matrix, and instead combine with others to reveal the complexity of the concept. The definition of Tekes, a Finnish funding agency for technology and innovation, is helpful in practical situations. They regard service innovation as a new or significantly improved service concept that is taken into practice. For example, it can be a new customer interaction channel, a new solution in the customer interface, a new distribution method or a distribution system, novel application of technology in the service process, new forms of operation with the supply chain, or new ways to organize and manage services (Tekes, www.tekes.fi/eng/).

This definition introduces three types of service innovation—namely, service products, service processes, and organizational and managerial structures. Miles (2007) emphasized in his studies that service innovation "will have to take on board the issue of organizational and market innovation, inter-organizational and client-facing innovation, and even aesthetic and cultural innovation" (p. 451). Accordingly, the three types of service innovation are not suitable in actual situations. Furthermore, product and process are difficult to distinguish because of the characteristics of intangibility and co-production. For example, a service delivery process in medical services can be regarded as a service product. We can also classify service innovation based on the level of innovation—namely, world-first, country-first, and market-first innovations (Riddle, 2008). World-first innovations are truly unique innovations. Country-first innovations are newly adapting world-first innovations in a new economic context. Market-first innovations are adapting country-first innovations in new geographical areas within the economy (Riddle, 2008). This classification scheme can be also applied to manufacturing products.

Integral model of service innovation

Innovation processes are examined in this section to develop an integral model of service innovation by considering the characteristics of service and service innovation. In the early 2000s, several authors presented theoretical perspectives on innovation in services (Gallouj, 2002; Bryson and Monnoyer, 2004; Tether, 2003). Howells (2007) provided conceptual and theoretical contributions by introducing three broad approaches to innovation studies—namely, "technologists," "service-oriented," and "integrative" approaches.

Gallouj summarizes the three approaches mentioned in literature as follows (2002, p. 1):

- A *technologist* approach equates with or reduces innovation in services to the introduction of technical systems (material transport, processing systems, and above all, information and communication systems) into service firms and organizations.
- A *service-oriented* approach seeks to identify any possible particu-larities in the organizational nature of innovation in services.

- An *integrative* approach considers a starting point in launching a trend toward convergence and in making the boundaries between goods and services indistinguishable, while favoring a similar analytical approach to innovation in both.

Tether (2003) also identified three similar basic approaches with different terminologies—namely, the "traditional view" of services, the "Lille School," and an emerging and less-defined view focused on "strategic positioning" (pp. 482–484), as summarized in Table 3.1.

Studies that adopt the "technologist" approach of innovation in services, which is comparable to Tether's traditional view, focus on introducing artifacts and hardware-driven technologies and systems to service firms. Tether identified the traditional view, which emphasized the supplier-dominated perspective, as adopting "externally developed technologies that facilitate new service provision and/or enhance service productivity" (Tether, 2003, p. 482).

In contrast to the "technologist" approach, the "service-oriented" approach handles "the peculiarities of service innovation and how this might lead to new conceptualizations of innovation processes in relation to service activity" (Howells, 2007, p. 38). This approach attempts to divert from the mere adoption of manufacturing or technology-centered innovation models and rejects the previous traditionalist view, which identified services as dependent, supplier-dependent, and noninnovative sectors. The French Lille School also moves away from the supplier and technologist-dominated models and is similar to the service-oriented approach. The Lille School was first characterized as a client-oriented service innovation and co-production of services. However, Tether (2003) highlights a variety of services in his empirical study, including standardized and low-technology service, and more in-house and independent basis of innovation in services.

The "integrative" approach develops an integrated theory to examine service innovation in the context of convergence of goods and services in their production and consumption in the economy (Howells, 2007). The integrative approach is similar to the strategic positioning approach of Tether (Gallouj, 2002; Tether, 2003). Both approaches emphasize close links between manufacturing and services in provision, consumption, and strategy formulation. Considering the close interconnection between goods and services, and the increasing indistinguishability between the boundaries of manufacturing and service firms, Gallouj (2002) reconciles goods and services under a single innovation theory. Gallouj and Tether stressed the combinational aspect of manufacturing and services, and hard and soft technologies; although the integrative approach focuses more on the innovation process itself, the strategic positioning approach views innovation within the wider realm of strategy and competitive positioning of a firm (Howells, 2007). Tether's comparison of the three approaches clarifies their progress and the evolutionary process of change occurring in studies on service activities, as shown in Table 3.1.

Table 3.1 Tether's three perspectives on innovation and technology in services

	Traditional, technology dependence	'Lille school's' interactive view	Strategic positioning (competition as a process)
Summary of conceptualization	Innovation essentially dependent on the adoption of externally developed 'hardware' technologies.	Strong emphasis on interaction, especially with users. Innovations tend to be jointly or co-produced, especially with users.	Positioning and innovation through creative combinations of 'hard' and 'soft' technologies. Self-determination of outputs and methods of provision
Source of innovation	Mainly developed by others (i.e. suppliers).	Developed jointly with others (i.e. customers).	Mainly developed internally.
R&D	Rare—not usually necessary for adoption of standard technologies.	May be undertaken, but not necessarily. (Often, R&D type activities are undertaken, but not recognized as such).	May be undertaken, but not necessarily. When undertaken, reinforces internal creativity.
Nature of expenditures for innovation	Dominated by the acquisition of externally developed technologies.	Mixed—includes internal activities and technological acquisitions.	Mixed—includes internal activities and technological acquisitions.
Collaborations for innovation	Rare, but most commonly with suppliers.	Common, especially with customers.	As needs be. Not necessarily confined to customers or suppliers.
Sources of information (ideas) for innovation	Principally suppliers, but also competitors (copying) and trade fairs.	Mainly customers (in combination with internal sources).	Mainly internal, but also customers and competitors.
Aims of innovation	Primarily cost reduction. Some scope for extending service (time and space) availability.	Principally oriented to quality and satisfying customers' requirements.	Wide variety. Reflects wide variety of strategic positions. (e.g. both cost saving and market expansion).

Source: Adapted from Tether, 2003, p. 486.

Tether's emphasis on evolutionary aspects and Gallouj's identification of the natural life-cycle in the theoretical development of service innovation suggest that the three approaches comprise a three-stage framework in the theoretical development of service innovation. However, the three aspects cannot be completely separated in practical service activities because they can exist in practice with a variety of service activities, from low level to advanced knowledge/technology requirements, as well as from relatively standardized to more complex and creative services.

The first and second views in both frameworks (Gallouj's and Tether's) are relatively clear in terms of the evolutionary aspects of research in services. However, the third approach, either "integrative" or "strategic positioning," remains emergent and not well defined (Howells, 2007). This study develops an integral model of innovation within a wider context, which may be regarded as an extension of the approaches of Gallouj (2002) and Tether (2003). The most important premise in the development of the integral model is the fact that innovation in services has not been limited in the service sector in recent years, but has extended to affect and connect all sectors of the economy and of society.

Using Tether's perspectives in Table 3.1, the key aspects of the integral model of service innovation in this study, which is different from the third approach on strategic positioning of Tether (2003), are identified in Table 3.2. The integral model of service innovation is illustrated in Figure 3.1. Eight propositions of the integral model are identified in Figure 3.1, which are described in the succeeding paragraphs.

Table 3.2 Key aspects of the integrative model of service innovation

Source of innovation	*Diverse from internally and jointly with customers and suppliers*
R&D	Undertaken, but not all the service firms.
Nature of expenditure for innovation	Mixed: includes internal activities and technological acquisitions.
Collaborations for innovation	Used to collaborate with diverse economic actors.
Information sources for innovation	Diverse sources from internally and externally.
Aims of innovation	Wide variety of strategic positions (e.g. quality, time/cost saving, safety, market expansion).
Summary of conceptualization	Innovation through networks of diverse actors, beyond customer and supplier. Creative combination of soft and hard technologies. Evolving chains of innovation over time and innovation systems in space.

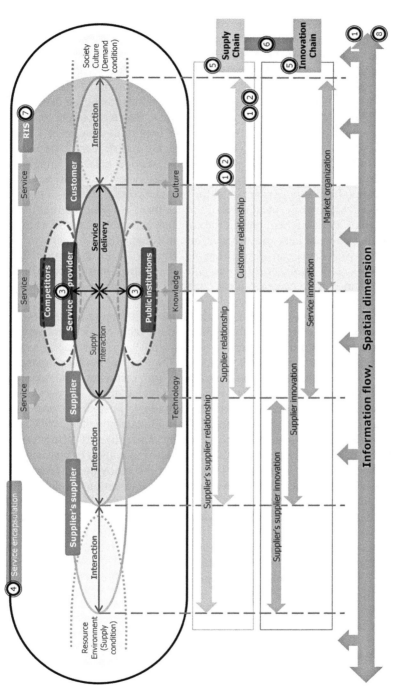

Figure 3.1 Integrative model of service innovation

Note: eight propositions: 1 Sources of information; 2 Collaboration with customers and suppliers; 3 Collaboration with competitions and public institutions; 4 Service encapsulation; 5 Innovation chain; 6 Path-dependent evolution; 7 Regional innovation system; 8 Spatial dimension.

First, the sources of information for innovation are diverse beyond internal sources. Networks with customers, suppliers, competitors, and public institutions, including universities and governments, are important sources for innovation (see Figure 6.1). Networks also extend spatially from local to national and international areas, along with the growth of a service firm. Networks are mainly intangible, and accumulating intangible assets is a critical factor in the innovation of services, such as those in manufacturing firms (Park, 2014). Unlike in the Lille School's interactive view, which considers customers as major sources of information, suppliers are important sources in Tether's traditional view (Gallouj, 2002; Tether, 2003). By contrast, our model is not one-sided. Suppliers tend to be dependent on service firms to improve or develop products. When service firms aim to develop new products, new ideas and innovation from suppliers are ideal for service firms to develop or improve their services. Meanwhile, customers of service firms are good sources of new information or ideas that will benefit the strategic activities of the service firm in generating new markets and services, and in enhancing the quality of their services. Service firms can also gather information from competitor firms. Collaborating with public institutions and universities, and participating in trade fairs and conferences are ideal channels in acquiring information for innovation in service firms.

Second, service firms continuously collaborate with suppliers and customers for innovation. Collaboration with suppliers in the technologist approach and with customers in the service-oriented approach has been regarded as a major networking factor for service innovation. In the integral model proposed in this study, collaborations are continuous with both customers and suppliers, which are critical actors for innovation in service firms. Networks and collaboration among suppliers, service providers, customers, and other economic actors form the service supply chain (Baltacioglu et al., 2007). The innovations of suppliers in the service supply chain directly affect service products or service delivery systems and stimulate innovation in service firms, whereas the innovation in service firms affects the innovation of suppliers, which reveals the two-way interactive network of innovation. Collaborations with customers are also critical for innovation in service firms in terms of testing or demonstrating innovative services and for participating in innovation activities, which suggest a continuous two-way interaction between service firms and customers. This approach is important in the practice of innovation. As Howells (2004) emphasized, consumption is not a one-time interaction when a product is being sold, but a continuing process involving a long-term relationship with customers through service delivery. In the process of consumption and continuous interaction with customers, customers seek novelty, which, in turn, creates incentives for innovation in service firms. Customers of service firms can also collaborate with suppliers of service firms for processes of innovation on the supplier side.

Third, collaborations with competitors and public institutions are important for service innovation. Collaboration in the strategic positioning approach is not confined to customers or suppliers. Collaborations with competitors and public institutions are emphasized in this study. Service firms can collaborate with public institutions and with competitors through strategic alliances. No eternal competitor or ally exists in service innovation. Firms may establish strategic alliances with competitors for joint innovation activities, joint development and sharing of patents, joint marketing, and others. These strategic collaborations help promote innovation in service firms. A clear boundary between allies and competitors does not exist in this aspect. Service firms collaborate with universities, research centers, local and national governments, and other public institutions for innovation. This collaboration is not just intended for information sharing, but also for parallel innovative activities. Vertical interactions, as illustrated in Figure 3.1, are more important than ever in service innovation. These propositions can be more prominent with the progress of Bathelt and Glückler's (2011) relational perspective in the knowledge-based economy.

Fourth, service encapsulation is an important concept for service innovation with the increasing role of services in the economy. Howells (2004) applied the concept of encapsulation during the life cycle of a good or service. An increasing trend of "servicization" is observed because manufacturing is becoming more service-like, and numerous manufacturing firms such as IBM, Siemens, and Samsung, are gaining a higher share of their turnover from selling services. Howells (2004) termed this process as the "servicization" of the manufacturing industry, wherein goods are not directly offered to privileged consumers, but are rather provided in terms of various service attributes. Howells regarded manufactured goods as part of a package that includes service components and termed this aspect of the servicization phenomenon as "service encapsulation." Various services, such as maintenance and repair, monitoring and diagnostic services, retrofitting and updating, obtaining related support activities and consultancies, purchasing finance and leasing facilities, and repurchasing, disposal, and recycling during the life cycle of a product, may be sold with a manufactured product during its lifetime (Howells, 2004). The concept of service encapsulation is associated with the interdependencies that exist among different sectors. Bryson and Monnoyer (2004, p. 216) suggested that the encapsulation concept "can also be considered as the ways in which services encapsulate manufacturing products and vice versa, and in several cases, this process leads to innovation." Bryson and Monnoyer (2004) also identified four types of encapsulation process. Each type represents a different manner, wherein innovation occurs in the production process. The four types of encapsulation process are encapsulation from manufacturing to services, services to manufacturing, manufacturing to manufacturing, and services to services. Service encapsulation resulting from the continuous relationship with suppliers can transcend to a supplier relationship management for service firms, whereas continuous services from service firms to customers establish customer relationship management.

Fifth, an innovation chain can be developed in line with supplier and customer relationship management, and with continuous innovations in services and goods. Selling of goods or service products is not a one-time interaction, but a continuous process of service delivery through customer and supplier relationships. The concept of encapsulation in the context of customer and supplier relationships forms the supply chain for services and goods, and promotes continuous innovation of services. Suppliers of goods or services can promote the development of new goods or services to the key service firm through close interaction with the supplier's supplier, which results in a supplier's supplier relationship and in suppliers innovating new goods or services for key service firms based on the result of their interaction. Subsequently, new goods or services developed by suppliers can affect key service firms in developing new service products or delivery systems for their customers under a close supplier relationship. Key service firms can develop new products or processes of service to satisfy the demand of customers based on customer relationship. The concept of encapsulation is meaningful during the process of innovation. The key service provider can promote innovation through encapsulation by various services outside the firm and through manufacturing activities. Similarly, encapsulation by services or manufacturing activities may affect the innovation of the supplier. The series of innovation can be regarded as the innovation chain of goods and services. The formation of the innovation chain is not only connected to the original supplier side, but also to the final end user side, which results in a two-way effect. Trends in the innovation chain may cause the boundaries between services and manufacturing to become indistinguishable.

Sixth, service innovation is the result of a path-dependent evolution with respect to a broader context of social, economic, cultural, and natural environments. Several firms reveal path movement as a dynamic process that involves layering, converting, and recombining knowledge and technology, whereas other firms reveal that path movement toward a stable state reinforces selected technologies, which results in a lock-in to the existing structure and networks (Martin, 2010). If firms accumulate and move toward the path of dynamic process by layering, converting, and recombining knowledge and technology along the supply chain of services and goods, then they can continuously develop new services or goods, as discussed in Chapter 4 of this book. In this study, a supply chain of goods and services represents "the context in which goods, services and information flow from the earliest supplier to the end user" (Baltacioglu et al., 2007, p. 106). However, several firms are resistant to shock and continue to create and accumulate intangible assets during crises or severe competitions in the global economy, but other firms are not. The latter are forced to restructure their organization, thus resulting in stagnation or even decline (Park, 2011). Accordingly, the innovativeness of firms can be related to their resilience under economic or environmental crises. The level of economic development and local culture may also affect the innovativeness of firms, thus suggesting that service innovation should be considered in the broader context of a global environment.

Seventh, innovation systems should also be considered with regard to policy issues, along with the broader context of the environment. This study emphasizes that the interaction of firms with diverse economic actors serve as sources through which information and knowledge, as well as collaboration for innovation, are acquired. Close interactions with diverse actors, including customers and suppliers, can promote the innovativeness of firms. Such interactions and relationships are influenced by the current rules, regulations, and institutions of a country. For example, the level of innovation and technological development in a nation is closely related to national innovation systems. Similarly, the innovation potential of a region may depend on the establishment of regional innovation systems, which effectively link diverse actors for innovation (Asheim et al., 2011; Cooke, 2004). Most studies on regional or national innovation systems have focused on innovations related to manufacturing. However, developing a regional innovation system in the service industry will enhance the level of service innovation in the region. Service supply chain combined with supplier and customer relationship management within a region can enhance the innovation of services (Baltacioglu et al., 2007). Collaborations, service supply chains, and chains of innovation in a region are closely linked with regional innovation systems.

Finally, service activities and service innovations have spatial dimensions, which show that the function of services and service innovation are linked with the hierarchy of urban areas. According to central place theory, higher order services tend to be located at the higher order center of urban areas, whereas lower order services tend to be located anywhere, including at the lower order center of urban areas (Christaller, 1966). This theory implies that the services located in the core areas of the metropolis serve higher order services and cover broader market areas, and market areas can be differentiated based on their locations. Given that several services cannot cover more expansive areas, service firms will consider a branch location for enlarging market areas and internationalizations. Moreover, age and gender can also affect the market of services. This spatial aspect suggests that appropriate policies and spatial strategies for services are necessary for regional development and further growth.

A case study of networked dermatology clinics

Most studies on service innovation have investigated knowledge-intensive or producer services (Bryson and Daniels, 2007; Doloreux et al., 2010; Miles, 2007; Park, 2005). Research should consider the heterogeneity of services to understand the processes of innovation in the service industry. Hence, more studies must be conducted in other fields beyond knowledge-intensive or producer services. Dermatology clinics were selected as a case study among other medical services for three reasons. First, studies on service innovation on medical services are few (Bryson and Daniels, 2007; Goes and Park, 1997). We need to extend our understanding of service innovation beyond producer services. Second, considerable innovations in medical services have been reported in recent years as a result of the advancement in technology and the increasing demand for medical services because of the growth in per capita income and the increase in the population of older adults. Furthermore, we have witnessed considerable changes in the spatial organization, and other inter- and intra-organizational aspects of medical services. Third, among medical service firms, dermatology clinics have exhibited dynamic changes in terms of technology and organization as a result of the increasing interest in beauty and anti-aging products and services, particularly in Korea.

Leaders Dermatology Clinic was selected because it continually introduces new technology, equipment, services, and organizational networks. The case study focuses on the evolution of activities in medical services in terms of the market, and the organization of clinics, the development and innovation of new services, and examination of the integral model of innovation. Dermatology, particularly cosmetic dermatology, primarily deals with anti-aging and skin rejuvenation. Unlike cosmetic surgery, cosmetic dermatology focuses on minimally invasive procedures such as Botox(tm) treatments, dermal fillers, and collagen injections. Laser-assisted treatment is one of the major procedures employed to reduce signs of aging because of the significant number of product and process innovations in the field of laser application. These procedures include wrinkle removal, skin tightening, collagen regeneration, skin resurfacing, and treatment of pigmentation disorders (Korea Medical Hub, http://kmhglobal.com).

Leaders Dermatology Clinic was organized by dermatological specialists who graduated from the medical school of Seoul National University. Leaders Dermatology Clinic has set up a nationwide network, with branches in Apgujung, Star City, Dogok, Mokdong in Seoul, Bucheon City in Gyeonggi, and Daegu City, among others. Each branch operates the clinic independently in both legal and financial aspects, but collaborate closely with other branches in terms of research, information, knowledge, technology, and others. These branches seem legally independent, but functions as one organization in the development of new services products and processes. The innovation of business organization of dermatology clinics, which efficiently performs the networked organization beyond the service product and process innovations, represents organizational innovation. In early 2013, the 12 clinics of Leaders Dermatology Clinic around the country employ 20 dermatological specialists and 170 staff and administration members who provide specialized and distinctive treatment services. The representative CEO of Leaders Dermatology Clinic suggests that Leaders Dermatology Clinic is the largest cluster of dermatology specialists in Korea, including large general hospitals. Leaders Dermatology Clinic, which is equipped with state-of-the-art laser treatment devices, offers a variety of dermatological treatments, medical skin-care services, and other dermatological procedures such as lipid insertion, liposuction, and hair transplantation. Since 2005, Leaders Dermatology Clinic has been designated as an educational hospital by the Korean Dermatology Medical Association. In the field of lipid stem cell development, Leaders Dermatology Clinic continuously succeeds in numerous treatments, such as those for dermatological disorders and depilation. Furthermore, Leaders Dermatology Clinic engages in developing leading clinical papers by actively conducting research and publishing new studies.

The rapidly increasing service innovation trend in dermatology focuses on anti-aging, which shares almost 90 percent of the dermatology market. Since the early 1990s, anti-aging medical treatment has focused on reducing discomfort without undergoing surgery and ensuring safety in treatment procedures. In Asia, Korea leads the development of service products. The CEO of Leaders Dermatology Clinic and the CEO of Lutronic, a supplier of laser equipment, assert that the skin of Asians is the most difficult to treat. Thus, Korea assumed the role of being the test bed for new service products, particularly in the field of anti-aging.

Examining the propositions of the integral model of service innovation

In-depth interviews with the CEO of Leaders Dermatology Clinic have been conducted several times from January 2012 to February 2013 to understand the processes of service innovation and service activities. An in-depth interview was also conducted with the CEO of Lutronic, one of the major supplier firms of Leaders Dermatology Clinic. Based on these interviews, the propositions of service innovation suggested in the integral model are examined using the following criteria.

First, the internal network within Leaders Dermatology Clinic is the most important source of information for innovation. Branch heads of Leaders Dermatology Clinic attend monthly meetings, during which they exchange information on how to develop new services. Similarly, suppliers and clients can provide information for innovation. To introduce new services, customers are engaged in launching new services that are only available in Korea. Branch heads continuously participate in lectures, conferences, and workshops that will enrich their learning, and attend national and international meetings. Participating clinics can share information for improving services and developing new services during such instances. Each clinic branch harbors no self-interest and shares important pieces of information based on their trust of each other. The branch heads are alumni of the medical school of Seoul National University, and they believe that sharing information and knowledge is one of the most important factors of their success of dermatology services and innovation.

Second, the collaboration between suppliers and customers are critical for service innovation in Leaders Dermatology Clinic. The clinic maintains close relationship with its suppliers by participating in demonstration treatments and tests for new equipment. The Leaders Dermatology Clinic also participates in the development of new equipment and in upgrading existing equipment of their suppliers' manufacturers. Leaders Dermatology Clinic used to be the first in introducing the latest equipment in the dermatology clinic market, thus making it the leader in innovating service products and delivery. Leaders Dermatology Clinic is regarded as a key player in the global equipment market. Customer relationship management is of primary importance as Korea is the bridgehead in the global cosmetic market. Maintaining close relationships of the staff with existing customers and establishing service management networks is necessary. The close relationship management for existing customers is attributed to the characteristics of maintaining anti-aging treatment procedures, which has a three-month cycle program.

Third, collaboration with domestic competitors is not extensive, but Leaders Dermatology Clinic has formed strategic alliances with leading global anti-aging clinics such as Clinique La Prairie and Laclinic in Switzerland. Leaders Dermatology Clinic collaborates with major hospitals in Korea, such as Seoul National University Hospital, Samsung Hospital, and Asan Medical Center, which are the leading polyclinic hospitals in Korea. Leaders Dermatology Clinic emphasizes networking with world-class dermatologists by inviting them to conduct seminars and exchanging the latest clinical information. They also collaborate closely with universities by participating in special lectures and treatments. One of the special characteristics of Leaders Dermatology Clinic is its focus on network management with other branches. Branches develop new forms of service delivery and services by sharing clinical experiences through weekly medical team meetings and live demonstrations of treatment. Moreover, representative staff members from each branch conduct monthly meetings, wherein they discuss customer responses to services and develop databases for detailed analyses. With regard to the role of doctors and staff members, intra-organizational collaboration within the networked clinics is also important for service innovation.

Fourth, Leaders Dermatology Clinic provides various services such as information and communications technology, maintenance, repair, and updating, among others. The encapsulation of service to service is evident in the case of Leaders Dermatology Clinic. However, encapsulation is not strong enough for manufacturing to service based on the four types of encapsulation identified by Bryson and Monnoyer (2004). Service encapsulation can be recognized in Lutronic, a manufacturer of dermatology laser equipment. The president of Lutronic maintains global networks by meeting with world-renowned dermatologists, professors, and dermatology clinics. Lutronic has an extensive collaboration networks with dermatology clinics for developing new equipment.

Fifth, a two-way innovation chain can be recognized in the case of Leaders Dermatology Clinic by collaborating and forming networks with suppliers and customers. New product innovation on the part of the supplier, such as Lutronic, can directly influence new service delivery or service products. When developing new equipment, the supplier closely interacts with Leaders Dermatology Clinic through consultation, direct participation, and demonstration of treatment. In turn, Leaders Dermatology Clinic develops new ideas for service products through close interaction with customers and through internal meetings. These new service products can stimulate suppliers to consider developing new, safe, and efficient equipment. Therefore, innovations by suppliers can affect Leaders Dermatology Clinic in developing new services, whereas service innovations from Leaders Dermatology Clinic can motivate suppliers to develop new equipment that will deliver the new service more efficiently and safely. Evidently, a two-direction innovation chain exists in the case of Leaders Dermatology Clinic. Moreover, with regard to the process of the two-way effects for an innovation chain, Leaders Dermatology Clinic directly participates in the innovation of goods, such as cosmetic products. Leaders Dermatology Clinic invests in developing cosmetic products through Leaders Cosmetic Corporation. Leaders Cosmetic Corporation focuses on developing quality products because the brand name "Leaders" may affect Leaders Dermatology Clinic. The boundaries between manufacturing and services are becoming difficult to distinguish along the innovation chain.

Sixth, the process of service innovation in Leaders Dermatology Clinic tends to be evolutionary in nature. Founded in 2001 at Mia-dong in the northern part of Seoul, Leaders Dermatology Clinic has continuously accumulated knowledge in dermatology through continuous collaborations with customers, suppliers, and universities, and through internal cooperation. For the past twelve years, Leaders Dermatology Clinic has pioneered organizational innovation, which continuously expanded the market by establishing new branches from the northern part of Seoul to the southern part of the city, including the core of Seoul, to Gyeonggi Province, which included the capital region, Daegu, and Jeju for foreign customers. This finding suggests continuous progress of spatial evolution. Leaders Dermatology Clinic continuously develops new services and terminates services, which are not guaranteed safe and suitable for customers. New services are mostly new medical treatments from new equipment developed in relation to technological development. New services based on newly developed equipment increase the effectiveness and reduce the pain of customers. The terminated services were related to the integration of dermatology services or services that did not belong to dermatology services formerly conducted in the dermatology clinics. From 2006 to 2011, Leaders Dermatology Clinic terminated 41 services while introducing 109 services, which resulted from the processes of layering, converting, and recombining services during that period.

Seventh, most of the branches of Leaders Dermatology Clinic and its major suppliers are located in the capital region. The capital region has several advantages with regard to customer relationship management, supplier relationship management, and collaboration with universities. Numerous research and development institutes, leading medical centers, and huge nationwide hospitals are found in the capital region. Medical teams from Leaders Dermatology

Clinic have established networks with professionals from diverse research institutes and hospitals in the capital region, which resulted in the growing potential for innovation. The relatively better development of regional innovation systems in the capital region, with an extensive network of diverse economic actors, compared with other regions in Korea, is a significant factor in the continuous development of new services in Leaders Dermatology Clinic. However, detailed analysis is needed to determine the importance of a regional innovation system for service innovation at Leaders Dermatology Clinic.

Finally, the spatial dimension of service and innovation is discussed in the subsequent section.

Spatial aspects of leaders dermatology clinic

To analyze the spatial evolution of service areas, approximately 48,000 customers in 2006 and 169,000 customers in 2011 from 11 branches of the networked dermatology clinics are studied in terms of service types, new services, sex, and ages by counties, and districts in the capital region of Korea. Dermatology services classified customers into three types:

* Type I: Patients with skin diseases covered by health insurance.
* Type II: Patients who do not have skin diseases, but are undergoing treatment for aesthetic purposes and are not covered by health insurance.
* Type III: A mix of Types I and II, with both diseases and aesthetics considered.

In 2006, Type I, Type II, and Type III share 38.4 percent, 59.2 percent, and 2.4 percent, respectively. However, the percentages by types changed to 30.7 percent, 67.3 percent, and 2.0 percent in 2011 respectively. These figures represent the increasing trend of the share of Type II services in 2011. The increase of the share of Type II services is related with the predominant development of new services in Type II, compared with the development of new services in Type I. In this study, new services refer to newly introduced service products after 2006. The result of the data analysis can be summarized as follows.

Figure 3.2 shows the location of branches of Leaders Dermatology Clinic. The figure only includes the capital region because most of the branches are in this region, and the two locations in Daegu and Jeju are recently established and cannot compare the data during the study period.

First, clinics in core locations in the capital region significantly serve more Type II customers than in other locations. For example, the branch in Apgujung, which is located in the new core of Seoul and is regarded as a high-class residential area in Seoul, exhibits the highest ratio of Type II customers at 82.9 percent in 2011. The branch in Myungdong, which is located in the traditional core of Seoul, also exhibits a higher ratio of Type II customers at 79.5 percent in 2011 compared with the branches in other locations

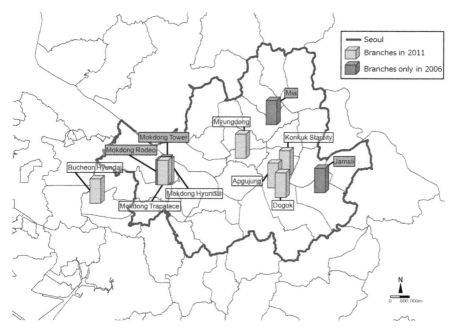

Figure 3.2 Location of branches of Leaders Dermatology Clinic

(Table 3.3). The branches in Apgujung and Mia showed a higher ratio of Type II customers in 2006. The Mia branch was the starting point of Leaders Dermatology Clinic, which serve a function that is similar to that of the Myundong branch, the traditional core of Seoul, because the Myungdong branch was not yet launched at that time. The Apgujung branch is regarded as the flagship marketing hub in Seoul. With an average ratio of 67.3 percent for Type II customers in all Leaders Dermatology Clinic branches in 2011, the aforementioned two branches received 82.9 percent and 79.5 percent for Type II customers, respectively.

Second, branches in core locations serve wider areas in Seoul beyond the relevant district. For example, the Apgujung and Mia branches demonstrated a lower share of the relevant district, which is equivalent to less than 30 percent points, in 2006 (Table 3.4). The Mia branch was a key location in Seoul in 2006 because it was the starting point of Leaders Dermatology Clinic. In 2011, the ratio of customers in the relevant district (Gangnam-gu) of the Apgujung branch to the total number of customers of the branch was 36.5 percent. The relevant district (Jung-gu) represented only 10.4 percent in the Myungdong branch. The former remains the only branch located in the central part of Seoul because the Myungdong branch replaced the Mia branch. Thus, this branch receives numerous nonlocal customers from outside the relevant district. The

Table 3.3 Share of services by service type and by branch (percent)

2006	All	Branches							
		Dogok	Bucheon Hyundai	Apgujung	Jamsil	Mokdong Hyundai	Mokdong Rodeo	Mokdong Tower	Mia
Type I	38.4	26.5	45.5	18.0	43.9	41.2	44.1	30.7	21.9
Type II	59.2	70.8	52.1	79.9	53.8	56.7	52.8	68.1	75.9
Type III	2.5	2.6	2.4	2.1	2.3	2.0	3.1	1.1	2.1

2011	All	Branches							
		Dogok	Bucheon Hyundai	Apgujung	Jamsil	Myungdong Shinsegae	Mokdong Hyundai	Mokdong Trapalace	Konkuk Starcity
Type I	30.7	27.9	43.6	15.9	22.7	18.9	32.0	34.2	32.8
Type II	67.3	69.5	54.2	82.9	76.0	79.5	65.4	64.1	65.6
Type III	2.0	2.6	2.2	1.2	1.3	1.6	2.7	1.8	1.5

Source: Calculated by the author from the internal data of Leaders Dermatology Clinics.

Table 3.4 Share of customers by region (percent)

2006	All	Branches							
		Dogok	Bucheon Hyundai	Apgujung	Jamsil	Mokdong Hyundai	Mokdong Rodeo	Mokdong Tower	Mia
Relevant district	63.2	64.1	62.1	36.5	63.6	60.9	63.2	71.9	38.8
Other areas of Seoul	12.4	26.1	4.5	46.3	25.5	31.7	28.2	20.8	55.5
Gyeonggi and Incheon	23.4	8.6	33.1*	14.3	9.1	6.5	7.4	7.1	4.9
Other regions	1.0	1.3	0.3	2.9	1.8	0.8	1.2	0.1	0.8

2011	All	Branches							
		Dogok	Bucheon Hyundai	Apgujung	Jamsil	Myungdong Shinsegae	Mokdong Hyundai	Mokdong Trapalace	Konkuk Starcity
Relevant district	66.7	74.0	62.9	45.5	69.3	14.4	64.8	69.9	63.2
Other areas of Seoul	9.8	19.0	3.9	43.2	22.8	75.4	27.7	24.4	29.6
Gyeonggi and Incheon	22.5	6.3	32.5*	9.0	6.9	8.8	6.9	4.8	5.4
Other regions	1.1	0.6	0.7	2.4	1.1	1.4	0.5	0.8	1.8

Source: Calculated by the author from the internal data of Leaders Dermatology Clinics.
Note: * Excluding Wonmi-gu in Bucheon city because it is regarded as a relevant district from Gyeonggi and Incheon.

customers of other branches are mostly from the relevant district, with 60–70 percent of the total customers coming from the relevant district (Table 3.4). A comparison of Types I and II customers in terms of the share of the relevant district to the total number of customers for each type shows that the share of Type I customers in the relevant district is significantly higher than that of Type II customers of the relevant district. This result shows that Type I customers tend to use nearby Leaders Dermatology Clinic compared with Type II customers. This trend is consistent with the central place theory that lower order services generally travel a shorter distance compared with higher order services.

This locational trend is demonstrated in Figures 3.3a, b, c, and d. The cases of Bucheon, Apgujung, Dogok, Mia, and Myungdong branches are depicted. A clear distance decay trend was observed in the case of Bucheon and a dispersing trend in Gyeonggi Province from 2006 to 2011 (Figure 3.3a). The relevant district of Bucheon shows a concentration of customers. However, the case of Apgujung, which is the new core area of Seoul, shows a different pattern with the case of Bucheon. No clear dominant share of customers was observed in the relevant district. In 2006, customers were dispersed to most of the districts in Seoul and dispersed to only a small portion of the customers to Gyeonggi Province, whereas customers were dispersed beyond the boundary of Seoul to Gyeonggi Province in 2011. The customers of Apgujung branch are mostly related to Type II services. The distinct leading role of the Apgujung branch can be identified in Figure 3.3b. A clear trend of the increase of customers was observed in the Dogok branch in Seoul in 2011 compared with that in 2006, but a considerable share of Type I customers was also found (Figure 3.3c). The customers of Myungdong branch dispersed considerably to Gyeonggi Province, as shown in Figure 3.3d. This result reveals the central position of the Myungdong branch. Despite the extension of the service area of Myungdong branch to Gyeonggi Province, a comparison of Figures 3.3b and 3.3d shows that Apgujung branch can be regarded as a top service center among dermatology clinics in Korea.

Third, an overall trend in the increasing share of Type II customers was observed from 2006 to 2011 (Table 3.5). Branches in Seoul exhibited a higher ratio of Type II customers and a lower ratio of Type I customers than the other branches in the capital region. This trend intensified over time, which demonstrates that more customers in Seoul fall under Type II. The ratio of Type II customers in other noncapital regions is relatively higher than those of Gyeonggi and Incheon. This finding may reveal that Type II customers tend to engage in relatively longer distance travel than Type I customers outside the capital region. The increasing trend of Type II services is related with the predominant development of new services in Type II. New services in 2011 were mostly for Type II customers at 88.9 percent, which is of higher value than the share of Type II in all the dermatology services customers in 2011. New services overwhelmingly belong to Type II, especially in Jamsil in the Gangnam area and in Myungdong, with a share of more than 95 percent (Table 3.6).

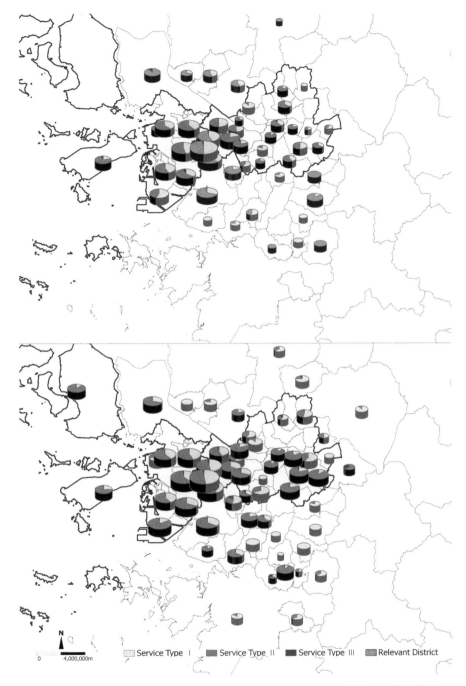

Figure 3.3a Share of services by service type in Bucheon Hyundai branch (2006 and 2011)

Note: Type I = skin diseases covered by health insurance; Type II = not related to the skin diseases but treatment for beauty, not covered by health insurance; Type III = mix of Type I and II considering both diseases and beauty.

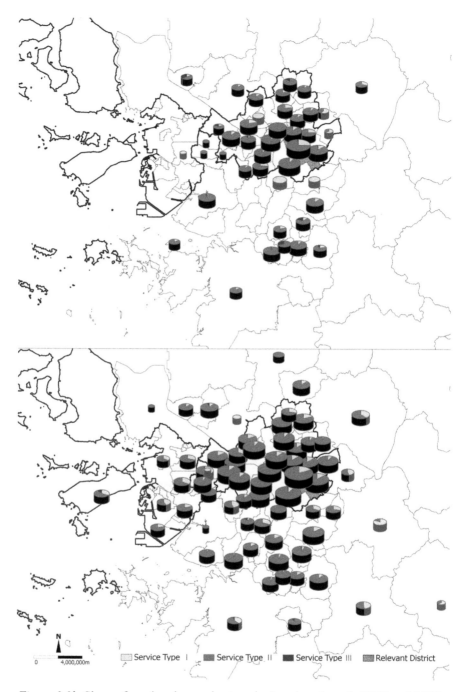

Figure 3.3b Share of services by service type in Apgujung branch (2006 and 2011)

Note: Type I = skin diseases covered by health insurance; Type II = not related to the skin diseases but treatment for beauty, not covered by health insurance; Type III= mix of Type I and II considering both diseases and beauty.

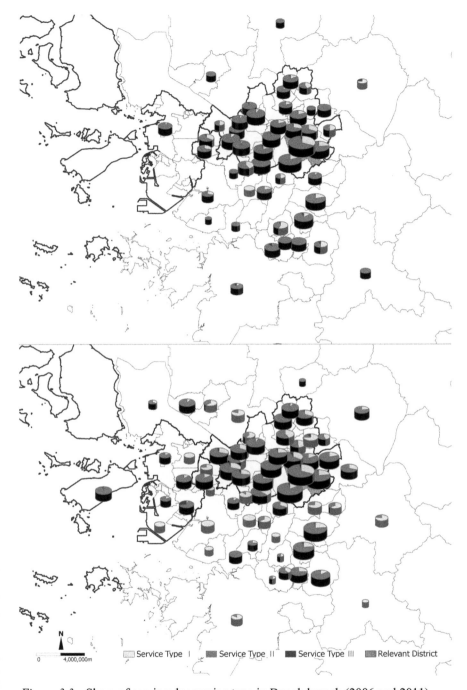

Figure 3.3c Share of services by service type in Dogok branch (2006 and 2011)

Note: Type I = skin diseases covered by health insurance; Type II = not related to the skin diseases but treatment for beauty, not covered by health insurance; Type III = mix of Type I and II considering both diseases and beauty.

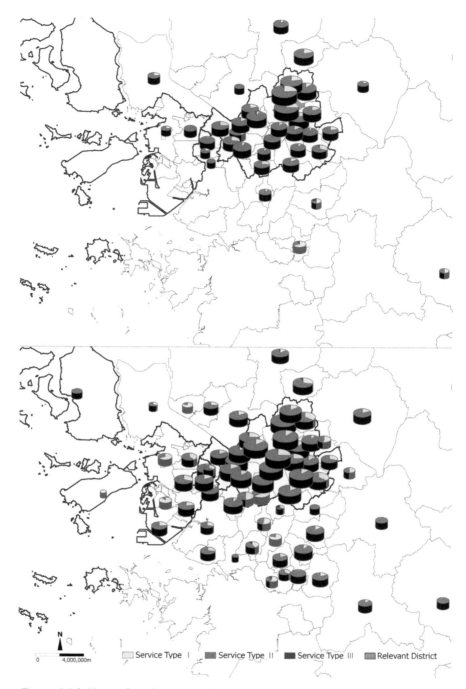

Figure 3.3d Share of services by service type in Mia (2006) and Myungdong branches (2011)

Note: Type I = skin diseases covered by health insurance; Type II = not related to the skin diseases but treatment for beauty, not covered by health insurance; Type III = mix of Type I and II considering both diseases and beauty.

Table 3.5 Region's sharing of customers by service type (percent)

Region	2006			2011		
	Type I	Type II	Type III	Type I	Type II	Type III
All	38.4	59.2	2.5	30.7	67.3	2.0
Seoul	37.3	60.3	2.5	28.0	70.1	1.9
Gyeonggi and Incheon	42.0	55.5	2.4	40.0	57.9	2.1
Other regions	36.6	60.8	2.6	29.9	67.8	2.2

Source: Calculated by the author from the internal data of Leaders Dermatology Clinics.

Fourth, customers of Leaders Dermatology Clinic, who avail new services, are predominantly female (84 percent), with males comprising only 16 percent (Table 3.7). A number of differences are observed in terms of type and region. For new services, the ratio of male customers of Type I (24.9 percent) is higher than that of male customers of Type II (14.9 percent), which indicates that female customers are more concerned with aesthetics or anti-aging treatments (Type II) than males. Several differences are also observed by age group. A general trend of increasing ratio of Type II customers is observed for each age group (Table 3.8). In 2006, the proportion of Type II customers was highest in the thirties age group (67 percent). However, the forties age group showed the highest ratio of Type II customers in 2011 (74.2 percent). Interestingly, the younger age group (customers under 20 years old) showed the most rapid increase in the ratio of Type II customers, although the share of Type II remains lower than that of Type I, which represents a rapid change in the trend of dermatology services.

Fifth, a trend of spatial evolution that shifts toward the market of higher income customers is observed. Starting from the northern part of Seoul, Leaders Dermatology Clinic expanded toward the higher class residential areas in Seoul, to one of the largest metropolises outside the capital region, and to Jeju, as a test market for foreign customers. Leaders Dermatology Clinic considers the central location of the relevant area, ease of access for high-income customers, and ease of parking as important location factors.

Summary and conclusion

Considering the significance of the service sector in the global economy and the integration of services into the dynamics of global economic spaces, service innovation has become an increasingly important research topic in recent years. This study develops an integral model of innovation in a broader context and conducts a case study. This preliminary study, which can be regarded as an extension of the approaches of Gallouj (2002) and Tether

Table 3.6 Share of new services by service type and by branch (percent)

| 2011 | All | Branches | | | | | | | |
		Dogok	Bucheon Hyundai	Apgujung	Jamsil	Myungdong Shinsegae	Mokdong Hyundai	Mokdong Trapalace	Konkuk Starcity
Type I	8.3	9.4	4.4	16.9	2.1	1.9	1.9	21.5	12.4
Type II	88.9	83.6	94.3	83.1	97.5	96.6	91.2	75.1	85.6
Type III	2.8	6.9	1.3	0.0	0.3	1.4	6.9	3.4	1.9

Source: Calculated by the author from the internal data of Leaders Dermatology Clinics.

Table 3.7 Region's sharing of new services by type and sex (percent)

Region	Total		Type I		Type II		Type III	
	Male	Female	Male	Female	Male	Female	Male	Female
All	16.0	84.0	24.9	75.1	14.9	85.1	22.3	77.7
Seoul	16.0	84.0	24.4	75.6	14.9	85.1	23.3	76.7
Gyeonggi and Incheon	15.5	84.5	26.7	73.3	14.8	85.2	14.2	85.8
Other regions	21.5	78.5	40.6	59.4	18.6	81.4	60.0	40.0

Source: Calculated by the author from the internal data of Leaders Dermatology Clinics.

Table 3.8 Sharing of service types by age (percent)

2006	Age 0–19	Age 20–29	Age 30–39	Age 40–49	Age 50
Type I	74.5	40.2	31.3	33.8	44.2
Type II	18.2	58.0	67.0	64.0	52.3
Type III	7.3	1.7	1.7	2.2	3.5

2011	Age 0–19	Age 20–29	Age 30–39	Age 40–49	Age 50
Type I	57.6	29.9	24.9	24.0	34.8
Type II	40.4	68.1	73.1	74.2	63.1
Type III	2.0	2.0	1.9	1.8	2.1

Source: Calculated by the author from the internal data of Leaders Dermatology Clinics.

(2003), develops a conceptual integral model of innovation. The most important premise in the development of the model is the fact that service innovation has not been limited to the service sectors in recent years, but has also extended to all sectors of the economy and society. In-depth interviews were conducted in the case study to identify the process of service innovation and the organizational changes in networked dermatology clinics with regard to the theoretical model developed in this study. Approximately 48,000 customers in 2006 and 168,000 customers in 2011 in eight networked dermatology clinics have been studied in terms of service types, new services, sex, and age to examine the evolutionary process of changes in medical service activities, with regard to the market and organization of clinics.

The major characteristics of services in this study are "intangibility," "co-production and interactivity," and "irreversibility." Service innovation, which is regarded as a new or significantly improved service concept, includes three types of innovation—namely, service products, service processes, and organizational and managerial structure. By considering the characteristics of services and the definition of service innovation, eight propositions of the integral model of service innovation can be summarized with regard to: (1) the sources of information for innovation; (2) collaboration with suppliers and customers for innovation; (3) collaboration with competitors and public institutions; (4) the importance of the concept of service encapsulation; (5) the development of an innovation chain; (6) path-dependent evolution; (7) innovation systems, and (8) spatial dimensions of service innovation.

Based on the result of the in-depth interviews with Leaders Dermatology Clinic and Lutronic, eight propositions for the integral model of service innovation have been discussed. Internal network within Leaders Dermatology Clinic is the most important source of information for innovation and collaboration. Suppliers and customers play critical roles in service innovation. Collaboration with domestic competitors is limited, but Leaders Dermatology Clinic maintains strategic alliances with leading international anti-aging clinics. Leaders Dermatology Clinic encapsulates various services such as ICT, maintenance, repair, and updating, among others. A two-way innovation chain is recognized by collaborating and establishing networks with suppliers and customers. The service innovation of Leaders Dermatology Clinic tends to be evolutionary in nature. Service innovation appears to be connected with a regional innovation system because most branches of Leaders Dermatology Clinic and its major suppliers are located in the capital region.

The spatial dimension of service and innovation of Leaders Dermatology Clinic is analyzed using customer data from 2006 and 2011. The branches of Leaders Dermatology Clinic that are located in the core of the capital region serve significantly more Type II customers than those in other locations. These branches also serve wider areas of Seoul beyond the relevant district. The customers of Leaders Dermatology Clinic are predominantly female, but both male and female have increased the share of Type II services from 2006 to 2011. A general trend of increasing ratio for Type II customers has been observed in each age group. A trend of spatial evolution that shifts toward the market of higher income customers has also been noted over time. The result of customer data analysis suggests that service types, service fields of clinics, and the distance decay effect of the services are related to the centrality of the clinics in the urban system. Moreover, a continuous spatial evolution has been found among the networked clinics with closures, new openings, and recombination of branches over time.

The case study supports the eight propositions of the integral model of service innovation proposed in this study. Evidently, the boundary between manufacturing and services has become indistinguishable because of the concept of a two-direction innovation chain. Such characteristics of the integral model are associated with the intensification of Bathelt and Glückler's (2011) "relational economy" in the knowledge-based economy. The concept of innovation chain shows that the theory of innovation should be considered in the broader context of the economy and society. Path-dependent evolution of service innovation and regional innovation systems are also significant considerations in the theory of innovation and policy salience of service innovation. Policy makers should consider the propositions of the integral model of service innovation beyond the traditional innovation policy, which focuses on the manufacturing perspectives of innovation processes. However, the case of Leaders Dermatology Clinic shows that the sources of innovation and collaboration are somewhat limited to customers and suppliers. Thus, a more in-depth analysis of the role of regional innovation systems in service innovation is necessary. These limitations suggest that the integral model of service innovation requires further elaboration by conducting more studies in other service sectors. Overall, this study covers more extensive issues of service innovation processes, although it sacrifices depth of analysis for these more extensive processes of innovation.

References

Asheim, B. T., Boschma, R. A. & Cooke, P. (2011). Constructing regional advantage: platform policies based on related variety and differentiated knowledge bases. *Regional Studies*, 45(7), 893–904.

Baltacioglu, T., Ada, E., Kaplan, M. D., Yurt, O. & Kaplan, Y. C. (2007). A new framework for service chains. *The Service Industries Journal*, 27(2), 105–124.

Bathelt, H. & Glückler, J. (2011). *The Relational Economy: Geographies of Knowing and Learning*. Oxford: Oxford University Press.

Bryson, J. R. & Daniels, P. W. (Eds.). (2007). *The Handbook of Service Industries*. Cheltenham and Northampton, MA: Edward Elgar.

Bryson, J. R. & Monnoyer, M. (2004). Understanding the relationship between services and innovation: the RESER review of the European service literature on innovation. *The Service Industries Journal*, 24(1), 205–222.

Christaller, W. (1966). *Central Places in Southern Germany* (C. W. Baskin, trans.). Englewood Cliffs, NJ: Prentice Hall.

Cooke, P. (2004). Introduction: regional innovation systems—an evolutionary approach. In P. Cooke, M. Heidenreich & H.-J. Braczyk (Eds.), *Regional Innovation Systems: The Role of Governance in a Globalized World* (pp. 1–18). London: Routledge.

Daniels, P. W. & Bryson, J. R. (2002). Manufacturing services and serving manufacturing: knowledge-based cities and changing forms of production. *Urban Studies*, 39(5–6), 977–991.

De Bandt, J. & Dibiaggio, L. (2002). Information activities as co-production of knowledge and values. In J. Gadrey & F. Gallouj (Eds.), *Productivity, Innovation and Knowledge in Services* (pp. 54–75). Cheltenham and Northampton, MA: Edward Elgar.

Doloreux, D., Freel, M. & Shearmur, R. (2010). *Knowledge-Intensive Business Services: Geography and Innovation.* Aldershot and Burlington, VT: Ashgate.

Gadrey, J. (2000). The characteristics of goods and services: an alternative approach. *Review of Income and Wealth*, 46(3), 368–387.

Gallouj, F. (2002). *Innovation in the Service Economy: The New Wealth of Nations*. Cheltenham and Northampton, MA: Edward Elgar.

Gallouj, F. & Weinstein, O. (1997). Innovation in services. *Research Policy*, 26, 537–556.

Goes, J. B. & Park, S. H. (1997). Interorganizational links and innovation: the case of hospital services. *The Academy of Management Journal*, 40(3), 673–696.

Hill, P. (1977). On goods and services. *Review of Income and Wealth*, 23(4), 315–338.

Howells, J. (2004). Innovation, consumption and services: encapsulation and the combinational role of services. *The Service Industries Journal*, 24(1), 19–36.

Howells, J. (2007). Services and innovation: conceptual and theoretical perspectives. In J. R. Bryson & P. W. Daniels (Eds.), *The Handbook of Service Industries* (pp. 34–43). Cheltenham and Northampton, MA: Edward Elgar.

Howells, J. (2010). Services and innovation and service innovation: new theoretical directions. In F. Gallouj & F. Djellal (Eds.), *The Handbook of Innovation and Services: A Multi-Disciplinary Perspective* (pp. 68–83). Cheltenham and Northampton, MA: Edward Elgar.

Illeris, S. (1997). *The Service Economy: A Geographical Approach*. Chichester: John Wiley & Sons.

Illeris, S. (2007). The nature of services. In J. R. Bryson & P. W. Daniels (Eds.), *The Handbook of Service Industries* (pp. 19–33). Cheltenham and Northampton, MA: Edward Elgar.

Martin, R. (2010). The Roepke lecture in economic geography—rethinking regional path dependence: beyond lock-in to evolution. *Economic Geography*, 86(1), 1–27.

Miles, I. (1993). Services in the new industrial economy. *Futures*, 25(6), 653–672.

Miles, I. (2007). Innovation in services. In J. Fagerberg, D. C. Mowery & R. R. Nelson (Eds.), *The Oxford Handbook of Innovation* (pp. 433–458). Oxford: Oxford University Press.

Park, S. O. (2005). Network, embeddedness, and cluster processes of new economic spaces in Korea. In R. Le Heron & J. W. Harrington (Eds.), *New Economic Spaces: New Economic Geographies* (pp. 6–14). Aldershot: Ashgate.

Park, S. O. (2011). Long-term strategies for regional development policies. In H. W. Richardson, C.-H. C. Bae & S. C. Choe (Eds.), *Reshaping Regional Policy* (pp. 302–320). Cheltenham and Northampton, MA: Edward Elgar.

Riddle, D. I. (2008). *Question & Answers: Service Iinnovation*. Service-Growth Consultants. Retrieved from www.servicegrowth.org/documents/Service%20Innovation%20Q%26As.org.pdf.

Tether B. S. (2003). The sources and aims of innovation in services: variety between and within sectors. *Economics of Innovation and New Technology*, 12(6), 481–505.

Website references

Korea Medical Hub (KMH): http://kmhglobal.com
Tekes: www.tekes.fi/eng/

4 Path dependence, regional resilience, and the evolution of the regional economy

Introduction

Several regions and countries have experienced recessions and severe natural and economic crises during the last two decades. Some regions have recovered from the crises and other regions have experienced a continuous decline in their economy. Such differences in the reaction to the crises in the global economy result in the dynamics of the global space economy. Along with the dynamic changes in the global space economy in the last two decades, increasing interest has been observed in two important themes—namely, "evolutionary turn" and "regional resilience" across the social sciences. The evolutionary turn has significantly affected geography, and evolutionary economic geography has developed as a significant field of research in geography (Boschma and Martin, 2007, 2010; Grabher, 2009; MacKinnon et al., 2009; Martin, 2010). Along with the evolutionary economic geography, Martin (2010) suggested an "alternative path dependent model" to understand the dynamic aspects of the local economic development.

Resilience has been increasingly interested in the social and environmental sciences in the last decades to understand the diverse reaction and recovery of regions to the recessions and crises (Foster, 2007; Walker et al., 2006; Pendall et al., 2010). Eventually, the concept of resilience entered into the discourse of regional studies and policies (Fingleton et al., 2012; Hill et al., 2008; MacArthur Foundation, 2009; Martin, 2012; Pendall et al., 2010; Pike et al., 2010; Reggiani et al., 2002; Simmie and Martin, 2010). However, there has been no consensus on the contribution of the notion of regional resilience because of the imprecision of definition and conceptualization, and application of the regional studies (Hanley, 1998; Pike et al., 2010, Hassink, 2010; Pendall et al., 2010). However, Martin (2012) contributes to the usefulness of the notion of resilience for understanding the reaction of regional economies to major recessionary shocks.

Martin (2010, 2012) significantly contributed to the development of a theoretical framework for understanding the dynamic regional economy by developing an "alternative path dependent model" and the concept of regional economic resilience in the last few years. The concepts of path dependence and regional resilience have been regarded as somewhat problematic in interpreting the dynamic features of a regional economy and policy implication for regional development. However, Martin attempted to develop an alternative model or interpretation to understand the dynamic regional economy and overcome the shortcomings of these concepts in their application of economic spaces. He recognized the interrelationship between the alternative path-dependent model and regional economic resilience in two recent papers, but he has not attempted to integrate the two models (Martin, 2010, 2012). The dynamics of economic spaces in the global economy result from complex processes, such as path dependence, self-reorganizing forces, restructuring, and resilience. The integration of the alternative path-dependent model and the notion of regional economic resilience apparently contributes more successfully to the understanding of the dynamic characteristics of the regional economy in the globalized knowledge-based economy.

As changes occur, some regions demonstrate resilience to the crisis or recession, thus achieving dynamic regional development, whereas other regions continue to experience prolonged difficulty. In the evolution or development of regions, resilience and evolutionary aspects are interrelated and contribute to the understanding of the changes in national and regional economies, and eventually to the understanding of the dynamics of the global economic space. In the evolutionary context, regional resilience pertains to the capacity of regional actors and institutions to adapt to change over time. Regional resilience and path dependence are both dynamic and evolutionary processes (Martin, 2012). Innovation network and restructuring governance are important in building successful regional resilience in this evolutionary process of path dependence. In the alternative path-dependence model, the path-development phase can be classified as path movement to a stable state and path as a dynamic process. The concept of resilience is associated with four themes—namely, equilibrium, systems perspective, path dependence, and long-term view (Pendall et al., 2007). This chapter focuses on the relationship between resilience and the evolutionary concept of path dependence in economic spaces.

The chapter integrates the notions of an alternative path-dependence model and regional economic resilience to understand the dynamic changes in the regional economy during economic crises or major economic challenges, and conducts case studies in the four industrial clusters in Korea. The conceptual framework of the chapter can be regarded as an extension and integration of the contributions of Martin to the notion of alternative path dependence and regional economic resilience (Martin, 2010, 2012). Addressing the notions of path dependence and resilience separately may be problematic to the understanding of contemporary dynamic regional economy. However, the integration of the two notions is more promising to the understanding of the dynamics and to the suggestion of policy issues because a local economy evolves over time through both continuous changes under global megatrends and changes to survive a global economic crisis or recession. Accordingly, path dependence and resilience are both ongoing processes for a region over time. The four industrial complexes to be analyzed are Guro (currently called Seoul Digital Complex), Banwol, Gumi, and Changwon, which were all established in the 1960s and 1970s and have led industrial development and economic growth in Korea over the last four decades.

Alternative path-dependent model proposed by Martin

Since the seminal work of Paul David (1985, 1986) on "QWERTY economics" that used the persistence of the standard typewriter keyboard to explain technological evolution more generally, interest in the path-dependent evolution in the field of social sciences, including economic geography, has substantially increased (David, 2001, 2005; Hirsch and Gillespie, 2001; Goldstone, 1998; Martin and Sunley, 2006; North, 1990; Pierson, 2000; Martin, 2010). The key concept of a path-dependent process is one whose outcome evolves as a result of the distinct history of the process. Three principal ideas of path dependence are interrelated in economics—namely, path dependence as technological "lock-in," as dynamic increasing returns, and as institutional hysteresis (Martin and Sunley, 2006). However, the concept of lock-in can be regarded as the core concept of path dependence. Network effects in the agglomeration of similar industries and the emergence of several related businesses in the same region can be considered the path dependence process.

However, in emphasizing the concept of lock-in in path dependence, the path-dependence process may not appropriately explain the dynamic aspects of regional economy. Regional economies dynamically change over time and never converge to equilibrium. Martin appropriately pointed out the problems of lock-in as follows:

> It is this (lock-in) notion that most fully captures the idea that the combination of historical contingency and the emergence of self-reinforcing effects steers a technology, industry, or regional economy along one "path," rather than another. It is the idea of lock-in that does not "evolutionary" work in the path dependence model. My argument, . . . , is that the concept of lock-in actually serves as a limited and restricted way of thinking about a path-dependent economic evolution. The idea of lock-in emphasizes continuity and stability, rather than change.
>
> (Martin, 2010, p. 3)

Martin (2010) criticizes the notion of lock-in emphasized by David in the technologies and technological standards in terms of "network externalities" and by Arthur in technologies and industrial location patterns in terms of the "increasing returns effects." Martin points out three defining features of the path- dependence model as the "accidental" origin of new paths, the notion of lock-in, and the appeal to exogenous shocks to delock paths (p. 5). Martin interprets the canonical path-dependence model proposed by David in terms of spatial industrial evolution with four stages—namely, historical accident, early path creation, path-dependent lock-in, and path delocking (Figure 4.1). In reviewing the contributions of David and Arthur, Martin argues that the three defining features of the canonical path-dependence model are problematic because they provide little insight into why and how new local industrial and technological paths emerge where they do. Martin specifically criticizes David's "path dependence equilibrium economics" in which David defines path dependence as "the historically contingent *lock-in to one of a multiplicity of possible equilibrium states*" (Martin, 2010, p. 7).

Martin criticizes the canonical path-dependence model because it represents equilibrium-dependent[1] rather than evolutionary aspects. In the canonical path-dependent model, lock-in pertains to the self-reinforcing process of collective behavior through which an economic system converges to a history-dependent equilibrium state from which it cannot escape. If industrial agglomerations and industrial clusters of the same industry in certain places can continue and persist over long periods, the phenomenon can be regarded as the continuity or stability of the economic landscape. However, the continuation of agglomeration and clustering cannot be regarded as equilibrium because it continuously evolves, although the system demonstrates self-organization (Foster, 2005). In economic spaces, "the idea of regional 'lock-in' has a strong intuitive appeal, but the appearance of simplicity may be deceptive" (Martin and Sunley, 2006, p. 415). Even industrial districts that specialize in a certain type of industry exhibit diverse development trajectories and do not demonstrate lock-in to a stable equilibrium (Park, 1996). The economic landscapes of clusters and industrial districts can be regarded as outcome path dependence, not a stable equilibrium (Martin, 2010). Most of the knowledge-based industrial clusters nowadays change and continuously evolve through innovation and cannot be regarded as moving toward an equilibrium. Economic landscapes continuously evolve rather than lock-in to

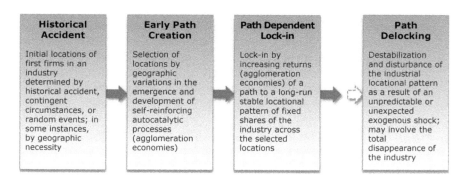

Figure 4.1 The canonical path-dependence model of spatial industrial evolution
Source: Adapted from Martin, 2010, p. 5.

a stable equilibrium because of the continuous innovation of firms, fusion of technologies, continuous external networks with globalization, and integration of service and manufacturing, as identified in Chapter 3, in modern knowledge-based industries.

Martin (2010) suggests an "alternative model of path dependence" beyond lock-in because of the problems and limitations of the canonical path-dependence model for the regional economy. Martin considers the recent development of the path-dependence model in political science and historical sociology, which focuses on ongoing evolution rather than stability, as reported by Crouch and Farrell (2004) and Boas (2007). Martin concurs with recent studies in political science and sociology (Boas, 2007; Stark and Bruszt, 2001) and argues the need for reworking the path-dependence model because institutions and socioeconomic systems are, unlike technologies such as the QWERTY keyboard, composite systems as follows:

> The argument is that, in contrast, most institutions are *composite* entities, made up of numerous microlevel institutions: organizational elements, structural arrangements, sociocultural norms, and individual rules and procedures. Furthermore, it is possible for many of these components to change without necessarily requiring change of all remaining components. By this process, it is possible for incremental change to occur in an institution as a whole, while it still exhibits path dependence and a significant degree of continuity. In addition, while basic path-dependence processes, such as increasing returns and network externalities, continue to prevent abrupt and radical shifts, incremental change at the microlevel can cumulate, resulting in fundamental institutional change over the long run, for example, in terms of structure, operation, scope, or even function. . . . ongoing mutation and adaptation of an institution is possible, and the institution may never become locked in to any stable or "equilibrium" configuration.
>
> (Martin, 2010, pp. 13–14)

Both institutions and technologies are composite because of various levels of standards and product components. Local industry can be considered an even more composite system because it is "composed of numerous individual firms, among which there are often detailed product variety and different market orientations, specific technologies, competencies, resources, routines, and business models, even though the firms all belong to the same overall industry" (Martin, 2010, p. 14). Local economies can be considered complex systems because they comprise numerous diverse firms that respond differently to the changing socioeconomic environment, "thereby allowing both continuity and change in the industry, the industrial district, or the business cluster as a whole" (Martin, 2010, p. 12). Complexities and varieties exist in the activities of economic actors in economic landscapes. The complexity and variety can result in a new path through local network externalities, global industrial and innovation networks, development of new technology, and fusion of technologies.

Martin adopts three processes that operate at the microlevel to allow change to a path-dependent institutional evolution identified in the political science and historical sociology—namely, layering, conversion, and recombination (Boas, 2007; Thelen, 2003). A *layering* process in an institution represents a gradual change "by adding new rules, procedures, or structures to what already exists" (Martin, 2010, p. 14). Local economy, similar to an institution, can be gradually cumulative and evolve with the addition of new firms, changes in industrial structure, and industrial policies, causing the mutation or sometimes transformation of the local economy. Several industrial districts and clusters evolve over time through the gradual layering process, and they may transform in terms of a long history, as seen in the traditional industrial districts in the United Kingdom and other developed regions (Park, 1996).

Conversion denotes "the reorientation of an institution in terms of form, function, or both" (Martin, 2010, p. 14). An institution can converge or reorient with the addition of new layers. An institution likewise converges with reorientation "to serve new purposes, in response to external pressures or developments, or as part of a learning process by which existing rules are improved" (p. 15). A local economy can converge with the introduction of new products, technology, or business organization to respond to market opportunities, knowledge spillovers, and innovation diffusion. In the local economy, layering and conversion can interact with each other, and the cumulative process changes the network externalities in the region. The conversion process path of the local economy evolves through the changes in the skills of the local labor force, in local suppliers, and supporting institutions. The recent change in the industrial cluster of Gumi in Chapter 7 of this book represents the interaction processes of layering and conversion.

Recombination is based on the idea that "any particular existing social-political-economic structure is, in effect, a system of resources and properties that actors can recombine and redefine, in conjunction with new resources and properties, to produce a new structure" (Martin, 2010, p. 15). The recombination of existing social and institutional resources allows an institution to evolve and become both path-dependent. Moreover, the recombination can occasionally cause radical change (Stark and Bruszt, 2001). Institutional paths are not uniform and are structurally diverse; thus, layering, conversion, and recombination can create a new path (Schneiberg, 2007). The recombination of elements or components from other coexisting institutions may create new paths. From the study of the economy in the first half of the twentieth century, Schneiberg suggests that the creation of new local paths can merge within existing pathways from the recombination or assembly of fragments of alternative industrial orders, "to the borrowing, transposition and elaboration of more or less coherent established secondary paths" (Schneiberg, 2007, p. 70). The idea of recombination is important for the evolution of a local economy. Economic agents can accumulate and recombine resources and experiences from within existing firms, through spin-offs, or from completely new ventures in a local area. This accumulation and recombination process can create new local industrial paths, which is frequently embedded in a local area (Nooteboom, 2000). High technology clusters specifically evolve and renew through the recombination of the knowledge resources of related industries, or the fusion of related technologies. For instance, Silicon Valley has been constantly evolving over time through the continuous creation of new industries and technologies via spin-offs, new firms, and restructuring of existing firms, and via various local and global networks (Park, 1996; Gray et al., 1998).

In real-world economic landscapes, some regions may be constrained to develop new paths because specific local knowledge and resources cannot be easily recombined or converted to create new competencies. Moreover, several regions, especially those of developing countries, where the local industrial base is relatively poor, the new trajectory of industrial development originates from nonlocal areas, including global resources, agents, and networks. Despite the positive or negative effects of path dependence on the local economy, Martin strongly criticizes David's history-contingent equilibrium process in the real-world economic landscape. The basic point of Martin is that "path dependence need not lead to or involve lock-in, or indeed lead to any form of equilibrium or stable state or trajectory" (Martin, 2010, p. 20).

Martin suggests an alternative path-dependence model of local industrial evolution, as depicted in Figure 4.2. He explains his alternative model as follows:

The emergence of new local industry may not be due to "chance" or "historical accident," but may be stimulated or enabled—at least in part—by the preexisting resources, competences, skills, and experiences that have been inherited from previous local paths and patterns of economic development. These inherited conditions shape the environment in which purposive or intentional experimentation and competition occur among local agents (or make the environment attractive to agents from elsewhere). Once a local industry begins to emerge, then provided that sufficient critical mass develops, it will stimulate the sort of autocatalytic network externalities that drive path-dependent growth. Simplifying the growth may then take one or another of two types of paths. One type of path is that emphasized by the standard canonical path-dependence model: convergence to a stable, self-reproducing form with the reinforcement of existing technology; little or no innovation; and little, if any, endogenous change—in effect, continuity and stasis. Such an outcome would render the industry highly prone to shifts in markets, to the rise of more productive (or cheaper) competitors elsewhere, and to atrophy or even decline. It is also likely to create a local environment that is inimical to entrepreneurial

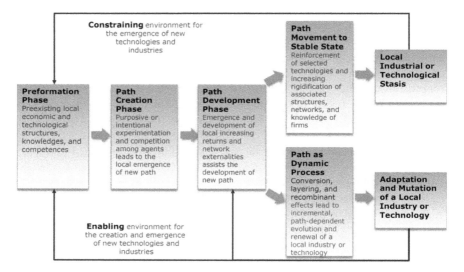

Figure 4.2 Toward an alternative path-dependence model of local industrial evolution
Source: Adapted from Martin, 2010, p. 21.

experimentations of new local industrial paths. The second type of trajectory is more open and allows for endogenous change and evolution. As a result of the processes of layering, conversion, and recombination, the industry changes slowly over time and traces out a developmental trajectory that is both path dependent *and* path evolving [italic is original].

(Martin, 2010, pp. 20–21)

Martin assumes that the speed or pace of adaptability varies from one region to another and may change over time. In his alternative model, Martin does not completely reject David's canonical path-dependence model, as shown in the upper path of Figure 4.2 (path as movement to a stable state). Martin includes the "path as movement to stable stasis" in his portrayed model; nevertheless, he is skeptical of the case of local industrial stasis in real economic landscapes—that is, he questions the actual existence of pure stasis. His alternative model of path dependence is accordingly focused on the lower path of Figure 4.2—that is, path as a dynamic process. Martin asserts that the alternative model contributes to the integration of path dependence into the evolution of regional and local economies, whereas the notion of lock-in is not related to the evolutionary concept. Martin emphasizes that the development trajectory of local industry includes both path dependence and path evolution. Despite Martin's criticism of David's notion of lock-in or stable stasis, he does not reject typical path-dependent processes, such as increasing returns and network externality effects. Rather, he emphasizes the concepts of layering, conversion, and recombination, which have been proposed by political science and historical sociology, along with the typical path-dependence processes, in the progress of ongoing changes and evolution. He likewise suggests the usefulness of integrating the notion of dynamic process into the evolutionary aspects as follows:

> Furthermore, the processes of layering, conversion, recombination, and structural variety resonate with many of the concepts and principles that help define a genuinely evolutionary perspective on the economic landscape, such as variety, novelty, selection, fitness, mutation, and adaptation.
>
> (Martin, 2010, p. 22)

Martin's alternative model has contributed to the understanding of the evolution of industrial districts, clusters or local economy, employing the dynamic aspects of path dependence. However, if the model is integrated with external or nonlocal factors, it can convey the more dynamic aspects of the local economy, as discussed in Chapter 2. Global megatrends significantly affect the local or regional economy in the twenty-first century. The progress of globalization and information society in the global knowledge-based economy significantly affects the local economy in two ways. First, external shocks such as the 2008 US financial crisis can severely affect the economy of certain countries or regions. The Wall Street crisis has caused the global economic crisis and recession due to the globally networked financial system. External shocks from natural disasters can likewise severely affect the path of the local economy. However, the effects of external shocks are not homogeneous to the regions or countries. Some regions can be resilient to the shocks and easily recover from the shock, whereas other regions may not be resilient and should restructure the economy to create new paths— that is, the stress on the changes of development trajectory or the creation of new paths of the local economy comes from outside the region, and exogenous forces rather than endogenous forces may have stronger effects on the creation of new paths in certain places and at certain times. Second, exogenous forces, such as strong national government policies, foreign direct investments, and the introduction of new technology from outside the region, can reshape the region and create paths. The exogenous forces can be integrated into Martin's alternative model. However, the external shocks should be reconsidered to understand the evolution of the local economy. To address this issue, the concept of regional resilience can be integrated into Martin's model. The integration of the notion of path dependence and regional resilience might certainly be fruitful to understand the evolution of a local or regional economy (Reggiani, 2002; Simmie and Martin, 2010; Martin, 2010).

Integrated model of path dependence and regional economic resilience

Regional resilience

The idea of "resilience" has been used in engineering and ecological sciences, and has gained attention in social sciences, such as psychology and organizational science. Interest in the notion of resilience has increased in the social and environmental sciences in the last decade, especially due to natural and environmental disasters, such as unexpected floods, tsunamis, and earthquakes. Economic geographers have been interested in the notion of resilience since Reggiani et al. (2002) explored the relevance of resilience in dynamic socioeconomic systems. However, consensus on the relevance and significance of the notion of resilience in economic geography is lacking, as reported in the special issue of the *Cambridge Journal of Regions, Economy and Society* (2010). The lack of consensus in the definition of resilience and problems in transferring developed in one system (i.e. ecosystem) to other systems (i.e. regional economic system) have caused contention in the resilience concept in economic geography (Martin, 2012). Consequently, several economic geographers, such as Hassink (2010), Hudson (2010), and Pike et al. (2010), are hesitant to agree on the usefulness of the notion of regional resilience.

Resilience refers to the capacity of an entity or system to "recover form and position elastically, following a disturbance or disruption of same kind" (Simmie and Martin, 2010). Regional resilience has attracted considerable interest in applying the concept of resilience on local socioeconomic systems. Since the catastrophic impact of Hurricane Katrina on New Orleans in 2005, universities and research centers have become interested in building a resilient region as a policy issue (e.g. MacArthur Foundation, 2007; Chapple and Lester, 2007). The MacArthur Foundation has established a research network on building a resilient region and seeks "to show how particular feature of regional governance—the actors, cultures, policies, and institutions of a region—contribute to resilience" (MacArthur Foundation, 2009). In building a resilient region, regional resilience is considered the ability of actors and institutions in a region to adapt to change over time. In a similar aspect, Foster (2007, p. 14) defines regional resilience as "the ability of a region to anticipate, prepare for, respond to, and recover from a disturbance." Thus, most of the recent uses of the term in regional or urban applications focus on recovering from a shock or disturbance. However, Simmie and Martin (2010) suggest "from an evolutionary perspective, the important attribute of regional economic resilience is the adaptive capacity of a local economy." They attempt to understand resilience as an evolutionary process in which variations in resilience exist across the adaptive cycle.

More recently, Martin (2012) has attempted "to explore how the notion of 'resilience,' for example as used in ecological work, can be combined with that of 'hysteresis,' as used in economics, to examine how regional economies react to recessionary shock" (p. 3). He has reviewed different interpretations of resilience according to three types—namely, engineering, ecological, and adaptive resilience (Table 4.1). Considering that engineering resilience and ecological resilience have been widely explored in the physical and ecological sciences, respectively, Martin has added adaptive resilience found in complex adaptive system theory.

Engineering resilience focuses on "stability at a presumed steady-state, and stresses resistance to a disturbance and the speed of return to the equilibrium point" (Berkes and Folke, 1998, p. 12). Returning to the pre-shock state and stability of a system in equilibrium is a key point in engineering resilience. However, different from physical systems, "a regional or local economy need never be in equilibrium, yet can be characterized by an identifiable, and relatively stable, growth trend or path" (Martin, 2012, p. 5). In the local economy, we may consider the level of employment, which is one of the most important variables for the local economy, prior to a shock as a basis for measuring the resilience after a shock—that is, measuring the speed and time to recover to the level of pre-shock can be used to describe one dimension of resilience.

In contrast to engineering resilience, ecological resilience focuses on "the role of shocks or disturbances in pushing a system beyond its 'elasticity threshold' to a new domain" (Martin, 2012, p. 7). If a shock is assumed to exceed the "elasticity threshold" of a system, the system moves to a different state. Martin assumes the relevance of the ecological resilience concept to the regional economic "hysteresis." The concept of hysteresis is often used in economics to describe a phenomenon that an economy can be moved from one domain to another as a result of recessionary shocks or disturbances

Table 4.1 Different interpretations of resilience

Interpretation/type of resilience	Main focus of interest
'Engineering' resilience (found in physical sciences)	Ability of a system to return to, or resume, its assumed stable equilibrium state or configuration following a shock or disturbance. Focus is on resistance to shocks and stability near equilibrium.
'Ecological' resilience (found in ecological sciences)	The scale of shock or disturbance a system can absorb before it is destabilized and moved to another stable state or configuration. Focus is on 'far from equilibrium' behavior of system.
'Adaptive' resilience (found in complex adaptive systems theory)	The ability of a system to undergo anticipatory or reactionary reorganization of form and/or function so as to minimize the impact of a destabilizing shock. Focus is on adaptive capability of system.

Source: Adapted from Martin, 2010, p. 5.

(Cross, 1993; Setterfield, 2010; Martin, 2012). Most of the discussions on hysteresis in economics focus on the negative effects of shocks; nevertheless, Martin suggests that positive hysteric reactions occur with regard to a shock on regional economy more than "rebounds" from the shock (Martin, 2012). Positive hysteric reactions may occur if the region can attract labor and capital from elsewhere, or witness the emergence of new sectors of activity and/or a new wave of growth-promoting innovation (Martin, 2012).

Martin likewise suggests that positive hysteric outcomes link with the notion of "adaptive resilience," which is derived from the theory of complex adaptive systems. Adaptive capacity is the focus of adaptive resilience. Adaptive capacity allows complex adaptive systems to spontaneously rearrange their internal structure in response to external shocks or in reaction to internal emergent mechanisms (Martin and Sunley, 2007). In this view of adaptive resilience, resilience is an evolutionary one and "a dynamic process, not just a characteristic or property, and it resonates closely with the Schumpeterian notion of 'gale of creative destruction'" (Martin 2012, p. 11). Dawley et al. (2010) similarly apply an evolutionary approach as an alternative and fuller conceptualization of regional resilience and "draw(s) attention to an evolutionary notion of resilience as a process, not pegged against movements to from single or multiple equilibria, but towards a more dynamic understanding of constant changes rather than stability" (p. 2). Regional resilience in this aspect focuses on the capacity of a regional economy to reconfigure its structure to sustain the economy with acceptable growth path over time. Martin suggests that the adaptive capability in the regional economic resilience is related to various factors as follows:

> Such adaptability will be depend on the rate of entrepreneurship and new firm formation in the region, on the innovativeness of existing firms, and their ability and willingness to shift into new sectors and product lines, on access to finance for investment, on the diversity of the regional economic structure, on the availability of labour of the right skills, and similar factors.
>
> (Martin, 2012, pp. 11–12)

Moreover, the metaphor from psychological resilience may be meaningful in adaptive resilience. In psychology, resilient individuals tend to view problems as opportunities for development. Accordingly, resilient individuals can effectively cope with unusual strains and shocks, and seem to experience such challenges as learning and development opportunities (Neill, 2006). Resilient people can successfully adapt to risks and shocks with a sense of dynamic self-renewing process (Neil, 2006). The metaphor of this psychological resilience on regional resilience suggests the self-organizing forces and evolution of a region over time.

Considering the interpretation of engineering, ecological, and adaptive resilience, Martin (2012) suggests four dimensions of regional resilience—

namely, *resistance* to disturbances or shock, speed and extent of *recovery*, structural *re-orientation*, and degree of *renewal* or resumption of the growth path (see Figure 4.3). The four dimensions may interact in various ways to produce different paths of regional economy. They are clearer than the adaptive cycles of system adaptation and change in ecological studies.[2] Martin argues that various factors, such as the prior economic growth performance of the regional economy, economic structure of the region, regional innovation systems, entrepreneurial culture, local policy bodies, and political economy, shape the resistance and response of a regional economy to a shock. He emphasizes the usefulness of hysteresis because external shocks can cause sudden and intense structural change and reorientation, resulting in hysteric change to the growth path of a regional economy. Martin's four dimensions of regional economic resilience are an aspect of the dynamics of regional economy to be considered under the evolutionary framework of the regional economy. He argues that the notion of resilience should be central to the understanding of the evolution of a regional economy as follows:

> Resilience is not a static feature of an economy, but a dynamic process, influenced both by the impact of major shocks and by the ongoing restlessness of structural economic change and adaptation. An evolutionary approach to regional economic resilience is thus called for which would

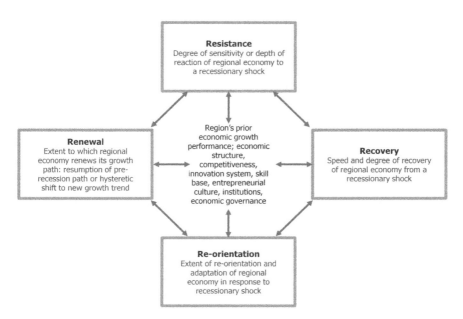

Figure 4.3 Four dimensions of regional economic resilience to a recessionary shock

Source: Adapted from Martin, 2012, p. 12.

permit such notion as variety, selection, path dependence and self-organization, as well as purposive adaptation by economic agents and policy-makers, to play an explanatory role. Indeed, the notion of resilience should itself be central to any conceptual framework for studying the evolution of the economic landscape.

(Martin, 2012, pp. 28–29)

As Martin suggests, the integration of the notion of path dependence and regional resilience seems to be important to the understanding of the dynamics of regional economy over time and space. The next section presents the integration of the notion of regional resilience into the alternative model of path dependence proposed by Martin.

Integration of path dependence and regional resilience

The integration of the notions of path dependence and resilience is required because these processes are place-dependent. In the integration model of this chapter, Martin's alternative model can be dealt with more flexibly to include additional alternative ways in the path-dependent phase. For instance, local industrial or technological stasis in the upper part of Figure 4.2 can move toward the path-creation phase in addition to move back to the performance phase. Moving toward the path-creation phase after the stasis phase may be possible if the local economy completely restructures to sustain the economy.

To integrate the notion of regional resilience into the path-dependent evolution, three premises are required in the path-dependent evolution. First, path-dependent evolution and regional resilience are affected by global megatrends. As discussed in Chapter 2, globalization, knowledge-based information society, service world, aging society, and climate change affect the local and regional economies in terms of economic structure, inter-firm and spatial networks, agglomeration, and technological change. The processes of conversion, layering, and recombination are different by region with the diverse and selective impact of global megatrends. Second, as discussed in the previous sections, path dependence and resilience are dynamic processes (Martin, 2010, 2012; Martin and Sunley, 2007). Third, the role of different factors, such as the firm, government, culture, institution, and social groups, is important for the path of local and regional economies and regional resilience because their characteristics and structure are related to the trajectory of regional economy and differ by region. The role of government in the newly industrialized and industrializing countries is more important than that of advanced industrialized countries.

Considering the three premises, the evolutionary process of regional resilience along the path-dependent evolution is depicted in Figure 4.4. Path-dependent evolution at any stage can be interrupted by external shocks, such as financial crisis, global recession, and environmental disaster, as well as severe competition and internal disturbance related to the global megatrends.

The effects of internal disturbance and stiff competition resulting from global megatrends, such as globalization and knowledge-based information society, are ongoing changes and not as severe as the effects resulting from the external crisis on the path-dependent evolution, and are not the principal focus of this chapter. Some regions confronted by an external shock are resistant to it, whereas others are not. Resistant regions can easily recover from the shock and evolve either through a dynamic process or a reinforcing path. In the case of the dynamic process, conversion, layering, and recombination will be continued to move toward the reorientation and renewal of the local economy; meanwhile, in the reinforcing path, competitive industrial and economic structure can be reinforced to sustain the economy either by specialization and diversification. The reinforcing path may result in the rigidification of the structure and industrial stasis or decline in the long term.

A nonresistant region may experience industrial restructuring to sustain the local economy and protect it from shock, or fail to restructure and decline. A firm should reorganize its internal structure in terms of labor, organization, technology, and/or location to sustain it during a crisis or in a competitive environment (Clark and Kim, 1995; Park, 1995). Similar to a firm, a region can restructure its economy to sustain itself during a crisis or in a competitive environment. A successful industrial restructuring can allow the regional economy to recover to the level of pre-shock and move toward reorientation with the development of new technology and the creation of a new path. A region that fails to restructure causes its economy to become vulnerable and decline, and creates the need to seek a new path. Under severe competition,

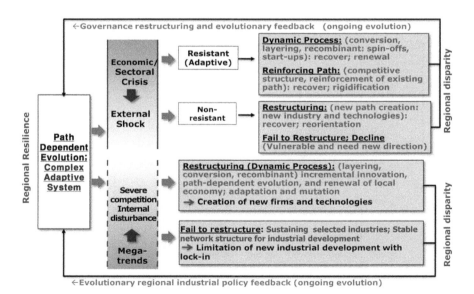

Figure 4.4 The evolutionary process of regional resilience

restructuring is the key approach to move toward a dynamic process and continue to undergo a path-dependent evolution. A region that fails to restructure its economy under a severely competitive environment causes its economy to decline and experience a lock-in.

The preceding evolutionary process of regional resilience can be integrated into the alternative path-dependent model proposed by Martin. Path-dependent evolution shows differently by the time of external shock—for instance, whether after the path-performance phase, after the path-creation phase, or after the path-development phase. In this chapter, two examples are described in Figures 4.5a and 4.5b as the cases of external shock after the path-development phase and after the path-creation phase, respectively.

If an external shock occurs after the path development phase of a regional economy, two path directions can be assumed based on the degree of resistance to shock (Figure 4.5a). A shock-resistant regional economy can continue its path development evolution as either a dynamic process or a reinforcing path as depicted in the evolutionary process of regional resilience in Figure 4.4. In the case of path as a dynamic process, a region can easily recover from the shock and shift toward renewal through conversion, layering, and recombination. In the case of a reinforcing path, the existing path can be reinforced and often experience lock-in resulting in a movement toward a stable state and industrial stasis or decline and may return to a performance phase in the long term. Returning to the path creation phase may likewise occur if the region restructures its economy to maintain competitiveness and reinforce its innovation potential to generate a new path (Figure 4.5a). A local economy that is not resistant to shock can cause the region to either restructure or fail to restructure the economy. A nonresistant region that successfully restructures

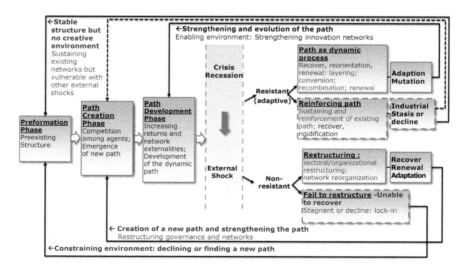

Figure 4.5a Path-dependent evolution of regional resilience

its economy through sectoral or organizational restructuring allows the region to recover from the external shock to the pre-shock level and move toward the evolving path creation phase and generate a new path. A nonresistant region that fails to restructure its economy prevents it from easily recovering from the shock to the pre-shock level; at the same time, the regional economy momentarily declines and restarts a new performance phase.

If an external shock occurs from either an economic crisis or a recession after the path creation phase, the path-dependent evolution somewhat differs from the case of an external shock after the path-development phase, as shown in Figure 4.5b. A shock-resistant region continuously moves toward the path-development phase. The region consequently experiences the path either as a dynamic process or a movement toward a stable state, as suggested by Martin's (2010) alternative model in Figure 4.2. The region with a dynamic process evolves with the strengthening of the path and continues to return to the path-development phase, with the strengthening innovation network and the processes of conversion, layering, and recombination. A region that stabilizes without a significant restructuring of the economy and with a reinforcement of the existing path experiences long-term decline. The path as movement to a stable state may revert to the path-creation phase when the region successfully restructures and sustains its economy.

A nonresistant region can either be successful in restructuring to maintain competitiveness or fail to restructure. The region with a successful restructuring can recover from the shock to the pre-shock level, as identified in the evolution of regional resilience, and evolve toward the new path-creation phase. A nonresistant region that fails to restructure causes its economy to decline and experience a lock-in, and should start a new performance phase.

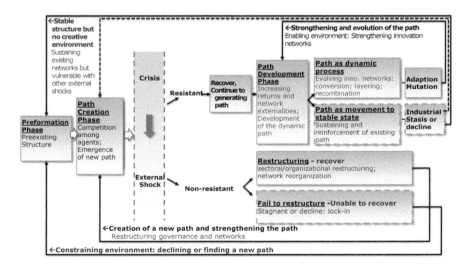

Figure 4.5b Path-dependent evolution of regional resilience

The integration of the notion of regional resilience into the path-dependent model shows the dynamics of economic landscapes more realistically through the display of alternative ways of the local economy after the external shocks. The integration model shows that the effects of external shocks depend on time or the phase of the path-dependence evolution of the local economy. This premise is consistent with the recent evolutionary theories that "suggest that whether agglomeration economies generate increasing returns or diminishing returns depends on time, and especially the evolution of the industry life cycle" (Potter and Watts, 2011, p. 417). In addition to the physical combination of Martin's (2010) alternative path-dependent model with the notion of regional resilience, the integration model considers the restructuring process of the regional economy. Despite the weakness of the regional economy in dealing with the external shock and its nonresistance to the shock, a region that successfully restructures its economy can move toward and follow the phases of the path-dependent evolution. Even under extremely competitive conditions resulting from the effects of the global megatrends, restructuring is the key approach to sustain and develop the region. Innovation, industrial structure, regional and national industrial policy, labor strategy, and industrial network, among other factors, are critical for the successful restructuring of the local economy. The integration of path dependence and regional resilience helps in understanding the dynamics of local economy evolution and in suggesting policy implications for local economic development. The integration model likewise implies the similarity of continuous adaptive evolution to the cluster adaptive cycle model suggested by Martin and Sunley (2011).

The case of four industrial clusters in Korea

The changes in the four industrial clusters in Korea are examined to explore the dynamics of local economic landscapes under a financial crisis and global economic recession. The four industrial clusters are Guro (Seoul Digital Complex)[3] in Seoul, Banwol in Gyeonggi Province, Gumi in North Gyeongsang Province, and Changwon in South Gyeongsang Province (see Figure 4.6). They were established from the mid-1960s to the late 1970s in the order of Guro, Gumi, Changwon, and Banwol, and assumed a pivotal role in the industrial development and economic growth of Korea in the last three decades. The major purpose of the case study is not to critically verify the integrated model, but to show how the paths differ by regional characteristics in terms of economic structure and location, and to depict the dynamics of path-dependent evolution and regional resilience in the real world.

Since the late 1980s, three significant periods in the Korean economy have affected the economic decline. First, Korea experienced a recession in the late 1980s and early 1990s, which was specifically characterized by severe labor disputes and a nearly 100 percent increase in labor cost from 1987 to 1989 (Park, 1993, 1994). Second, Korea was shocked by the severe East Asian financial crisis in 1997. Similar to Indonesia and Thailand, the GDP growth

Figure 4.6 Location of study areas (four industrial clusters) in Korea

rate of Korea sharply decreased from 1997 to 1998. Third, the Korean economy was in recession during the 2008 global financial crisis. These financial crises and economic recessions have affected differently the economic sectors and regions in Korea. This chapter focuses on the 1997 financial crisis and the more recent global recession. The employment growth pattern by economic sectors and regions is examined initially in this section, and the patterns for industrial clusters are explored subsequently in terms of employment growth and economic structure.

Employment growth by regions of Korea

The capital region has demonstrated a substantially higher growth than any other region in the last two decades. The dominance of the capital region over the other regions in terms of growth caused a higher growth pattern of the national average compared with the rest of the region (see Figure 4.7a). The southwest region, which includes Gwangju City, Jeolla-buk and -nam Provinces, and Jeju Province, has been considered the peripheral region in Korea and demonstrated the lowest growth pattern.

The 1997 financial crisis severely affected all of the regions. However, the effects of the crisis by region differed in three aspects. First, in terms of the employment level after the crisis, that of the capital region significantly decreased from 1997 to 1998 compared with those of the other regions. Second, there are some variations of the period of recovering to the pre-shock employment level. Overall, the nation required three years to recover to the pre-shock level in 1997. Most of the region recovered to the pre-shock level within three years after the financial crisis; however, the southwest region did not recover to the pre-shock level until 2011. Third, a significant variation occurred in the growth rate after recovering to the pre-shock level. The capital region has demonstrated a considerably higher growth than any other region since recovering to the pre-shock level, and showed a level of annual growth rate almost similar to that during the pre-shock period. Gyeonggi Province led the growth of the capital region (Figure 4.7b). The middle region, which includes Daejeon City, Chungcheong-buk and -nam Provinces, and Gangwon Province, showed a relatively high growth rate, but slightly lower than that during the pre-shock period. The relative growth of the middle region, which is near the capital region, is related to the locational effects and filters down

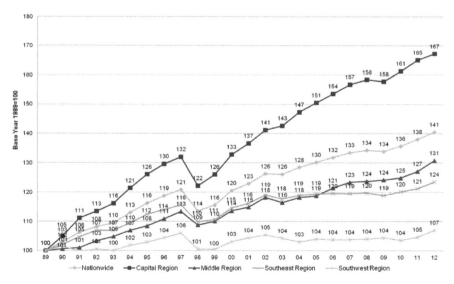

Figure 4.7a Changes in the total number of employees by region

Source: Korean Statistical Information Service.

the process of manufacturing firms from the capital region. Within the middle region, Daejeon City showed a significant growth performance (Figure 4.7b). Other regions demonstrated a substantially lower growth pattern compared with that during the pre-shock period. No significant increase in employment level occurred in the southwest region from 2011 to 2012. Within the southwest region, Gwangju has displayed a considerably high growth rate since the financial crisis; however, the growth rate of Jeonam Province, which surrounds Gwangju City, has continuously decreased since the early 1990s (Figure 4.7b).

The regional effect of the global recession resulting from the US financial crisis was not severe compared with that of the 1997 financial crisis. Only the southeast region showed a slight decline and shortly recovered to the pre-shock level in 2010 (Figure 4.7a). However, a variation by provinces occurred. Overall, the nation exhibited a slight decrease in employment level from 2008 to 2009 and recovered before 2010 to the pre-shock level. The capital region likewise showed a negligible decline but shortly recovered. Jeju Island, which is a Special Province similar to a free trade zone, was severely affected and required almost three years to recover to the pre-recession level (Figure 4.7b). This result revealed that Jeju Special Province was relatively sensitive to the global recession. Interestingly, the poor regions of Jeolla-nam and -buk Provinces and Gangwon Province showed an increase in employment from 2008 to 2009 and a decrease from 2009 to 2010, which was the opposite trend nationwide (Figure 4.7b). This opposite trend of these provinces may be related

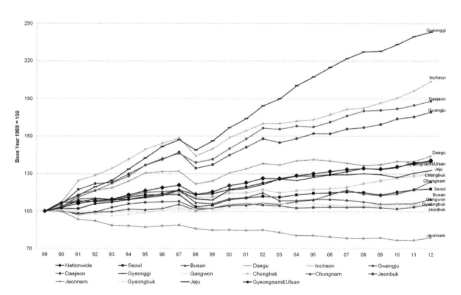

Figure 4.7b Changes in the total number of employees by provinces

Source: Korean Statistical Information Service.

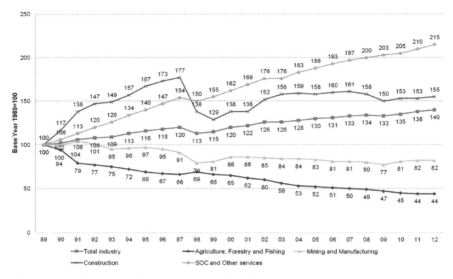

Figure 4.8 Changes in the total number of employees by industry
Source: Korean Statistical Information Service.

to the characteristics of their economic structure, which indicated the relatively high share of the agricultural sector in provincial areas; nevertheless, this outcome requires a more detailed analysis to obtain an accurate conclusion.

The effects of crisis or recession differ by industrial sector and by region. The differences by region may be related to the differences in economic structures. Figure 4.8 shows that the shock effect on construction is considerably more severe than on other sectors. Construction has never recovered to the pre-shock level of the 1997 crisis, and the growth rate has been significantly lower than that during the pre-shock period. The service sector was slightly affected by the 1997 crisis, but shortly recovered and maintained a similar trend of growth rate compared with that during the pre-shock period. Manufacturing was considerably affected, but the general trend of the manufacturing employment level decreased even before the financial crisis. Interestingly, the employment level of the agricultural sector increased from 1997 to 1998, which is opposite to the trend in the other sectors. This opposite trend is related to returnees to the agricultural sector from job losses in the other sectors. This phenomenon explains the absence of a decrease in employment in Jeolla-nam and -buk Provinces and Gangwon Province from 1997 to 1998 (Figure 4.7b). The recent global recession did not severely affect the service sector, but it considerably decreased the employment in the construction sector. The recession likewise affected the manufacturing sector, but not as severely (Figure 4.8).

In addition to the regional history and economic structure, industrial policies have significantly affected the path-dependent evolution. Industrial policies have evolved since the launch of the First Five-Year Economic Development Plan in 1962 in Korea. In early industrial development policies, industrial district development was the major policy in Korea, shifting the strategic industries from labor-intensive industries, to heavy and chemical industries, and to knowledge-intensive high-tech industries. High-tech industries, such as semiconductors and personal computer-related products, have been increasingly favored since the mid-1980s. Beginning in the 1990s, especially after the financial crisis in November 1997, the Korean government has considerably promoted the development of knowledge-intensive industries to open up the country to trade and capital movements, restructure the economy, including the financial sector, and to develop a flexible labor market. Regional innovation was the key policy in the first decade of the twenty-first century (see Figure 4.9 for different key industrial policies).

Figures 4.7a, 4.7b, 4.8, and 4.9 show the different effects of crises and recessions by region and economic structure in terms of industrial policies. These differences suggest the variation in the path-dependent evolution and regional resilience by regional history, regional economic structure, and regional policy. The differences by region and by economic sector may provide the underlying background of the differences in the path-dependent evolution and regional resilience of four clusters in the next section.

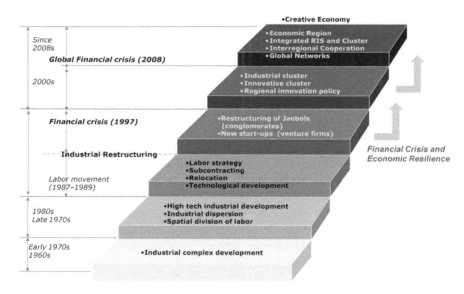

Figure 4.9 Evolution of industrial policy in Korea
Source: Revised from Park, 2010.

Growth pattern of four industrial clusters

Four industrial clusters are selected because they represent different development histories and regional characteristics. These industrial complexes were developed by the national government. Two are located in the capital region— namely, Guro complex in Seoul and Banwol industrial complex in Gyeonggi Province (Figure 4.6). The other two are located in the southeast region, which is the industrialized area in Korea—namely, Gumi in Gyeongsangbuk Province and Changwon in Gyeongsangnam Province. Small- and medium-sized enterprises (SMEs) are mostly located in Kuro and Banwol complexes, whereas large branch plants, which are mostly headquartered in Seoul, are located in Gumi and Changwon complexes.

Guro industrial cluster is the first industrial complex of Korea, which was established as an export base and considered a symbol of the export-oriented industrial policy of the government in the mid-1960s. Since the First Five-Year Economic Development Plan in 1962, the government started to develop an export-base industrial complex for labor-intensive industries. The complex had rapidly grown in the 1970s, but experienced remarkable fluctuation in employment and export. Approximately 11,100 firms are located in the complex, which employed 142,300 workers and accounted for exports worth US$2.7 billion in 2012.

Guro industrial complex has dramatically changed since its establishment (Koo, 2012). In the late 1980s, employment in Guro complex increased, but it began to decrease from 1988 when labor disputes were severe in Korea. Annual labor disputes from 1987 to 1989 were more than 100 times compared to those in 1986, and the industrial wage rate increased to nearly twice the rate in 1986 (Park, 1994). The labor movement caused most of the SMEs in the capital region to struggle with restructuring in the early 1990s (Park, 1995). Since the recession, coupled with labor disputes in the late 1980s, the Guro complex had continued to decrease its employment until the beginning of the financial crisis in 1997; moreover, the average firm size had dramatically decreased during the same period (Figures 4.10a and 4.11a).

The 1997 financial crisis was a critical turning point for the industrial restructuring of Guro complex. The employment level considerably decreased in 1997 to 1998, but it began to turn into a new direction toward a continuous increase in employment coupled with recovery within two years to the pre-shock level. The resurgence of the Guro complex in terms of the increase in employment was a historical event because its employment level had continuously decreased from 1987 to 1998. In the early and mid-1990s, new small firms continuously entered the Guro complex, whereas relatively large- or medium-sized firms left the complex.

However, the financial crisis triggered the industrial restructuring of the Guro complex. Export-oriented manufacturing activities were replaced by non-manufacturing activities. The number of new small firms in the Guro complex dramatically increased, from 442 firms in 1997 to 11,092 firms in 2011;

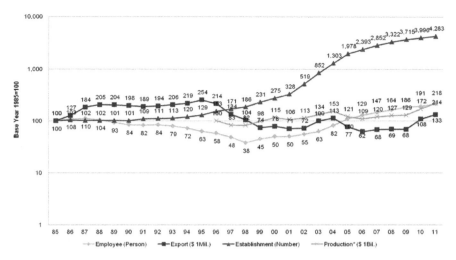

Figure 4.10a Changes in the Guro industrial cluster, 1985–2011
Source: Korea Industrial Complex Corporation.

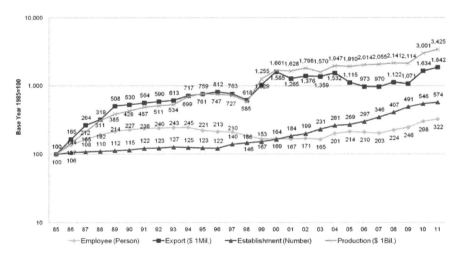

Figure 4.10b Changes in the Banwol industrial cluster, 1985–2011
Source: Korea Industrial Complex Corporation.

meanwhile, the average firm size in terms of employment decreased from 278 in 1987 to 72 in 1997 and to 12 in 2011 (Figure 4.11a). The trend of industrial restructuring, coupled with labor disputes and recession, occurred in the late 1980s, but a complete restructuring has progressed since the 1997 financial crisis. A turning point occurred in 1998, in which the ten-year declining trend completely changed into an increasing trend from 1998 with the creation of a new path—that is, the financial crisis triggered a new path for the local economy of Guro complex.

The creation of a new path reinforced the continuance of path creation during the recent global recession. Employment, number of firms, and export and production values have continuously increased since 2007 (Figure 4.10a). The evolution of the Guro complex followed the nonresistance path during the recession in the late 1980s and advanced to a restructuring process (Figure 4.5a). Guro continuously generated a new path and moved toward a dynamic process during the 1997 financial crisis (Figure 4.5b). By contrast, Guro has evolved from a government-led industrial agglomeration to an industrial cluster with diverse inter-firm and interorganizational networks.

Banwol industrial cluster was created in the late 1970s to decentralize industry from Seoul. Its establishment was initially the result of a deliberate policy to relocate polluted industries from Seoul. In the late 1970s, Seoul struggled with congestion caused by an extraordinary population growth and thus became unacceptably crowded and polluted. Ansan City, where Banwol industrial complex is located, likewise experienced an extraordinary population growth. Banwol complex consisted of approximately 5,500 firms that employed 136,000 workers and accounted for exports worth US$6.6 billion in 2012.

Banwol industrial complex, which is located outside Seoul within the capital region, showed a different trend from the Guro complex after the recession in the late 1980s. In contrast, the number of employees and firms increased in the early 1990s (Figure 4.10b). Medium-sized firms relocated from Seoul, including the Guro complex to the Banwol complex during the recession period, resulting in the growth of the Banwol complex in the early 1990s. The economic structure of the Banwol complex, which is different from that of the Guro complex, and the locational advantage for industrial firms in the far suburban Seoul allowed Banwol to continue its growth pattern in the recessionary period of the late 1980s and the early 1990s.

However, the 1997 financial crisis hit the complex in terms of its employment level. Employment decreased by more than 10 percent from 1997 to 1998, and recovery to the pre-shock level lasted for nearly eight years. Banwol has increased its employment level and number of firms since 2005. The number of firms has increased more than twice since 2005, and showed a decreasing trend in the size of firms in terms of employment. The average firm size decreased from 35 employees in 2005 to 25 employees in 2011 (Figure 4.11a).

The resurgence of Banwol during the late half decade of 2000 is related to government policy to support innovative clusters (Presidential Committee on Balanced National Development, 2007). Worldwide recession has not affected the economic performance of Banwol. From 2008 to 2009, employment, number of firms, and export and production values continuously increased, whereas exports slightly declined (Figure 4.10b). Compared with the other three complexes, Banwol has been relatively stable, which indicates neither a severe change nor a restructuring. Banwol complex followed the combined paths of reinforcement and dynamic process due to the continuous entry of new firms from Seoul. Banwol has likewise evolved from simply an agglomeration of SMEs to an industrial cluster in recent years.

Gumi and Changwon industrial clusters, located in the southeast region, have evolved differently from the Guro and Banwol complexes that are located in the capital region. Gumi industrial complex was established in the early 1970s and designed as an electronics district. Gumi industrial complex, which was a small agricultural village in 1969, fits into the government economic strategy of a new round of export-oriented industrial developments at the time (Park and Markusen, 1995). Gumi city has grown rapidly since the establishment of the Gumi industrial complex. Rousghly 1,600 firms are located in the complex, and these firms employed 86,000 workers and accounted for exports worth US$33.2 billion in 2012.

Changwon industrial complex was established in "a barren tract of rice paddies and muddy shores" (Markusen and Park, 1993, p. 167). Changwon industrial complex was designed as a special case of a military industrial district, entirely the creature of an ambitious national government initiative in heavy industry, especially machinery industry, in the mid-1970s. Changwon has grown rapidly since its establishment, and it has approximately 2,200 firms that employed 87,500 workers and accounted for exports worth US$23.4 billion in 2012.

Gumi and Changwon complexes demonstrate a similar pattern of path-dependent evolution and resilience because they are composed of large branch plants mainly headquartered in Seoul and are specialized industrial clusters in the electronics and machinery industry, respectively. Both Gumi and Changwon started as satellite industrial districts (Markusen, 1996; Park, 1996), which were originally composed of branch plants of large firms headquartered in Seoul. They exhibited a similar employment change pattern until 2003— that is, both complexes decreased their employment numbers after the late-1980s recession due to the labor disputes until 1993, but increased them from 1993 to 1996. The 1997 financial crisis significantly decreased the employment from 1997 to 1998 (Figures 4.10c and 4.10d). Gumi and Changwon required six and eight years to recover to the pre-shock employment level, respectively. However, the employment growth patterns of Gumi and Changwon have been different since 2004. Employment in Changwon considerably decreased until 2009 and has sharply increased since the time, whereas that in Gumi has continuously increased. The 1997 financial crisis and 2008 global economic recession slightly decreased the production in Changwon, whereas production in Gumi was not significantly affected.

In terms of export value, that of Gumi slightly decreased during the financial crisis but it shortly recovered, whereas that of Changwon increased in the same period. However, the export value of both complexes considerably decreased during the 2008 global economic recession. The exports of Changwon sharply

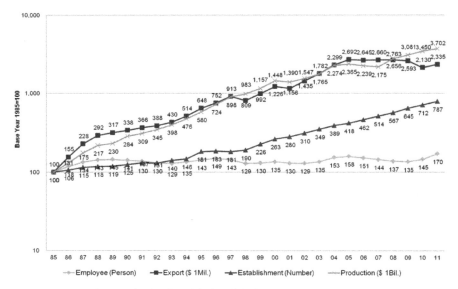

Figure 4.10c Changes in the Gumi industrial cluster, 1985–2011

Source: Korea Industrial Complex Corporation.

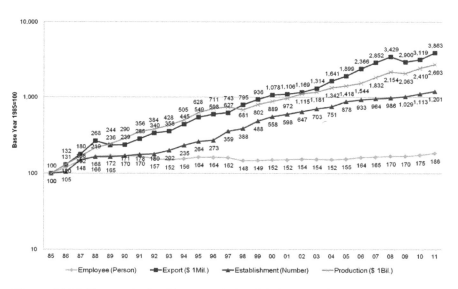

Figure 4.10d Changes in the Changwon industrial cluster, 1985–2011

Source: Korea Industrial Complex Corporation.

decreased from 2008 to 2009 and recovered within 1.5 years to the pre-shock level, whereas those of Gumi sharply decreased from 2009 to 2010. This difference in the export growth pattern during the global recession is closely related to the industrial structure of the two complexes, which is examined in the subsequent section.

The number of firms in both complexes continuously increased, which suggested the continuous evolution of the local economy with the emergence of new firms and recombination. Both complexes have reinforced their paths even after the 1997 financial crisis. Gumi and Changwon have evolved through the "dynamic process path" (Figure 4.5b) after the 1997 financial crisis and the "reinforcing path" (Figure 4.5a) in the recent global recession. This outcome suggests that the future of Gumi and Changwon is uncertain because they may move toward the path development, path creation, or performance phases with complete decline. Several new strategies, such as the accumulation and use of local intangible assets, strengthening competitiveness with external innovation networks, and the development of human capital, are accordingly critical to the destiny of both complexes. Both complexes have likewise evolved from an agglomeration of large branch plants, which is originally considered a satellite industrial district, to an industrial cluster.

Economic structure of four industrial clusters

The economic structure of a region is one of the key variables that shape the resistance, recovery, and response of a regional economy to a shock (Martin, 2012). Leading industrial types, role of services in general and producer services in particular, and firm size of a cluster may show the major characteristics of the economic structure of a cluster.

Four industrial clusters represent distinctive industrial structures in terms of leading industrial sectors (Table 4.2). Guro initially specialized in textile and clothing industries, but electronics has become the leading industry since the 1980s. Electronics, textiles, and machinery remained the three important industries in Guro until 2004. Machinery has been a leading industry in Banwol since the end of the 1990s; the share of textile and clothing has relatively decreased, whereas that of electronics has continuously increased since the late 1990s. The electronics industry has been continuously predominant in Gumi, whose shares comprised more than half of the total employment. Nonmetallic and textile industries were the next leading groups, but the share of the latter continuously decreased. The machinery industry has been predominant in Changwon. Transport equipment, and electric and electronics industries were constantly the second and third major industries in Changwon, respectively. The industrial structure of Changwon has been the most stable compared with the other three clusters. The industrial structure of Gumi has been relatively stable, but that of Guro has drastically changed. The industrial structure of Banwol continuously changes, but it is relatively stable compared with that of Guro.

Table 4.2 Leading industries in four industrial complexes (percent)

Industrial complexes	Industry	1999	2002	2004	2006	2008	2010	2012
Guro	Textiles/clothing	22.82	18.05	14.81	9.97	8.33	6.32	5.56
	Machinery	11.41	15.08	13.89	10.39	4.70	4.82	2.91
	Electric/electronics	35.57	38.23	35.35	22.75	24.02	21.42	19.63
	Nonmanufacturing	**0.00**	**5.53**	**17.87**	**45.63**	**52.88**	**59.81**	**65.92**
Banwol	Textiles/clothing	19.38	16.76	14.36	12.45	11.32	8.32	8.56
	Machinery	20.91	22.02	27.82	28.84	28.76	17.84	21.95
	Electric/electronics	**16.11**	**14.99**	**19.25**	**19.38**	**23.81**	**33.36**	**36.52**
	Nonmanufacturing	0.00	0.00	0.00	0.07	0.12	0.50	3.75
Gumi	Textiles/clothing	16.19	14.21	11.47	8.51	6.28	4.75	3.87
	Nonmetallic	13.00	14.94	12.49	11.34	13.80	8.11	6.15
	Machinery	4.03	3.89	5.24	4.17	11.97	15.02	16.75
	Electric/electronics	**55.43**	**55.30**	**61.44**	**66.23**	**58.70**	**60.36**	**62.32**
	Nonmanufacturing	0.00	0.00	0.00	0.00	0.05	0.09	0.07
Changwon	**Machinery**	**54.39**	**50.37**	**48.50**	**49.41**	**56.09**	**57.50**	**58.93**
	Electric/electronics	9.15	11.64	11.33	11.58	11.20	11.73	13.73
	Transport/equipment	24.44	24.91	26.25	27.64	23.27	21.66	19.14
	Nonmanufacturing	0.00	0.02	0.05	0.08	0.38	0.39	0.39

Source: Korea Industrial Complex Corporation, each year.

The share of nonmanufacturing activities has demonstrated a sharp contrast between Guro and the other three clusters in recent years (Table 4.2). The Guro complex has dramatically changed since the financial crisis, especially after its post-crisis recovery; two-thirds of the total employment of the cluster comprise the nonmanufacturing sector in Guro, whereas the nonmanufacturing sector in the other three complexes accounted for less than 4 percent of total employment. Guro had been an industrial complex specializing in manufacturing with no service activities within the complex prior to the 1997 financial crisis. Large manufacturing plants in Guro relocated to Gyeonggi Province or to non-capital regions during the restructuring period of the financial crisis. Since the beginning of the twenty-first century, the land of the location of former Guro large manufacturing plants that relocated to other areas has been converted into high-rise apartment or office buildings. In the same period, several small firms that were recovering from the financial crisis began to locate in apartment-type plants; these plants were newly built high-rise buildings converted from the former location of manufacturing plants in the Guro complex.

The majority of the nonmanufacturing sectors in the Guro complex are ICT-related services and knowledge-based services (Table 4.3). The number of nonmanufacturing firms and their employment increased more than twice from 2006 to 2013. Software development and supply accounted for approximately

Table 4.3 Contents of nonmanufacturing in the Guro industrial cluster (count, person, percent)

Industry types	December 2006		October 2013	
	Establish-ments (count, %)	Employees (person, %)	Establish-ments (count, %)	Employees (person, %)
ICT-related services	1,513 (65.2)	28,359 (62.2)	3,515 (68.5)	59,395 (62.1)
Data-base activities and on-line information provision services	88 (3.8)	1,592 (3.5)	144 (2.8)	3,016 (3.2)
Software development and supply	1,296 (55.8)	24,175 (53.0)	2,818 (54.9)	45,936 (48.0)
Data processing, hosting and related service activities	15 (0.6)	215 (0.5)	41 (0.8)	1,817 (1.9)
Telecommunications	20 (0.9)	229 (0.5)	49 (1.0)	552 (0.6)
Computer programing, system integration, and management services	94 (4.0)	2,148 (4.7)	463 (9.0)	8,074 (8.4)
Knowledge-intensive services	809 (34.8)	17,229 (37.8)	1,616 (31.5)	36,248 (37.9)
Architectural, engineering and other scientific technical services	317 (13.7)	5,866 (12.9)	632 (12.3)	11,191 (11.7)
Activities of management consultancy	– (0.0)	– (0.0)	10 (0.2)	79 (0.1)
Advertising preparation	42 (1.8)	545 (1.2)	91 (1.8)	1,283 (1.3)
Motion picture, video, broadcasting Programmes production	48 (2.1)	1,502 (3.3)	132 (2.6)	2,903 (3.0)
Research and experimental Development on natural sciences	147 (6.3)	5,712 (12.5)	280 (5.5)	13,915 (14.5)
Specialized design services	186 (8.0)	1,388 (3.0)	339 (6.6)	2,817 (2.9)
Publishing of books, magazines and other publications	69 (3.0)	2,216 (4.9)	129 (2.5)	4,048 (4.2)
Packaging and filling activities	– (0.0)	– (0.0)	3 (0.1)	12 (0.0)
Total	2,322 (100.0)	45,588 (100.0)	5,131 (100.0)	95,643 (100.0)

Source: Korea Industrial Complex Corporation, 2013.

half of the nonmanufacturing employment, but a diversification trend occurred. Engineering and technical services represented the next important sector, but research and experimental development on natural sciences accounted for a 14.5 percent share in terms of employment in 2013, which implied that knowledge-intensive basic research is likewise conducted in the Guro complex.

The Guro complex was nonresistant to the external crisis in the late 1990s and began to completely restructure its economic base from the beginning of the twenty-first century. Guro has completely restructured and created a new trajectory for the local economy, focusing on ICT and knowledge-intensive services using high-rise office buildings or apartment-type, multifloor plants, revealing the evolution of a new path involving a new path-creation phase in the integrated model (Figure 4.5a).

The role of the service sector in the local economy reveals interesting aspects. Table 4.4 shows the share of service sector to total employment and the share of producer service to employment in services of four cities, where the four clusters are located. Overall, Ansan, Gumi, and Changwon represent specialized industrial cities with a significantly smaller share of the service sector, compared with Guro District in Seoul and Seoul City. However, the share of producer services to total services sharply increased in Guro District after the financial crisis, which is even larger than that of Seoul. This change in Guro District is related to the restructuring and regeneration of the new path of the Guro complex.

The shares of the producer services in the other three cities are much smaller than those of Guro District and Seoul, but are relatively large compared with those of other cities in the region, representing the formation of considerable networks between manufacturing firms in the cluster and producer service firms in the relevant city. Although several fluctuations occurred in the share of producer services in Ansan, Gumi, and Changwon, the share of producer services increased in the last decade, especially after the financial crisis. The relatively high ratio of producer services in the industrial cities suggests the evolution of the local economy with the formation of local industrial networks within the cities and economic varieties in the local economy.

The results of the comparison of average firm size in terms of employment and export suggest another dimension of the evolution of industrial clusters (Figures 4.11a and 4.11b). Significant differences exist in the average firm size based on two variables—namely, employment and export. Since the economic recession due to the labor movement in the late 1980s, average employment size has continuously and remarkably decreased, except in the Banwol cluster, which began to decrease after 2004 (Figure 4.11a). The average employment figures in the Guro, Gumi, and Changwon clusters before the labor movement were almost similar, whereas in Banwol they were substantially smaller than in the other three clusters. Downsizing in terms of employment was not remarkable for Banwol, but that in the other three clusters was dramatic from the late 1980s to the end of the twentieth century. The downsizing of Guro

Table 4.4 Changes in the employment structure of Seoul and four industrial cities (person, percent)

Region	Industry	1995	1997	2000	2005	2008	2010
Seoul	Services* (%)	78.6	78.1	80.0	83.5	90.0	91.0
	Producer services** (%)	36.9	36.6	37.2	40.9	41.6	40.6
	Total employment (Person)	3,784,597	3,758,459	3,574,824	3,843,010	4,079,277	4,487,357
Guro-gu (District) in Seoul	Services	–	68.0	73.3	79.4	84.4	86.4
	Producer services	–	12.7	13.4	30.5	22.6	42.9
	Total employment	118,786	111,936	113,619	143,568	150,552	180,311
Ansan City (location of Banwol)	Services	–	46.5	47.8	52.0	56.9	64.3
	Producer services	–	16.7	15.9	16.8	21.6	24.6
	Total employment	191,055	188,410	200,125	232,109	258,881	269,816
Gumi City	Services	37.1	42.7	45.2	44.9	46.9	47.9
	Producer services	14.2	16.9	16.1	18.5	24.6	25.7
	Total employment	135,944	142,314	142,768	171,492	169,220	185,102
Changwon City>	Services	44.3	47.3	48.5	51.8	54.0	64.9
	Producer services	18.0	19.7	18.4	20.7	23.6	25.3
	Total employment	187,186	188,181	197,407	226,775	230,552	399,143

Source: Korean Statistical Information Service, census on establishments, each year; local government statistics, each year.
Note:
* Share of services to total employment.
** Share of producer services to employment in services.
> In 2010, the three neighboring cities, Changwon, Masan, and Jinhae, were consolidated into the Unified Changwon City.

Consumer services:
Electricity, gas, steam and water supply (35–36); construction (41–42); wholesale and retail sale (45–47); transportation (49–52); accommodation and food service activities (55–56); publishing, video, broadcast communications and information services (58–63); education (85); human health and social work activities (86–87); arts, sports and recreation-related services (90–91); membership organizations, repair and other personal services (94–96).
Producer services:
Financial services and insurance activities (64–66); real-estate activities, and renting and leasing (68–69); professional, scientific and technical activities (70–73); business facilities management and business support services (74–75); sewage and waste treatment, material recovery and restoration activities of environment (37–39).

was the most dominant, from the largest, with an average of 256 employees in 1985, to the smallest, with an average of 13 employees in 2011, from the four clusters.

Despite the significant decrease in the average employment size of a firm, its average export size did not significantly decrease, except in the case of Guro. The average export size of Guro sharply decreased from 1995 to 2009. The average export size of a firm likewise indicates the impact of the financial crisis and global recession. Guro, Banwol, and Changwon clusters recovered from the recession, but Gumi did not recover until 2011 in terms of the average export value of firms (Figure 4.11b). Changes in the average firm size in terms of employment and export suggest continuous changes, and the evolution of the clusters even in periods without a recession or crisis.

Conclusion

In this chapter, the notions of path dependence and resilience have been examined, and the integration of the notion of regional resilience to Martin's alternative path-dependent model has been attempted. Economic landscapes continuously evolve over time because of the continuous innovation of firms, fusion of technologies, external networks with globalization, and the integration of service and manufacturing. Integrating the notion of path dependence and regional resilience is apparently fruitful to the understanding of the evolution of the local or regional economy. In the integration model, the notion of regional resilience can be applied at any phase of the path-dependence

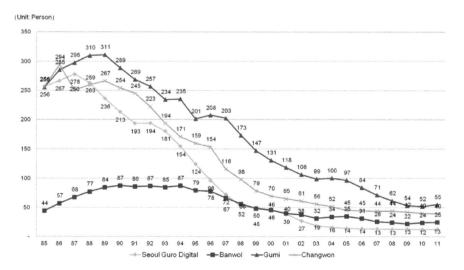

Figure 4.11a Changes in a firm's average employment size, 1985–2011

Source: Korea Industrial Complex Corporation.

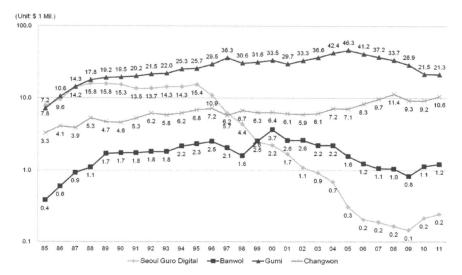

Figure 4.11b Changes in a firm's average export value, 1985–2011

Source: Korea Industrial Complex Corporation.

evolution, and Martin's alternative model can be interpreted more flexibly to include additional alternative ways of moving toward a new stage. In the integration model, restructuring has been considered an important process for the evolution of the local economy after a crisis or recession. Regional resilience and path dependence are considered dynamic and evolutionary processes in the integration model. However, incorporating the notion of resilience into the path-dependence evolution provides additional alternative ways for the local economy to move toward the next phase of the path-dependence evolution. Innovation network and industrial restructuring are important in successfully building regional resilience in this evolutionary process of path dependence.

The principal aim of the case study is not to verify the integrated model, but to demonstrate how the paths differ by regional characteristics in terms of economic structure and location, and to depict the dynamics of path-dependent evolution and regional resilience in the real world. The responses and paths of four Korean industrial clusters to external shocks support the conceptual framework of the path-dependence evolution and regional resilience. The four cases exhibited different paths and degrees of regional resilience, such as the reinforcement of paths, regional economic restructuring, and dynamic processes. The local economy can evolve through the path-dependence evolution via the dynamic process or reinforcing path over a long period. The analysis of growth patterns and changes in the economic structure of the four complexes likewise reveals that they evolved from agglomerations without innovation networks in the earlier development phases to industrial clusters with intensifying networks and innovation activities in both local and nonlocal contexts—that is, the mere co-locations of manufacturing plants or industrial complexes have evolved into industrial clusters through different evolutionary processes. Guro started with no innovation in the past and then restructured to a new path; Banwol started with simply an agglomeration of SMEs and continuously evolved as an industrial cluster; and Gumi and Changwon evolved from co-locations of branch plants to sustaining the industrial cluster through strong innovation strategies.

Incorporating the notion of regional resilience into the path-dependence evolution aids in understanding the changes in the local economy along the path- dependence evolution under crisis and recession conditions. Furthermore, the local economy has a larger opportunity to restructure and create a new path in a short period under an economic crisis or recession, as illustrated by the Guro industrial cluster. Overall, the evolutions of four industrial clusters are closely related to the integration of the path-dependent model and regional resilience. This chapter contributes to explaining the spatial forces in the dynamics of economic landscapes with the new theoretical framework and the concepts of path dependence and regional resilience. However, how various factors, such as innovation strategies, collaboration among economic actors, and external innovation networks, contribute to regional resilience and the path of the local economy should be empirically investigated.

Notes

1　Page (2006) points out two types of path dependence—namely, "outcome-dependent" and "equilibrium-dependent." If the outcome in a period depends on past outcome, the process is outcome-dependent, whereas if a convergence occurs in a long-run stable distribution over outcomes, which depends on past outcomes, the process is equilibrium-dependent.
2　For the adaptive cycle of system adaptation and change, see Pendall et al., 2010.
3　Guro industrial complex was initially named Korea Export Promotion Complex in the mid-1960s and was later called Seoul Digital Complex.

References

Berkes, F. & Folke, C. (Eds.). (1998). *Linking Sociological and Ecological Systems: Management Practices and Social Mechanisms for Building Resilience*. New York: Cambridge University Press.
Boas, T. C. (2007). Conceptualising continuity and change: the composite-standard model of path dependence. *Journal of Theoretical Political Science*, 19(1), 33–54.
Boschma. R. & Martin, R. (2007). Constructing an evolutionary economic geography. *Journal of Economic Geography*, 7(5), 537–548.
Boschma. R. & Martin, R. (Eds.). (2010). *The Handbook of Evolutionary Economic Geography*. Cheltenham and Northampton, MA: Edward Elgar.
Cambridge Journal of Regions, Economy and Society. (2010). Special issue on The Resilient Region. *Cambridge Journal of Regions, Economy and Society*, 3(1).

Chapple, K. & Lester, B. (2007). Emerging patterns of regional resilience (Working Paper 2007–13). Institute of Urban and Regional Development, University of California, Berkeley, CA.

Clark, G. L. & Kim, W. B. (Eds.). (1995). *Asian NIEs & the Global Economy*. Baltimore, MD and London: The Johns Hopkins University Press.

Cross, R. (1993). On the foundations of hysteresis in economic systems. *Economics and Philosophy*, 9(1), 53–74.

Crouch, C. & Farrell, H. (2004). Breaking the path of institutional development? Alternatives to the new determinism. *Rationality and Society*, 16(1), 5–43.

David, P. A. (1985). Clio and the economics of QWERTY. *American Economic Review*, 75(2), 332–337.

David, P. A. (1986). Understanding the economics of QWERTY: the necessity of history. In W. N. Parker (Ed.), *Economic History and the Modern Economics* (pp. 30–49). Oxford: Blackwell.

David, P. A. (2001). Path dependence, its critics and the quest for "historical economics." In P. Garrouste & S. Ioannides (Eds.), *Evolution and Path Dependence in Economic Ideas* (pp. 15–40). Cheltenham: Edward Elgar.

David, P. A. (2005). Path dependence in economic processes: implications for policy analysis in dynamical systems contexts. In K. Dopfer (Ed.), *The Evolutionary Foundations of Economics* (pp. 151–194). Cambridge: Cambridge University Press.

Dawley, S., Pike, A. & Tomaney, J. (2010). Towards the resilient region? (Discussion Paper). Centre for Urban and Regional Development Studies (CURDS), Newcastle University.

Fingleton, B., Garretsen, H. & Martin, R. (2012). Recessionary shocks and regional employment: evidence on the resilience of UK regions. *Journal of Regional Science*, 52(1), 109–133.

Foster, J. (2005). Self-organisational perspective on economic evolution: a unifying paradigm. In K. Dopfer (Ed.), *The Evolutionary Foundations of Economics* (pp. 367–390). Cambridge: Cambridge University Press.

Foster, K. A. (2007). A case study approach to understanding regional resilience (Working Paper 2007–08). Institute of Urban and Regional Development, Berkeley, CA.

Goldstone, J. A. (1998). Initial conditions, general laws, path dependence and explanation in historical sociology. *American Journal of Sociology*, 104(3), 829–845.

Grabher, G. (2009). Yet another turn? The evolutionary project in economic geography. *Economic Geography*, 85(2), 119–127.

Gray, M., Golob, E., Markusen, A. & Park, S. O. (1998). New industrial cities? The four faces of Silicon Valley. *Review of Radical Political Economics*, 30(4), 1–28.

Hanley, N. (1998). Resilience in social and economic systems: a concept that fails the cost-benefit test? *Environment and Development Economics*, 3(2), 244–249.

Hassink, R. (2010). Regional resilience: a promising concept to explain differences in regional economic adaptability? *Cambridge Journal of Regions, Economy and Society*, 3(1), 45–58.

Hill, E. W., Wial, H. & Wolman, H. (2008). Exploring regional economic resilience (Working Paper 2008–2004). Institute of Urban and Regional Development, Berkeley, CA.

Hirsch, P. M. & Gillespie, J. J. (2001). Unpacking path dependence: differential valuations accorded history across disciplines. In R. Garud & P. Karnøe (Eds.), *Path Dependence and Creation* (pp. 69–90). London: Lawrence Erlbaum.

Hudson, R. (2010). Resilient regions in an uncertain world: wishful thinking or practical reality? *Cambridge Journal of Regions, Economy and Society*, 3(1), 11–25.

Koo, Y. (2012). An analysis of cluster life cycle on the dynamic evolution of the Seoul digital industrial complex in Korea. *Journal of the Korean Association of Regional Geographers*, 18(3), 283–297 (in Korean with English summary).

MacArthur Foundation. (2007). *Network on Building Resilient Regions*. MacArthur Foundation. Retrieved from www.macfdn.org/media/article_pdfs/2BRR_NETWORK 8.5X11_0307.PDF.

MacArthur Foundation. (2009). *Building Resilient Regions*. Retrieved from www. macfound.org/site/ (accessed October 14, 2009).

MacKinnon, D., Cumbers, A., Pike, A., Birch, K. & McMaster, R. (2009). Evolution in economic geography: institutions, political economy, and adaptation. *Economic Geography*, 85(2), 129–150.

Markusen, A. (1996). Sticky places in slippery space: a typology of industrial districts. *Economic Geography*, 72(3), 293–313.

Markusen, A. & Park. S. O. (1993). The state as industrial locator and district builder: the case of Changwon, South Korea. *Economic Geography*, 69(2), 157–181.

Martin, R. (2010). The Roepke lecture in economic geography—rethinking regional path dependence: beyond lock-in to evolution. *Economic Geography*, 86(1), 1–27.

Martin, R. (2012). Regional economic resilience, hysteresis and recessionary shocks. *Journal of Economic Geography*, 12(1), 1–32.

Martin, R. & Sunley, P. (2006). Path dependence and regional economic evolution. *Journal of Economic Geography*, 6(4), 395–437.

Martin, R. & Sunley, P. (2007). Complexity thinking and evolutionary economic geography. *Journal of Economic Geography*, 7(5), 573–601.

Martin, R. & Sunley, P. (2011). Conceptualizing cluster evolution: beyond the life cycle model? *Regional Studies*, 45(10), 1299–1318.

Neill, J. (2006). What is psychological resilience? Retrieved from www.wilderdom. com/psychology/resilience/PsychologicalResilience.html (accessed April 16, 2006).

Nooteboom, B. (2000). *Learning and Innovation in Organizations and Economies*. Oxford: Oxford University Press.

North, D. (1990). *Institutions, Institutional Change and Economic Performance*. Cambridge: Cambridge University Press.

Page, S. E. (2006). Path dependence. *Quarterly Journal of Political Science*, 1, 87–115.

Park, S. O. (1993). Industrial restructuring and the spatial division of labor: the case of the Seoul metropolitan region, the republic of Korea. *Environment and Planning A*, 25(1), 81–93.

Park, S. O. (1994). Industrial restructuring in the Seoul metropolitan region: major trigger and consequences. *Environment and Planning A*, 26(1), 527–541.

Park, S. O. (1995). Seoul, Korea: city and suburbs. In G. L. Clark & W. B. Kim (Eds.), *Asian NIEs & the Global Economy, Industrial Restructuring & Corporate Strategy in the 1990s* (pp. 143–167). Baltimore, MD and London: The Johns Hopkins University Press.

Park, S. O. (1996). Network and embeddedness in the dynamic types of new industrial districts. *Progress in Human Geography*, 20(4), 476–493.

Park, S. O. (2010). Dynamics of economic spaces and spatial inequality in East Asia. *Journal of Korean Geographical Society*, 45(4), 478–501.

Park, S. O. & Markusen, A. (1995). Generalizing new industrial districts: a theoretical agenda and an application from a non-Western economy. *Environment and Planning A*, 27(1), 81–104.

Pendall, R., Foster, K. A. & Cowell, M. (2007). Resilience and regions: building understanding of the metaphor (Working Paper 2007–2012). Macarthur Foundation Research Network on Building Resilient Regions, Institute for Urban and Regional Development, University of California, Berkeley, CA.

Pendall, R., Foster, K. A. & Cowell, M. (2010). Resilience and regions: building understanding of the metaphor. *Cambridge Journal of Regions, Economy and Society*, 3(1), 71–84.

Pierson, P. (2000). Increasing returns, path dependence and the study of politics. *American Political Science Review*, 94(2), 252–267.

Pike, A., Dawley, S. & Tomaney, J. (2010). Resilience, adaptation and adaptability. *Cambridge Journal of Regions Economy and Society*, 3(1), 59–70.

Potter, A. & Watts, H. D. (2011). Evolutionary agglomeration theory: increasing returns, diminishing returns, and industry life cycle. *Journal of Economic Geography*, 11(3), 417–456.

Presidential Committee on Balanced National Development. (2007). Balanced national development policy in Korea: theory and practice. Seoul: Presidential Committee on Balanced National Development.

Reggiani, A. (2002). Resilience: an evolutionary approach to spatial economic systems. *Networks and Spatial Economics*, 2(2), 211–229.

Reggiani, A., Graff, T. & Nijkamp, P. (2002). Resilience: an evolutionary approach to spatial economic systems. *Networks and Spatial Economics*, 2(2), 211–229.

Schneiberg, M. (2007). What's on the path? Path dependence, organizational diversity and the problem of institutional change in the US economy (1900–1950). *Socio-Economic Review*, 5(1), 47–80.

Setterfield, M. (2010). Hysteresis (Working Paper 10–04). Department of Economics, Trinity College, Hartford, CT.

Simmie, J. & Martin, R. (2010). The economic resilience of regions: towards and evolutionary approach. *Cambridge Journal of Regions, Economy and Society*, 3(1), 27–43.

Stark, D. & Bruszt, L. (2001). One way or multiple paths? For a comparative sociology of east European capitalism. *American Journal of Sociology*, 106(4), 1129–1137.

Thelen, K. (2003). How institutions evolve: insights from comparative historical analysis. In J. Mahoney and D. Rueschemeyer (Eds.), *Comparative Historical Analysis in the Social Sciences* (pp. 208–240). New York: Cambridge University Press.

Walker, B., Cunderson, L., Kinzig, A., Folke, C., Carpenter, S. & Schultz, L. (2006). A handful of heuristics and some propositions for understanding resilience in socio-ecological systems. *Ecology and Society*, 11(1), 13.

Website references

Korea Industrial Complex Corporation: www.kicox.or.kr/

Korean Statistical Information Service (KOSIS), Census On Establishments: http://kosis.kr/eng/database/database_001000.jsp?listid=Z

Local Government Statistics: www.guro.go.kr/; www.iansan.net/; www.gumi.go.kr/; www.changwon.go.kr/

5 Global megatrends and spatial economic inequality in East Asia[1]

Introduction

Global economic spaces have been considerably reshaped in the last two decades. Uneven development is prevalent, and spatial inequality is unlikely to be eliminated or may even be substantially reduced in these environments. Two contrasting views on spatial inequality exist—namely, convergence and divergence. In the neoclassical equilibrium economics model, the general trend of regional convergence over time is challenged through the flow of labor and capital toward the direction of equilibrium over space, in an integrated national space economy. In the neoclassical model, migration might be expected to reduce spatial inequality, resulting in regional convergence. However, such migration is selective and especially common among higher skilled workers, and might cause regional divergence instead of convergence (Kanbur and Rapport, 2005). The new empirics of regional convergence in industrialized countries recently revealed a much slower regional convergence rate than that proposed by the orthodox neoclassical model (Martin and Sunley, 1998).

Accordingly, concern has grown regarding spatial inequality patterns and levels and the underlying processes that give rise to these patterns and levels (Rey and Janikas, 2005). Uneven development with regional divergence trends is suggested with regard to the cumulative concentration of capital, labor, and output. Endogenous growth theories suggest that uneven development results from the fact that the key factors of economic growth, such as localized collective learning, accumulation of skills, and technological innovation, develop unevenly across the economic space (Martin, 2001; Rey and Janikas, 2005). Spatial externalities and technology spillovers are considered the primary factors in shaping regional economic growth and spatial disparity, in both endogenous growth theory and the new economic geography model (Fujita et al., 2001; Ravallion and Jalan, 1996; Rey and Janikas, 2005). However, the endogenous growth model has limitations in the context of a globalized knowledge-based information society. According to Martin and Sunley (1998), "its reliance on formal models which fail to capture the importance of the socio-institutional context and embeddedness of regional economic development," and it has been "overwhelmingly abstractly theoretical and its key conditions have been insufficiently investigated empirically" (p. 220). Rey and Janikas (2005) likewise pointed out the limitations of the endogenous regional inequality model in terms of spatial scale choice, level of spatial concentration, and relationship between overall inequality and spatial autocorrelation.

Spatial inequality is another principal issue in reshaping economic spaces in the globalized economy, especially when viewed against the recent global financial crisis. The World Bank (2009) attempted to interpret the reshaping or transformation of economic spaces in terms of three dimensions (3Ds)—namely, density, distance, and division. The 3Ds are easy metaphors, because density, distance, and division summon images of human, physical, and political geography, respectively. Understanding the transformations along these dimensions helps identify the main market forces and appropriate policy responses at each of the three geographical scales—namely, local, national, and international. "Density," which is related to agglomeration economies, is the most important dimension in a local context. "Distance" to density is the most important dimension at the national scale, whereas "Division" is the principal dimension in an international context. Density and scale economies have become exceedingly important in the progression of the service world and knowledge-based economy. The development of information society and globalization has contributed to the easy flow of information and materials over space, and then to the decreasing impact of distance and division. However, the differentiations of 3D impacts over global economic spaces are significant. The theoretical framework of the World Bank can be considered as a starting point or an initial basis for understanding the transformation of economic spaces. Additional frameworks are therefore required to explain the dynamics of economic spaces and understand the spatial inequalities that occur in a knowledge-based economy.

Spatial inequalities can be considered as resulting from the dynamics of economic spaces that have evolved along with the advancement of the four global megatrends—namely, globalization, knowledge-based economy, information society, and the service world (Bryson et al., 2004; Park, 2009b; Regional Studies, 2008). The four global megatrends of change are interrelated. Globalization and information society are related to dispersion and long-distance networks, whereas knowledge-based economy and the service world are mostly correlated with agglomeration and localized networks. In the real world, the forces and processes resulting in inequalities in space are complex and dynamic due to the contrasting spatial trends that govern economic spaces. Economic spaces and spatial inequalities cannot evolve through a single criterion of economic rationality.

The processes of shaping economic spaces and economic inequalities have been diverse over time periods and regions. The changes in economic spaces have been well recognized at various spatial scales through the emergence of "new industrial spaces" (Scott, 1988) or "sticky places in a slippery space" (Markusen, 1996), the shift of the economic gravity center (Park, 1997), regional world (Storper, 1997), the development of spatial innovation systems (Oinas and Malecki, 1999), industrial restructuring (Park, 1993; Clark and Kim, 1995), and diverse clusters, including the temporary and the virtual (Park, 2005; Torre, 2008). These dynamics are likewise closely related to the techno-economic paradigm shifts that have distinctive characteristics in production, business, and innovation systems (Hayter, 1997; Park, 2003).

This chapter is a preliminary examination for understanding spatial economic inequality under the framework of the dynamics of economic spaces with regard to the four global megatrends previously identified. The four megatrends of change are not independent of nor separate from each other. Rather, they are interrelated in the processes of concentration and dispersion. This study analyzed both the international economic inequalities in East and Southeast Asia and the interregional economic inequalities within a nation. The inequalities within a nation were analyzed using cases from Japan, Korea, and Thailand, whereas the trends of international inequalities were interpreted through the changes of major variables related to the four megatrends and macroeconomic events, such as financial crises and industrial restructuring.

This chapter used three different empirical methodologies to analyze spatial economic inequality in East and Southeast Asia. First, relative entropy index was measured to analyze international inequalities in East and Southeast Asia, as well as interprovincial inequalities within selected countries in terms of GDP and major economic activities. Considering the level of economic development and reliable data, Japan, Korea, and Thailand were selected for regional inequality analysis. Relative entropy indices were used for comparison because the number of observations (countries and provinces) differed. Second, multiple regression analysis was employed to examine the impact of the four global megatrends on the spatial variation of international per capita GNI in East and Southeast Asia. Regression analysis was likewise applied to countries that are members of the Organization for Economic Cooperation and Development (OECD) to understand the impact of the differences in the four global trends on the respective economic developments of countries. Third, the impact of the four megatrends on regional inequality within a nation was examined using Korea as the sample. Only the case of Korea was analyzed due to the lack of reliable data in relation to the four megatrends.

This chapter is organized as follows. The subsequent section discusses the four global megatrends with regard to the dynamics of economic spaces. The impact of the megatrends on spatial economic inequality is also discussed. The third section analyzes the international inequalities in East and Southeast Asia. The impact of the four megatrends on the international variation of per capita GNI is analyzed for the East and Southeast Asian countries as well as for those that are part of the OECD. The fourth section analyzes the inter-regional inequalities within Japan, Korea, and Thailand. It likewise explores the impact of the four megatrends on the regional variation of per capita GDP. Finally, the fifth section concludes with policy implications on both developing and developed economies.

Four global megatrends and the dynamics of economic spaces

Changes in spatial economic inequalities result from the changes in economic spaces on the regional, national, and global scale. Changes in economic spaces at various spatial scales in the last two to three decades seem to be closely related to the progress of the four global megatrends. Considering that this study is a segment of the research on the broader theme of the dynamics of economic spaces, the relationship between the four global megatrends and the dynamics of economic spaces are briefly examined.

New spatial processes and forms of economic practices have evolved in the global society in the last two decades. These processes and forms result from the four global megatrends previously mentioned. The spatial dynamics of the economy has been strengthened by the contrasting forces of the megatrends in the twenty-first century. The trend of economic inequality over space is inconsistent because this trend causes different effects on global economic spaces. For instance, knowledge-based economy and the service world may generally facilitate divergence with increasing spatial inequality, through the concentration of high quality human resources and innovation via intensive knowledge exchange on a local scale. In contrast, information society and globalization may promote convergence with decreasing spatial disparity through the easy circulation of codified knowledge, capital, and technology in the global space economy. However, the dynamics of spatial inequality is more complex in reality, because knowledge-based economy may likewise be related to dispersion and spatial convergence with brain circulation and global knowledge networks. Moreover, contrasting spatial processes in the organization of economic activities are related to diverse actors, which may display behavioral and strategic conflicts.

Networking is one of the most important processes for knowledge creation in a knowledge-based economy. The transfer of tacit knowledge is often regarded as being confined to the local milieu, whereas codified knowledge may exist ubiquitously. Spatial proximity for face-to-face contact is important in ensuring the effective sharing of tacit knowledge; thus, concentration reinforces the importance of innovative clusters and regions in a knowledge-based economy (Polenske, 2007). In this view, learning processes occur among actors residing in a community by being there—local buzz, contributing spatial divergence with increasing spatial inequalities. Meanwhile, recent studies suggest that knowledge can be attained and created by investing in communication channels, called pipelines, with selected providers located outside the local milieu (Bathelt et al., 2004; Rychen and Zimmermann, 2008). Therefore, firms develop global pipelines not only as venues in which they can exchange products or services, but also to benefit from novel ideas and knowledge learned from outside sources. Accordingly, a high level of local buzz and selected global pipelines coexist, providing firms located in clusters with a string of particular advantages unavailable to outsiders. These contrasting processes may cause regional divergence within a nation, while promoting spatial convergence among other countries.

The knowledge-based economy has facilitated the progress of the service world (Bryson et al., 2004). In a knowledge-based economy, advanced services are very important in reorganizing economic spaces. Diverse services, especially producer services, are closely linked to every stage of manufacturing, from production to distribution. Consequently, producer services, such as R&D activities, finance, advertising, engineering, computer software services, and design, have become increasingly important in a knowledge-based economy (Harrington and Daniels, 2006). These advanced services tend to concentrate overwhelmingly in large metropolitan areas because face-to-face contact is important for sharing and creating new information and knowledge. The development of producer services in a nation may therefore cause regional inequalities within it because the concentration of producer services results in a concentration of a high quality labor force in a given area and a new spatial division of labor (Park, 2006).

The development of ICT and the Internet has contributed to the progress of the information society or digital era. The Internet has a significant impact on codified knowledge transfer over the global space. It has likewise significantly contributed to rapid globalization. However, the existence of knowledge and information that cannot be traded through the Internet has produced a paradox in speculation on the spatial impact of ICT. On one hand, the rapid development of ICT in the last decade and the increase in the number of Internet users have been considered the important impetus for reducing spatial disparities and promoting the spatial convergence of economic activities over space. On the other hand, several geographical studies have indicated that spatial proximity and the nodality of cities retain their importance in economic development, even as communication has improved and the economy has become globalized with ICT development (Florida, 1995, 2002; Gertler, 1995; Malecki, 2002; Zook, 2002). Along with the development of the Internet, the creation of knowledge for innovation, and the flow of knowledge, information, and materials are critical to the dynamics of economic spaces. The Internet infrastructure, knowledge-intensive manpower, innovation clusters and networks, and a "cluster of wants" are unevenly distributed over space, and thus become significant factors in reorganizing economic spaces (Park, 2003).

Globalization has likewise considerably affected the spatial dynamics of economic activities. As globalization progresses, the processes in and emergence of new forms of economic spaces have extended beyond local and national boundaries over time. The global flows of capital, labor, technology, engineering, and even policies, are now extremely important to changes in economic spaces (Alvstam and Schamp, 2005). The foreign direct investments that transnational corporations (TNCs) infuse in developing countries certainly contribute to international convergence, aided by technology and knowledge transfer that extends beyond the dispersion of manufacturing activities at the international scale. However, the progress of globalization may have different effects at the regional level within a nation. For instance, TNCs will prefer to locate their branch plants or offices at the core area of developing countries due to geographical advantages, including transportation and communication infrastructure, labor markets, and living environments, thereby revealing regional divergence with increasing inequalities. However, the regional impact of globalization may not be unidirectional and may be different depending on the respective characteristics of each country (Coulombe, 2007).

As previously discussed, the global megatrends significantly affect the dynamics of economic spaces and spatial economic inequalities. However, the spatial effects of the four megatrends are multidirectional and complex. The reason for the existence of this complexity in the spatial manifestation of megatrend effects to economic spaces is closely related to the disparities existing in physical space. The social, material, and environmental conditions of the physical space are unevenly distributed. Linguistic, cultural, and institutional differences likewise exist, along with significant variations in the characteristics of local labor markets, culture, and social relations. These disparities significantly affect the spatial manifestation of electronic space because the latter is intrinsically embedded in physical space. Furthermore, differences in local cultures, institutions, and labor markets in the physical space significantly affect innovations in a knowledge-based economy. Despite their considerable differences, physical and electronic spaces are complementary in the economic space process. Thus, the ICT infrastructure cannot be separated from the social, political, economic, and cultural contexts in which the technological infrastructure is embedded (Li et al., 2001). These complexities cause spatial economic inequalities to become persistent even under globalization and in an information society. Furthermore, the spatial dynamics have both spatial and temporal dimensions because the inequalities diversify by spatial scale and change over time.

International economic inequalities in East Asia

East Asian countries have experienced significant economic changes with industrial restructuring, financial crisis, and dynamic economic growth in the last four decades. East Asian countries have diverse histories and cultures, but have experienced dynamic economic growth in the same period. Examining the dynamic economic spaces despite their diverse cultural and historical backgrounds is appropriate because of the dynamic changes in the East Asian countries. This study covers thirteen East and Southeast Asian countries, as shown in Table 5.1. Mongolia and Taiwan were supposed to be included in East and Southeast Asia, but were excluded in the analysis due to the unavailability of serial data in international statistical records. Although the thirteen countries have experienced rapid economic growth, they likewise suffered sharp economic declines during the financial crisis that occurred some time at the end of the twentieth century. From 1971 to 2007, China showed

Table 5.1 Average annual GDP growth rates, 1971–2007 (percent)

	Mean (%)	SD (%)	N (1971–2007)
Korea	6.8951	3.59957	37
China	9.0076	3.51864	37
Japan	2.9192	2.32741	37
Hong Kong	6.2935	4.44289	37
Singapore	7.5605	3.70477	37
Malaysia	7.1200	4.61589	37
Philippines	3.8689	3.45485	37
Indonesia	6.0205	3.94122	37
Vietnam	6.0897	3.31647	37
Thailand	6.1868	4.04972	37
Cambodia	3.3303	8.18772	37
Laos	5.6451	3.72439	37
Myanmar	4.7657	7.22470	37

Source: UN Statistics Division (UNSD), National Accounts Main Aggregates Database, each year.

the highest average annual GDP growth rate with 9.0 percent, whereas Japan showed the lowest average GDP growth rate with 2.9 percent (Table 5.1).

To measure the trend of spatial economic inequality in East and Southeast Asia, relative entropy index was measured. Considering that the entropy value (H) is sensitive to the number of subgroups, it is not comparable when the number of subgroups changes by variable. To compare the spatial disparities of different economic activities or variables with different numbers of subgroups, the "relative entropy value" (RH) was used in this paper. The coefficient of variation (CV) was examined as well. However, RH shows the trend of spatial disparity more clearly and CV shows trends similar to that of RH; thus, spatial economic disparities were explained through different variables based on the changes of RH over time.

The entropy value in this chapter is measured as follows.

$$H = -\sum_{i}^{n} q_i \log_2 q_i$$

where

H = entropy value,

q = a set of nonnegative numbers, whose sum is unity, and

$$\left(\sum_{i}^{n} q_i = 1.0\right)$$

n = number of subgroups.

If any $q = 1$ and all other qs are zero, then H is equal to zero.
For a given n, H is at its maximum when all qs are equal, thus:

$$H = -n\left(\frac{1}{n} \log_2 \frac{1}{n}\right) = \log_2 n$$

Relative Entropy (RH) = $H/\log_2 n$

The major variables used to explain the spatial disparity in nations are selected as a represented variable for each global megatrend. Gross domestic production (GDP) is used for measuring the spatial economic disparity. The number of patent applications filed under the PCT (PATENT), the ratio of Internet users (INTERNET), service value-added (SERVICE), and export sales (EXPORT) are selected as surrogate variables for knowledge-based economy, information society, service world, and globalization, respectively. In addition to the preceding variables, population (POPULATION) and manufacturing value-added (MANUFACTURING) are used to compare the spatial disparity. The two variables of PATENT and INTERNET were measured from 1995 to 2007. The other five variables were measured from 1970 to 2007.

Several important characteristics of the spatial disparities in East Asia at the international level were observed. First, overall, a trend of convergence of all variables occurred. This trend was consistent with the general trend analyzed by the World Bank (Hamaguchi, 2009). The convergence can likewise be recognized by actual per capita GDP (Figure 5.1). The decline of the per capita GDP of Japan since 1995 has significantly contributed to the general trend of convergence in East Asian countries.

The RH values of POPULATION slightly increased in a continuous manner from 1970 to 2007 (Figure 5.2). The RH indices of GDP, EXPORT,

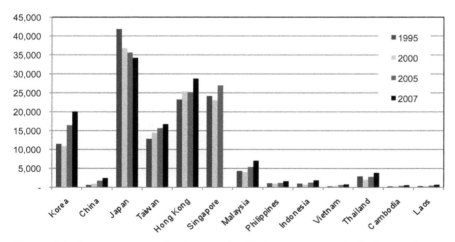

Figure 5.1 Convergence trends of per capita GDP among countries in East and Southeast Asia (dollars)

Source: IMF, International Financial Statistics; World Bank, World Table; UN (http://esa.un. org/unpp); Taiwan National Statistical Office, each year.

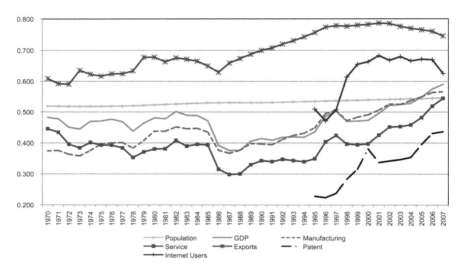

Figure 5.2 Change of relative entropy values in East and Southeast Asia

Source: IMF, International Financial Statistics; World Bank, World Tables; UN (http://esa.un.
org/unpp); Taiwan National Statistical Office, each year.

Note: For relative entropy value of patent, Cambodia, Myanmar, Laos, and Vietnam are not
included and Taiwan is included (ten countries).

For other relative entropy values, thirteen countries are measured.

MANUFACTURING, and SERVICE revealed a general trend of convergence
with an increase in the relative entropy value from 1970 to 2007 from 0.482,
0.609, 0.375, and 0.445 to 0.590, 0.745, 0.567, and 0.545, respectively. The
RH values of PATENT and INTERNET likewise generally increased from
1995 to 2007, from 0.228 and 0.509 to 0.436 and 0.626, respectively. This
general trend of convergence over time among the countries seemed to be
related to the international flow of manufacturing investments as well as the
transfer of technology and knowledge. The most rapid increase in the RH value
of PATENT since 1995 suggested a clear dispersal trend. At the international
level, the flow of technology and investment among nations contributed to the
overall trend of convergence among East Asian nations.

Second, divergence trends with increasing international inequality occurred
during the global crises. Thus, the impact of global crises caused some
exceptions in the overall trend of convergence. Consistent fluctuations occurred
during the two oil crises in 1973 and 1978, as well as the East Asian financial
crisis at the end of the twentieth century. A divergence trend occurred with a
consistent decrease in the RH values of GDP, MANUFACTURING, and
SERVICE in 1973, 1978, and from 1998 to 1999 (Figure 5.2). Moreover, the
RH values of GDP, MANUFACTURING, and SERVICE considerably
decreased from 1986 to 1988. EXPORT RH values likewise decreased in 1986.

The considerable decrease in RH values reveals the divergence trend or increase in spatial inequalities among East Asian countries. The global oil crises in the 1970s and the Asian financial crisis in 1997 appear to have affected developing countries more negatively. The relative contraction of these countries contributed to the decrease in the RH values and increase in spatial inequalities. The rapid decrease in the RH values in the late 1980s seemed to be related to the temporary contraction of investments, compounded by labor dispute difficulties in the Asian NIEs, and later in the early 1990s, both of which increased the value with increasing investments to low-cost developing countries and industrial restructuring of the Asian NIEs (Clark and Kim, 1995; Park, 1993).

Third, considerable differences emerged in the degree of spatial disparities among the variables. The RH value of EXPORT was the largest, whereas that of PATENT was the smallest. The sharp increase in the PATENT RH value after the East Asian financial crisis in 1997 indicated the considerable dispersion of technology and knowledge to East and Southeast Asian countries, with the trend of globalization and knowledge-based economy. The GDP RH value rapidly increased after the financial crisis, and this outcome was related to the relative decline of the Japanese economy and relative growth of developing countries.

What are the most significant variables with regard to the four megatrends that can explain the international economic inequalities in East and Southeast Asia? To answer this question, multiple regression analyses were conducted, with per capita GNI as the dependent variable and EXPORT, INTERNET, SERVICE, and PATENT as the independent variables of the four megatrends as follows.

$$\text{Per capita GNI} = f(\text{EXPORT, INTERNET, SERVICE, PATENT}) \quad (1)$$

This regression analysis is considered an initial attempt and a preliminary analysis of the effect of four megatrends. A more detailed analysis of the impact of the four megatrends will be conducted through in-depth interview surveys in the next step following this research.

Data availability for East Asian countries was the most substantial in the 1995 and 2005 cases; hence, the analyses focused on these periods. Similar analyses were conducted for OECD countries to compare the results. The four variables may not be representative of the four megatrends. However, only one representative variable for each megatrend was used due to the consistent availability of reliable data. EXPORT, INTERNET, and PATENT seemed to sufficiently represent globalization, information society, and knowledge-based economy, respectively. Producer service was more appropriate as a representative variable for the service world. However, the SERVICE variable was used in this study because of the availability of reliable data.

Four models were employed—namely, models for the East and Southeast Asian countries and the OECD countries, respectively, for both 1995 and 2005.

Except for the 2005 East and Southeast Asia model, the other three models were significant at the 0.000 level. The 2005 East and Southeast Asia model was significant at the 0.1 level (0.053). In East and Southeast Asia, the model explained 99 percent and 80 percent of the variations of per capita GNI in 1995 and 2005, respectively; meanwhile, in the OECD, the model explained 54 percent and 73 percent of the variations in dependent variables, respectively (Tables 5.2 and 5.3). Out of four variables for explaining the dependent variable, only INTERNET was statistically significant at the 0.05 level in the 1995 and 2005 in the East Asia models (Table 5.2). The rate of Internet users dramatically increased in the first half decade of this century, but considerable differences in the Internet user rate can be observed (Figure 5.3).

However, in the OECD cases, both SERVICE and INTERNET were statistically significant. The results of the multiple regression analysis suggested that information society significantly affected the spatial conversion

Table 5.2 Result of regression analysis for "per capita GNI," ASIA

Independent variable	Dependent variable			
	Per capita GNI, 1995		Per capita GNI, 2005	
	B	p-value	B	p-value
(Constant)		.079		.642
Export	.010	.960	−.169	.639
Internet	.641>	.000	.779**	.027
Service	−1.394	.317	1.547	.424
Patent PCT	2.036	.138	−1.097	.544
R^2	.992>	.802*		

Note: *Significant at the 10% level; **significant at the 5% level; >significant at the 1% level.

Table 5.3 Result of regression analysis for "per capita GNI," OECD

Independent variable	Dependent variable			
	Per capita GNI, 1995		Per capita GNI, 2005	
	B	p-value	B	p-value
(Constant)		.790		.087
Export	.130	.660	−.191	.309
Internet	.379**	.013	.524>	.000
Service	.571>	.001	.545>	.000
Patent PCT	−.007	.982	.076	.676
R^2	.541>	.733>		

Note: * Significant at the 10% level; ** significant at the 5% level; > significant at the 1% level.

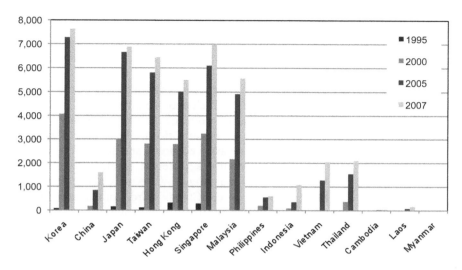

Figure 5.3 Internet users of Asian countries (per 10,000)

Source: International Telecommunication Union, World Telecommunication/ICT Indicators Database, each year.

trend of international per capita GNI in East and Southeast Asia. In contrast, the service world and information society significantly affected the spatial conversion trend of international per capita GNI in OECD countries. The significance of the INTERNET variable in both OECD countries and East and Southeast Asia seemed to indicate the meaningful effect of the information society in the global economic space. This result likewise suggested that the service world was more advanced in OECD countries, whereas it was in the initial stage of impact in East and Southeast Asia. Considering the trend of spatial inequality in SERVICE in recent years, as shown in Figure 5.2, the effect of the service world will soon become important in explaining the spatial inequality of per capita GNI in East and Southeast Asia.

Interregional inequalities in Japan, Korea, and Thailand

Overall pattern of changes in GDP growth rate

The overall converging international trend in East Asia for the last four decades may not represent the interregional convergence trend within a nation. The reason is that regional inequality trends may differ due to the level of economic development and economic structural characteristics of a nation. In this chapter, the regional inequalities of economic activities were examined for selected countries.

The author selected three appropriate nations to examine the trend of interregional inequalities in East Asian countries. Using the annual growth rate data of the thirteen countries from 1971 to 2007, factor analysis was initially conducted (Table 5.4). Four factors were extracted from the analysis. Korea, Japan, Hong Kong, Singapore, Malaysia, Indonesia, and Thailand contributed to Factor 1, which was labeled as "market economy." The rest of the factors were labeled as "socialist country," "developing country," and "emerging socialist country." Case study countries from the "market economy" group were selected for three reasons. First, the examination of the impact of the four megatrends seemed appropriate for a market economy and not for a relatively less open economy, which may require a different framework. Second, appropriate data regarding the four megatrends were unavailable from the countries of the other three groups, except China. Third, comparison among the market economy countries seemed appropriate in comparing the changes in spatial inequality over time according to development levels.

From the "market economy" group, Japan, Korea, and Thailand were selected, and the selection considered the economic development in these countries. Japan, Korea, and Thailand were considered advanced country, newly developed country, and newly industrializing country, respectively. Given that Japan and Korea are in East Asia, Southeast Asia seemed to have been underrepresented. Accordingly, Indonesian examples were discussed, although the data analysis for Indonesia could not be fully conducted.

Considerable fluctuations in the GDP growth rates of the four selected countries have occurred since 1971. The first oil crisis in the early 1970s

Table 5.4 Result of factor analysis

| | Factor | | | |
	Market economy	Socialist country	Less developed	Emerging social, economy
Korea	.748	.099	−.284	.064
China	.044	.838	.022	.078
Japan	.559	−.210	−.233	−.531
Hong Kong	.667	−.233	−.322	−.112
Singapore	.760	−.205	−.058	−.139
Malaysia	.790	−.303	.062	.057
Philippines	.340	−.640	−.154	.096
Indonesia	.879	−.137	.216	−.119
Vietnam	.048	.177	−.134	.852
Thailand	.864	.105	−.096	−.055
Cambodia	−.137	.675	−.110	.295
Laos	−.023	.090	.880	−.130
Myanmar	−.233	−.155	.560	.492
Eigenvalue	4.228	1.901	1.444	1.424
% Variation	32.527	14.627	11.106	10.952

critically hit the Japanese economy, and the second oil crisis in the late 1970s critically affected the Korean economy, resulting in negative growth rates (Figure 5.4). The two oil crises in the 1970s did not significantly affect the Indonesian and Thai economies. However, the Asian financial crisis in the late 1970s was more critical for Indonesia and Thailand, in which GDP growth rates were both less than – 10 percent. At the time, Korea, Thailand, and Indonesia suffered from a bailout situation. Japan likewise showed a negative growth rate, although it was not involved in a bailout. Among the three bailout countries, Korea recovered the most rapidly and achieved a growth rate of more than 9 percent in 1999.

Based on the RH indices of the regional GDP, the regional inequality levels in the three countries differed, but the overall trend of inequality in these nations moved toward convergence. Before the mid-1990s, the regional inequality level in Thailand was much higher than those in Japan and Korea; however, the differences in regional inequality among the three countries have decreased, and a converging trend of regional inequality levels among them has occurred since 2001 (Figure 5.5).

The three countries generally showed common short-term cyclical trends after 1985. First, trends of increasing regional inequalities occurred in Japan until 1990, in Korea in 1993, and in Thailand in 1990. Second, a trend of decreasing regional inequality occurred from 1990 to 1996 in Japan, 1993 to 1998 in Korea and Thailand, until the period prior to the Asian financial crisis. Third, a slight increase in inequality has occurred in Japan since 1996, an overall increasing inequality trend in Korea since 1998, and a decreasing inequality trend in Thailand since 2001. Moreover, Korea and Thailand, both of which experienced bailouts in 1998, showed common trends around the financial crisis— that is, both countries showed decreasing regional inequalities

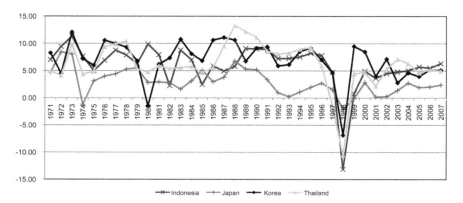

Figure 5.4 Changes of GDP growth rate in Korea, Indonesia, Japan, and Thailand, 1971–2007, percent

Source: UNSD, National Accounts Main Aggregates Database, each year.

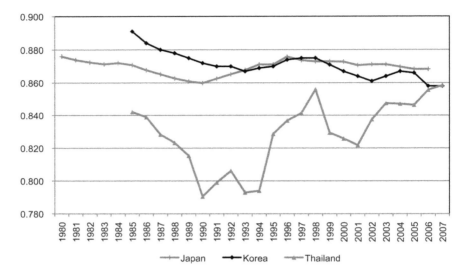

Figure 5.5 Relative entropy values of GRDP in Korea, Japan, and Thailand, 1980–2007

Source: Japan Statistics Bureau; Korea National Statistical Office; Thailand National Accounts Office, each year.

prior to the financial crisis. Regional inequality in these countries increased for three to four years after the financial crisis, and regional inequality in GDP decreased with increasing RH values (Figure 5.5). Such changes in regional inequality before and after the financial crisis in Korea and Thailand indicated the significant regional effect of a global crisis within a nation. A global crisis affects the increasing spatial inequality both at the international and interregional levels. Such a crisis would have more negative effects on less developed countries at an international level and peripheral regions within a nation. This trend may be applicable to the current global economic crisis resulting from the US financial disaster.

Thailand has shown an overall trend of convergence in the regional inequality of regional GDP since the early 1990s, and this trend differs from the cases of Japan and Korea. If we consider the regional inequality of POPULATION, a converging trend in regional inequality of the per capita GDP may occur even in Japan and Korea, because the regional inequalities of POPULATION in these countries have increased, whereas no significant change in the regional inequality of POPULATION in Thailand has occurred (Figure 5.6). A continuously increasing regional disparity of POPULATION has occurred, with concentration in the core regions of Japan and Korea, with that in Korea being particularly remarkable (Figure 5.6).

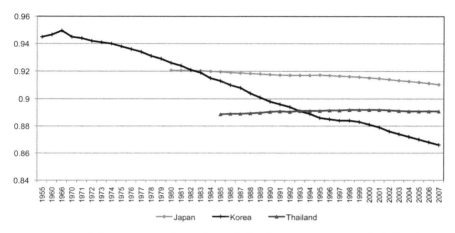

Figure 5.6 Relative entropy values of population in Korea, Japan, and Thailand, 1955–2007

Source: Japan Statistics Bureau; Korea National Statistical Office; Thailand National Accounts Office, each year.

Comparison of the regional disparities in the key variables

The comparison of the level and trend of regional disparities in POPULATION, GDP, MANUFACTURING, and SERVICE reveals the different national characteristics of regional inequality in the three countries.

In Japan, the level of regional inequalities in the last three decades was the highest in SERVICE, followed by GDP, MANUFACTURING, and POPULATION (Figure 5.7). In the last four decades, GDP, SERVICE, and POPULATION showed only a slight overall concentration trend with a slight increase in regional inequality, whereas only MANUFACTURING showed a continuous regional convergence trend with a decrease in the level of regional inequality. The change trend in the regional inequality of GDP was similar to that of SERVICE, which suggested that service activities significantly affected the trend of regional inequality of GDP and depicted the progress of the service world in Japan as an advanced country. The different trends of regional inequalities in economic activities seemed to be related to the spatial dispersion trend of manufacturing activities within a country, whereas the regional concentration trend of service activities in Japan. The RH index of regional GDP was significantly related to the RH index of SERVICE, whereas the relationship was insignificant, even negative, with regard to the RH index of MANUFACTURING (Table 5.5). Moreover, large metropolitan areas play a leading role in the service world with the agglomeration of service activities in these areas, especially in the core area of Japan.

In Korea, the overall trend of regional inequality in the last four decades increased with the regional concentration of economic activities. This overall

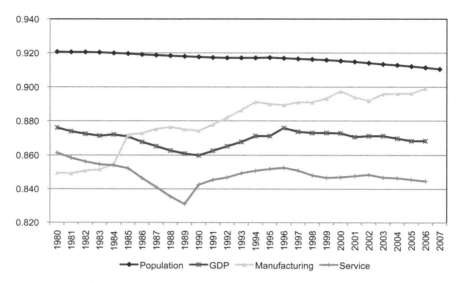

Figure 5.7 Relative entropy values of population, GDP, manufacturing production, and service production in Japan, 1980–2007

Source: Japan Statistics Bureau, each year.

Table 5.5 Correlation between "RH of regional GDP" and "RH of other variables"

RH of other variables	RH of regional GDP		
	Japan	Korea	Thailand
MANUFACTURING	−0.038	0.682	0.627
SERVICE	0.794	0.840	0.823
Per capita regional GDP	0.912	0.128	0.721
Population	0.068	0.872	0.055

trend was similar in the four variables, although the level of regional inequalities differed by variable. The level of regional inequality of SERVICE was the highest, but almost similar to that of MANUFACTURING, whereas the level of regional inequality of POPULATION was the lowest (Figure 5.8). A considerable trend of regional concentration of manufacturing activities occurred with the increasing level of regional inequality in the 1980s, whereas slight fluctuations have occurred since the late 1980s. Nevertheless, the overall trend can be regarded as a steadily increasing level of inequality of MANUFACTURING. Compared to Japan, manufacturing activities in Korea are important to the level of regional inequality of GDP, and the service world in Korea has not progressed as considerably as it has in Japan in recent years (Figure 5.8). In contrast to the case of Japan, data from Korea indicated that the RH index of regional GDP remained significantly correlated with MANUFACTURING (r=0.682) (Table 5.5), which suggested that manufacturing remains important to the changes in regional inequality in the country.

The case of Thailand showed quite a different story. In Thailand, the regional inequalities of GDP, SERVICE, and MANUFACTURING considerably fluctuated, whereas the inequality of POPULATION showed almost no change (Figure 5.9). MANUFACTURING showed both the highest level of regional inequality and a considerable decrease in regional inequality compared with other variables in the last three decades. The increasing regional inequality with decreasing values of RH from 1998 to 2001 for GDP, SERVICE, and MANUFACTURING indicated the impact of the financial crisis and the converging trend after 2001, which resulted from the recovery from the crisis.

Despite a slight trend of increasing regional disparity in regional GDPs in Japan and Korea, the disparity in per capita regional GDP may not significantly change because of the trend of increasing regional inequality of POPULATION. The level of regional disparity in the per capita GDP has been extremely low, and slight changes in the last three decades have been observed for both Japan and Korea (Figure 5.10). This result indicated that the regional disparity in regional GDP has been considerably offset by the migration of a population toward the core area. An overwhelming concentration of economic activities in the capital region has been observed, but an overall trend has occurred regarding per capita regional GDP convergence by offsetting with the continuous overwhelming concentration of a population to the capital

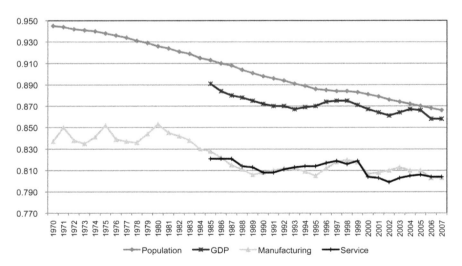

Figure 5.8 Relative entropy values of population, GDP, manufacturing production, and service production in Korea, 1970–2007

Source: Korea National Statistical Office, each year.

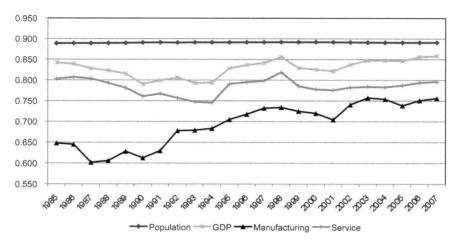

Figure 5.9 Relative entropy values of population, GDP, manufacturing production, and service production in Thailand, 1985–2007

Source: Thailand National Accounts Office, each year.

region in Korea (Park, 2009a). Thus, a converging trend of per capita regional GDP has occurred, and the correlation between the RH indexes of regional GDP and per capita regional GDP is insignificant in Korea (Table 5.5). In the case of Thailand, the trend of changes in regional inequality of the per capita regional GDP showed similar patterns with the changes in the regional inequality of GDP because of the lack of significant changes in the level of regional inequality of POPULATION (Figure 5.10).

The cases of the three countries suggest several implications. Japan has been clearly involved in the service world, and service activities are extremely important for regional economic growth and inequalities in Japan. Manufacturing agglomeration remains critical for regional economic growth and inequalities in Korea, and Korea is currently in the initial stage of the progress of the service world, initiated by the agglomeration of advanced service activities in the capital region. In Thailand, both manufacturing agglomeration and dispersion are progressing in recent years and are important for regional economic growth and change. The differences in the significant variables for explaining the regional inequalities among the three countries may indicate the differences in the level of economic development, on one hand, and the various effects of the four global megatrends, on the other hand.

Impact of the four megatrends in Korea

As examined in East and Southeast Asia at the international level, the effects of the four megatrends were analyzed by multiple regression analysis for 2000 and 2007 in Korea as follows.

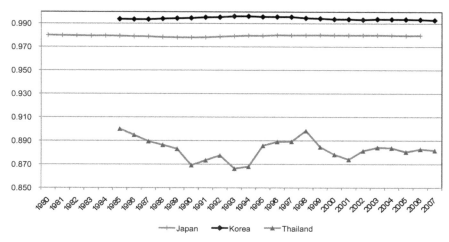

Figure 5.10 Relative entropy values of per capita GRDP in Korea, Japan, and Thailand, 1980–2007

Source: Japan Statistics Bureau; Korea National Statistical Office; Thailand National Accounts Office, each year.

Regional GDP = f (PATENT, BUSINESS SERVICE,
INTERNET, EXPORT) (2)

Per capita regional GDP = f (PATENT, BUSINESS SERVICE,
INTERNET, EXPORT) (3)

Both "regional GDP" and "per capita regional GDP" are used as dependent variables. BUSINESS SERVICE is used instead of SERVICE because the former is a more appropriate variable for representing the "service world." BUSINESS SERVICE in this chapter includes computer and related services, professional, scientific and technical services, and business support services.

Models 2 and 3 are statistically significant at the 0.01 level. As expected from the previous discussion of the offsetting effect of POPULATION, the explained variations in model 2 (approximately 98 percent for 2000 and 2007) are considerably higher than those in model 3 (approximately 70 percent for 2000 and 81 percent for 2007). The reason is that the regional disparity in the per capita regional GDP decreased by offsetting the regional GDP disparity through the regional disparity in POPULATION. The statistical significance of the models with regard to the regional and per capita regional GDPs reveals the importance of the four megatrends in understanding the dynamics of economic spaces in Korea in the twenty-first century. However, the importance of each megatrend differs and changes over time.

Globalization and knowledge-based economy are significant for both the regional disparities of regional and per capita regional GDPs at the beginning of the twenty-first century. The PATENT and EXPORT variables are statistically significant at the 0.01 level to explain the regional disparity in both regional and per capita regional GDPs in the model for 2000 (Tables 5.6 and 5.7). The BUSINESS SERVICE variable is not significant because the service world has not yet progressed significantly in 2000. The INTERNET variable is the most important for the international disparity in per capita GDP in East and Southeast Asia, as previously examined. However, the INTERNET variable is not significant in explaining both the regional disparities in regional and per capita regional GDPs in Korea. This difference in the impact of the INTERNET seems to be related to two aspects. First, considering that Korea is a small country in terms of physical land, it already had a well-developed Internet infrastructure in 2000. The regional disparity in the rate of Internet

Table 5.6 Result of regression analysis for "GRDP," by region, Korea

Independent variable	Dependent variable			
	GRDP, 2000		GRDP, 2007	
	B	p-value	B	p-value
(Constant)		.146		.054
Export	.261$^>$	.009	.247$^>$	.000
Internet[1]	−.074	.199	−.089	.101
Business service	.108	.300	.346$^>$	.001
Patent	.700$^>$	.000	.618$^>$	.000
R^2	.983$^>$	.979$^>$		

Note: * Significant at the 10% level; ** significant at the 5% level; $^>$ significant at the 1% level.
[1] Internet variable in 2000 used Internet user data from 2001.

Table 5.7 Result of regression analysis for "per capita GRDP," by region, Korea

Independent variable	Dependent variable			
	Per capita GRDP, 2000		Per capita GRDP, 2007	
	B	p-value	B	p-value
(Constant)		.962		.724
Export	1.488$^>$	.001	1.015$^>$	.000
Internet[1]	.059	.802	.093	.546
Business service	.490	.175	.836$^>$	.006
Patent	−1.668$^>$	.002	−1.166$^>$	.001
R^2	.699$^>$	.814$^>$		

Note: * Significant at the 10% level; ** significant at the 5% level; $^>$ significant at the 1% level.
[1] Internet variable in 2000 used Internet user data from 2001.

users is not significant at the provincial level (Park, 2004). Second, a limitation exists in the impact of Internet user rates when Internet diffusion reaches the mature stage, because the maximum value is 100 percent. Accordingly, despite the critical importance of the development of an Internet infrastructure and information society to the economic growth of Korea, the effect on regional disparity at the provincial level within Korea is not statistically significant.

The standardized coefficient β of PATENT is a strong negative value for the model of per capita regional GDP in Table 5.7. PATENT is highly concentrated in Seoul (approximately 40 percent of the nation) and in the capital region (more than three-quarters of the nation). This PATENT concentration is much higher than the concentration of the population in Seoul (approximately 21 percent of the nation) and in the capital region (about 48 percent of the nation). In contrast to the overwhelming PATENT concentration in Seoul, the share of PATENT in most of the industrial cities, which show higher per capita regional GDP, is extremely low. Convergence in the regional disparity of the per capita GDP is caused by the offset effect of the concentration of regional GDP through population concentration; thus, the overwhelming PATENT concentration in the capital region yields statistically negative effects on the regional variation in per capita GDP.

The effect of BUSINESS SERVICE represents an interesting story about the progress of the service world in Korea. In both models for regional and per capita regional GDPs, BUSINESS SERVICE was not statistically significant in 2000. However, BUSINESS SERVICE in the 2007 models was statistically significant in both models for regional GDP and per capita regional GDP at the 0.01 significant level (Tables 5.6 and 5.7). This change in the effect of BUSINESS SERVICE in 2007 indicates the rapid progress of the service world in Korea in recent years. The shares of business and producer services to the total services of Korea in terms of employment increased from 4.7 and 26.7 percent in 2000 to 7.6 and 28.5 percent in 2007, respectively (Park et al., 2007). As previously discussed, however, Korea has not yet fully entered the service world similar to most advanced countries, with manufacturing still significantly contributing to the regional disparity in regional GDP.

Conclusion and policy implications

This chapter is a preliminary result of the analysis of spatial economic inequality in East Asia with regard to the four global megatrends—namely, knowledge-based economy, globalization, information society, and the service world, under the broad framework of the dynamics of economic spaces. The international inequalities of per capita GNI at the national scale in East and Southeast Asia, as well as interregional inequalities at the regional scale within the national space economies of Japan, Korea, and Thailand, were analyzed with regard to the four megatrends. The major findings of this study are as follows.

First, the four megatrends as a whole have clearly explained the variations in international inequalities among the countries in East and Southeast Asia, and interregional inequalities at the regional scale within a nation, revealing that the four megatrends significantly affected the dynamics of economic space in East and Southeast Asia. However, the individual effects of the four megatrends on spatial inequalities are significantly different depending on the spatial scale of analysis and national characteristics. The progress of the information society significantly affects international inequalities at the national scale, whereas it is not statistically significant in explaining the regional inequalities at the regional scale within a nation. These findings support the importance of spatial scale in the analysis of spatial inequalities, as suggested by Martin and Sunley (1998), Rey and Janikas (2005), Yamamoto (2008), and so on.

Second, a trend of international convergence of per capita GNI of East and Southeast Asian nations has occurred, whereas different trends have been observed in countries at the regional scale within a nation. For instance, a slightly increasing trend of regional inequality of regional GDP has occurred in Japan and Korea, but an overall converging trend with decreasing regional inequalities in Thailand has occurred in the last two decades. These differences have caused the level of regional inequality to converge even though the level of regional inequality has been higher in Thailand than in Japan and Korea. Despite a slight increase in the regional inequality of regional GDP in Japan and Korea, the regional inequality of per capita GDP was extremely low, and no significant change had been observed over time due to the offset effects of the concentration of population to the core region.

Third, global crises had a significant effect, which extended beyond the effect of the four megatrends, on the changes in spatial inequalities. Two global oil crises in the 1970s and the East Asian financial crisis in the late 1990s had a discontinuity effect in the general trend, thus increasing the international inequality of economic activities. This finding suggests that despite the contrasting effects of the global crisis in each country, poor countries are generally more vulnerable in a global crisis. The previous negative effects of the global crisis on developing economies at the international level and on peripheral regions within a nation suggest that the current global economic crisis resulting from the US financial crisis may increase the international inequalities and interregional inequalities within a nation. According to a recent research on inequality in Korea, the regional inequality has been expected to increase in 2009, with the closure of marginal firms in the region and the concentration of new start-ups in the capital region (Hyundai Research Institute, 2010).

The findings of the current study suggest several policy implications. Considering the significance of the information society at the international level, developing countries should primarily improve their Internet infrastructures to catch up with newly industrialized countries. The Internet user rates of the Philippines, Indonesia, Cambodia, Laos, and Myanmar are currently extremely low; thus, the improvement of Internet infrastructures in these countries will certainly contribute to the diffusion of knowledge and technology and to the converging trend in East Asian countries. In developing countries, the agglomeration of manufacturing activities seems to be critical for national economic development and international convergence of per capita GNI. The cluster of manufacturing activities in developing countries may initially increase regional disparity within a nation, but the regional disparity of per capita GDP will decrease over time with spillover effects, as shown in Korea. In developing countries, in addition to the improvement of information infrastructure and manufacturing cluster strategy, the development of human resources is critical to the global trends of a knowledge-based economy.

Variables related to the knowledge-based economy (PATENT) are significant for the variation in per capita regional GDP in Korea; thus, brain circulation within a nation will be critical in promoting regional development in the peripheral areas of newly industrialized and advanced countries. Regional innovation systems should likewise be promoted in the aforementioned areas. Considering the high rate of Internet users in these countries, new forms of economic spaces such as temporary clusters and virtual innovation networks (Park, 2005, 2009b) can be promoted in the peripheral areas to enhance the utilization of regional resources and potentials. In view of the importance of the service world (SERVICE) and information society (INTERNET) for the variation in per capita GNI in OECD countries, newly industrialized countries should develop appropriate policies for promoting the service world. In particular, considering the inclusion of the BUSINESS SERVICE variable for explaining the 2007 per capita GDP of Korea (which was excluded in 2000), the development of producer services in the peripheral areas seems to be a critical policy issue in the future of newly industrialized countries.

A new system should be established for brain circulation and labor retraining within the context of the dramatic social changes in advanced and newly industrialized countries resulting from low birth rates and rapid population aging trends. To support the development of a creative region, retired experts can take on consulting activities for local SMEs and participate in the local retraining programs as teachers. Employing the expertise of retired professionals is an efficient and inexpensive means of enhancing the competitiveness of the local labor market and brain circulation for regional development in an aging society.

Finally, rather than "picking-the-winner" policy for regional development and innovation in the less favored regions of East Asia, region-specific assets and potentials should be developed by improving the absorbing power of knowledge through diverse networks at various scales, from local and regional to national and global. Significant differences exist in the spatial dynamics of innovation between China and India in industrializing countries (Crescenzi et al., 2012) as well as between the United States and Europe in advanced countries (Crescenzi et al., 2007). Considering the organizational, institutional, and structural differences by country, policy makers should be careful in copying best practices in the advanced countries or successful cases in East Asia.

Note

1   This chapter is based on a revision of the following paper: Park, Sam Ock (2010). Dynamics of economic spaces and spatial inequality in East Asia. *Journal of Korean Geographical Society*, 45(4), 478–501.

References

Alvstam, C. G. & Schamp, E. W. (2005). *Linking Industries Across the World*, Aldershot: Ashgate.

Bathelt, H., Malmberg, A. & Maskell, P. (2004). Clusters and knowledge: local buzz, global pipelines and the process of knowledge creation. *Progress in Human Geography*, 28(1), 31–56.

Bryson, J. R., Daniels, P. W. & Warf, B. (2004). *Service Worlds: People, Organizations, Technologies*. London and New York: Routledge.

Clark, G. L. & Kim, W. B. (Eds.). (1995). *Asian NIEs & the Global Economy*. Baltimore, MD and London: The Johns Hopkins University Press.

Coulombe, S. (2007). Globalization and regional disparity: a Canadian case study. *Regional Studies*, 41(1), 1–17.

Crescenzi, R., Rodriguez-Pose, A. & Storper, M. (2007). The territorial dynamics of innovation: a Europe–United States comparative analysis. *Journal of Economic Geography*, 7(6), 673–709.

Crescenzi, R., Rodriguez-Pose, A. & Storper, M. (2012). The territorial dynamics of innovation in China and India. *Journal of Economic Geography*, 12(5), 1055–1086.

Florida, R. (1995). Towards the learning region. *Futures*, 27(5), 527–536.

Florida, R. (2002). *The Rise of the Creative Class*. New York: Basic Books.

Fujita, M., Krugman, P. & Venables, A. J. (2001). *The Spatial Economy: Cities, Regions, and International Trade*. Cambridge, MA: MIT Press.

Gertler, M. S. (1995). "Being there": proximity, organization, and culture in the development and adoption of advanced manufacturing technologies. *Economic Geography*, 71(1), 1–26.

Hamaguchi, N. (2009). Regional integration, agglomeration, and income distribution in East Asia. In Y. Huang & A. M. Bocchi (Eds.), *Reshaping Economic Geography in East Asia* (pp. 1–18). Washington, DC: The World Bank Publications.

Harrington, J. W. & Daniels, P. W. (Eds.). (2006). *Knowledge-Based Services, Internationalization and Regional Development*. Aldershot: Ashgate.

Hayter, R. (1997). *The Dynamics of Industrial Location*. Chichester, New York, Weinheim, Brisbane, Singapore and Toronto: Wiley.

Hyundai Research Institute. (2010). Stagnation and promotion issues of regional economy. *Weekly Review of Economy*, Vol. 10–03.

Kanbur, R. & Rapoport, H. (2005). Migration selectivity and the evolution of spatial inequality. *Journal of Economic Geography*, 5(1), 43–58.

Li, F., Whalley, J. & Williams, H. (2001). Between physical and electronic spaces: the implications for organizations in the networked economy. *Environment and Planning A*, 33(4), 699–716.

Malecki, E. J. (2002). The economic geography of Internet's infrastructure. *Economic Geography*, 78(4), 399–424.

Markusen, A. (1996). Sticky places in slippery space: a typology of industrial districts. *Economic Geography*, 72(3), 293–313.

Martin, R. (2001). EMU versus the region? Regional convergence and divergence in Euroland. *Journal of Economic Geography*, 1(1), 51–80.

Martin, R. & Sunley, P. (1998). Slow convergence? The new endogenous growth theory and regional development. *Economic Geography*, 74(3), 201–227.

Oinas, P. & Malecki, E. J. (1999). Spatial innovation systems. In E. J. Malecki & P. Oinas (Eds.), *Making Connections: Technological Learning and Regional Economic Change* (pp. 7–34). Aldershot: Ashgate.

Park, S. O. (1993). Industrial restructuring and the spatial division of labor: the case of the Seoul Metropolitan Region, the Republic of Korea. *Environment and Planning A*, 25(1), 81–93.

Park, S. O. (1997). Rethinking the Pacific Rim. *Tijdschrift voor economische en sociale geografie* (*Journal of Economic and Social Geography*), 88(5), 425–438.

Park, S. O. (2003). Economic spaces in the Pacific Rim: a paradigm shift and new dynamics. *Papers in Regional Science*, 82(2), 223–247.

Park, S. O. (2004). Knowledge, networks and regional development in the periphery in the internet era. *Progress in Human Geography*, 28(3), 283–286.

Park, S. O. (2005). Network, embeddedness, and cluster processes of new economic spaces in Korea. In R. Le Heron & J. W. Harrington (Eds.), *New Economic Spaces: New Economic Geographies* (pp. 6–14). Aldershot: Ashgate.

Park, S. O. (2006). Service world and the dynamics of economic spaces. In J. W. Harrington & P. W. Daniels (Eds.), *Knowledge-Based Services, Internationalization and Regional Development* (pp. 15–40). Aldershot: Ashgate.

Park, S. O. (2007). Industrial restructuring and changes of economic spaces. In U.-C. Chung & H.-S. Cho (Eds.). *Financial Crisis + 10, How Has It Changed Korea?* (pp. 59–101). Seoul: SNU Press (in Korean).

Park, S. O. (2009a). A history of the republic of Korea's industrial structural transformation and spatial development. In Y. Huang & A. M. Bocchi (Eds.), *Reshaping Economic Geography in East Asia* (pp. 320–337). Washington, DC: World Bank Publications.

Park, S. O. (2009b). Long-term Visions and strategies for the regional development policies of Korea. In *Proceedings, Reshaping Regional Policy: Co-prosperity and Competitiveness* (pp. 75–103). Seoul: Presidential Committee for Regional Development.

Polenske, K. R. (Ed.). (2007). *The Economic Geography of Innovation*. Cambridge: Cambridge University Press.

Ravallion, M. & Jalan, J. (1996). Growth divergence due to spatial externalities. *Economic Letters*, 53(2), 227–323.

Regional Studies. (2008). Special issue: Clusters in the global knowledge-based economy: knowledge gatekeepers and temporary proximity. *Regional Studies*, 42(6), 767–904.

Rey, S. J. & Janikas, M. V. (2005). Regional convergence, inequality, and space. *Journal of Economic Geography*, 5(2), 155–176.

Rychen, F. & Zimmermann, J. B. (2008). Clusters in the global knowledge-based economy: knowledge gatekeepers and temporary proximity. *Regional Studies*, 42(6), 767–776.

Scott, A. J. (1988). *New Industrial Spaces: Flexible Production Organization and Regional Development in North America and Western Europe.* London: Pion.
Storper, M. (1997). *The Regional World.* New York and London: The Guilford Press.
Torre, A. (2008). On the role played by temporary geographical proximity in knowledge transmission. *Regional Studies*, 42(6), 869–889.
World Bank. (2009). *World Development Report 2009: Reshaping Economic Geography.* Washington, DC: World Bank Publications.
Yamamoto, D. (2008). Scales of regional income disparities in the USA (1955–2003). *Journal of Economic Geography*, 8(1), 79–103.
Zook, M. A. (2002). Hubs, nods and by-passed places: a typology of e-commerce regions in the United States. *Tijdschrift voor Economische en Sociale Geografie*, 93(5), 509–521.

Website references

IMF, International Financial Statistics: http://elibrary-data.imf.org/FindDataReports.aspx?d=33061&e=169393
ITU, World Telecommunication/ICT Indicators Database: www.itu.int/en/ITU-D/Statistics/Pages/publications/default.aspx
Japan Statistics Bureau: www.stat.go.jp/english/
Korea National Statistical Office: http://kostat.go.kr/portal/english/index.action
OECD, patent database: www.oecd.org/sti/inno/oecdpatentdatabases.htm
Taiwan National Statistical Office: http://eng.stat.gov.tw/mp.asp?mp=5
Thailand National Statistical Office: http://web.nso.go.th/index.htm
UN: http://esa.un.org/unpp
UN Statistics Division (UNSD), National Accounts Main Aggregates Database: http://unstats.un.org/unsd/snaama/Introduction.asp
UN, Population Division: www.un.org/en/development/desa/population/
World Bank, World Table: www.worldbank.org/

6 Interaction between corporate and urban systems for the accumulation of intangible assets[1]

Introduction

Globalization has been one of the significant megatrends in changes in global economic spaces in the last three decades. Increase in foreign direct investments (FDIs) beyond the increase in international trade has dramatically shaped and reshaped the global space economy, especially in emerging East Asian economies. The progress of a knowledge-based economy and an information society has overlapped with globalization, and has resulted in the remarkable global flows of both intangible assets, including knowledge, human capital, technological know-how, and brand, as well as tangible assets through FDIs and the international trade of products and resources. Accompanying the progress of a knowledge-based information society are two trends—namely, (1) the relatively decreasing importance of physical resource endowment as drivers of regional development and firm growth, and (2) the increasing importance of intangible assets related to personal knowledge for both firm and region (Surinach and Moreno, 2012).

Intangible asset accumulation by firms and regions has become a critical factor in gaining competitiveness. In particular, the accumulation of some kind of intangible asset in a given city or region is very important in attracting FDIs for industrializing countries because the externalities gained through knowledge spillover from firms can influence the accumulation of regional intangible assets, which results in a positive relationship between a firm and a region in the knowledge-based economy (Artis et al., 2012). Accordingly, the creation, accumulation, and flow of intangible assets in the global space economy have become significant factors influencing the changes in global economic spaces along with the changing competitiveness and productivity of firms and regions. In the processes involved in the intangible asset accumulation of a firm, cities and regions outside the internal organization of the firm become important in the acquisition and integration of external knowledge beyond the internal knowledge base of the firm. These processes reflect the interaction of the firm with diverse regions to access region-specific knowledge and thus imply the importance of regions as the key driver of innovation (Asheim et al., 2011).

The interaction between a firm and a region in an industrial location has long been traditionally included in the theories of economic and urban geography. In the long history of firm–region interaction, the relative emphasis has recently shifted from the access to tangible assets to the access to intangible assets (Regional Studies, 2012). In corporate geographic research, the focus has shifted from manufacturing activities to knowledge and information flows and corporate networks with financial institutions (Gong and Wheeler, 2002; Park and Wheeler, 1983; Wheeler, 1981, 1986, 1999). Wheeler (1986, 1988a, 1988b) emphasized the corporate role in the urban systems of the USA in terms of the relationship between firms and urban areas.

This chapter extends the relationship between corporate systems and urban systems to the global space economy beyond the USA, as well as to the intangible assets, by considering the two global megatrends of globalization and a knowledge-based information society. The relationship between corporate and urban hierarchies is examined within the context of intangible asset accumulation to increase the competitiveness of firms and regions. Several studies have explored the importance of intangible assets in the competitiveness and productivity of firms (e.g. Artis et al., 2012; Bianchi and Labory, 2004; Lev, 2001; Marrocu et al. 2011; O'Mahony and Vecchi, 2009; Revilla Diez, 2000; Surinach and Moreno, 2012). The role of intangible assets in regional economic growth has been broadly examined in a special issue of *Regional Studies* (2012). However, the function of corporate and urban systems has not been well examined relative to intangible asset accumulation to increase the competitiveness of both firm and region. Given Wheeler's pioneering research on corporate system and urban hierarchy in terms of headquarters location in the USA, the current study can be regarded as an extension of his work through its focus on intangible assets.

The major purpose of this chapter is to investigate the conceptual framework of the processes of intangible asset accumulation through the interaction of corporate and urban systems. To understand the interaction process between corporate and urban systems, as well as intangible asset accumulation, two cases of distinctive and contrasting Korean firms, which include more than 200 establishments, are historically analyzed using various materials and firm report statistics on the spatial and structural strategies for growth employed by the firms. In-depth interviews are also conducted to clarify such interaction and the processes of intangible asset accumulation. Qualitative methods serve an important function in understanding the complex plurality of contexts and the networks between firms and their environment (Birkinshaw et al., 2011). Following the Introduction, the second section examines the firm–region relationship relative to intangible assets. In the third section, the conceptual framework of the interaction between corporate and urban systems is discussed. In the fourth section, the two cases of Samsung Electronics Corporation (SEC) and Lutronic Corporation are examined based on the conceptual framework. The final section presents the concluding remarks.

Firm–region relationship and intangible assets

Firm–region relationship has been a long-standing focus of research in geography since the works of traditional location theorists, Alfred Weber and August Lösch (Weber, 1929; Lösch, 1952). However, most early studies on firm–region relationship have focused on the organization of tangible assets relative to location factors, such as access to material sources and market, transportation, and labor. Firms interact with the region in the process of making location decisions, considering the accessibility to input materials and markets, as well as to sources of cheap labor. In a firm–region interaction, transportation cost is a critical factor in the spatial organization of production activities. With the progress of the knowledge-based economy over the last few decades, intangible assets, such as knowledge, technological innovation, and brand, have become more important than ever in firm–region interaction because these assets can improve productivity and generate competitiveness (Bianchi and Labory, 2004; Fey and Birkinshaw, 2005; Surinach and Moreno, 2012).

An intangible asset is not physical in nature. Such an asset is regarded as a "non-material factor to enterprise performance in the production of goods or the provision of services, or that are expected to generate future economic benefits to the entire or individual that control the deployment" (Tommaso et al., 2004, p. 76). Intangible assets are generally considered as "all the possible sources of competitive advantages for firms that have no physical substance" (Tommaso et al., 2004, p. 77). In the financial report of a firm, identifiability is emphasized to distinguish an intangible asset from goodwill, as well as for practical use in financial reports. Intangible assets are widely recognized as the driving force behind the productivity growth of the knowledge-based economy and are becoming increasingly crucial for firm survival and productivity (Fey and Birkinshaw, 2005; Marrocu et al., 2011). Furthermore, intangible assets are regarded as sources of competitive advantage, not only for firms, but also for cities and regions in the globalized economy (Bianchi and Labory, 2004; Kramer et al., 2009). Intangible assets can be categorized into diverse bundles. Anson (2007) categorized intangible bundles with the marketing, IT, and technical bundles, among others. For convenience, these bundles are used conceptually in the present work to describe the relationship between firms and urban systems.

Understanding firm behavior in terms of seeking and exploiting intangible assets is helpful in understanding the firm–region relationship in the knowledge-based economy. Theoretically, two motives exist for locating FDIs abroad: asset exploiting and asset exploring (Dunning and Narula, 1995; Verspagen and Schoenmakers, 2004). Asset-exploiting R&D denotes that "firms seek to exploit their existing technological capabilities (developed by home-based R&D) by means of performing R&D that is aimed at adapting products and technologies to local circumstances in a foreign country" (Verspagen and Schoenmakers, 2004, p. 25). In exhibiting asset-seeking behavior, the firm "aims at utilizing the local knowledge-base to develop new capabilities that are complementary to its existing capabilities" (Verspagen and Schoenmakers, 2004, p. 25). Traditionally, the FDIs of firms are regarded as the exploitation or transfer of firm-specific advantages, assuming that the firms possess certain types of proprietary resources that can be exploited in the host country (Hymer, 1976; Makino et al., 2002). However, recent international business studies suggest that firms invest in foreign countries to develop their firm-specific advantages or to seek necessary intangible assets, as well as to exploit their firm-specific advantages in a host country (Dunning, 1995; Kumar, 1998). Firms engage in FDIs to accumulate intangible assets by learning and gaining access to the necessary assets available in the host country. A study suggests that firms in newly industrialized economies gain access to established brand names, novel product technology, and extensive distribution networks by investing in advanced countries (Kumar, 1998). Such asset-seeking and asset-exploiting behavior is consistent with one of the many enduring ideas in organization science—that is, the long-term success of an organization depends on its capability to explore new competencies and exploit its current capabilities (Raisch et al., 2009). Another study suggests that superior performance is expected from ambidextrous organizations "that are capable of simultaneously exploiting existing competencies and exploring new opportunities" (Raisch et al., 2009, p. 685). In the present study, we assume that firms interact with various cities through both asset-seeking and asset-exploiting behavior relative to intangible assets by differentiating cities and regions in the global space economy.

Owing to their asset-seeking behavior, firms carefully select their local area of investment by considering local industrial clustering, regional innovation systems, local culture, and environment according to their investment function. For example, supplier networks specializing in input material, labor, and so on in the local area will be highly considered in the selection of a local area for manufacturing plants, whereas innovation networks and a pool of scientists and engineers are important for the location of R&D institutes. The characteristics of the local labor market, regional technology, and knowledge bases can be carefully considered in investments in R&D centers because each region may have different knowledge and technology bases—that is, exploring and seeking intangible assets are important in investments in R&D centers. In production investment, asset-exploiting behavior may be considered in establishing local production networks. Firms exploit knowledge through foreign sales and marketing on one hand and seek knowledge to develop new products and processes on the other hand (Dunning, 1995; Makino et al., 2002). However, the asset-seeking and asset-exploiting behavior of firms cannot be regarded as independent. Firms move from asset exploiting to asset seeking and vice versa in their investments. Through the continuous cycle of asset exploiting and asset seeking, firms can accumulate intangible assets. In the knowledge-based information society, multinational firms (MNFs) should continuously progress through investments of different functions in various cities and regions. Accordingly, MNFs are hypothesized to pursue both asset-seeking and asset-exploiting behavior concurrently by differentiating the cities and regions in the global space economy. Schematically, the interaction and networks of firms with suppliers, customers, competitors, universities, governments, and communities result in the accumulation of knowledge, technology, human capital, brand value, and so on. Knowledge spillover through networks within firms and interorganizational networks is an important component of the intangible asset accumulation of firms.

Cities and regions are fields of the collective action of individuals, organizations, and social institutions. Actors in cities and regions mobilize heterogeneous resources from both private and public institutions. Through such collective action and mobilization, cities and regions function as a setting in which physical, human, and social capital can be combined to create competitive environments, where high productivity, innovativeness, and adaptability coexist. Cities and regions evolve through the accumulation of local intangible assets. Local knowledge spillover, access to knowledge capital, local knowledge base for intangible asset seeking, and local market base for intangible asset exploiting are the processes involved in the accumulation of regional intangible assets. In these processes, the socioeconomic characteristics of firms, such as embeddedness, networks, and reciprocity, are important (Dicken and Malmberg, 2001; Taylor and Asheim, 2001).

Firm–region interaction can develop through the accumulation of regional assets. Intangible assets are continuously accumulated in certain regions with a well-developed industrial cluster, regional innovation system, or qualified local labor market (Kramer et al., 2011). Firms can concentrate in environments that are favorable for seeking new knowledge and information on new products and process technology, pooling qualified labor, establishing innovation networks, and so on. Industrial clusters are the result of close formal and informal networks that aim to acquire information on and knowledge of new products and process innovations, marketing, and sales beyond merely material linkages. Beyond the material linkages of supplier and customer relations, intangible asset accumulation in industrial clusters is important in locating firms within the clusters. The establishment of innovation systems in a region through continuous formal and informal networks of firm–university–R&D centers, favorable institutions and culture, social capital, and so forth can attract firms that seek knowledge and technology assets for innovation and R&D activities. Industrial clusters and innovation centers can accumulate regional intangible assets through the continuous interaction of firms, whereas firms can accumulate intangible assets through their participation in formal and informal networks within regions.

Interactions between corporate systems and urban systems

The systems approach is helpful in the clear identification of the firm–region relationship. Dicken and Malmberg (2001) conceptualized the firm–region relationship by adopting the systems approach. They suggested the firm–territory nexus as a schematic framework in which industrial and governance systems are interlinked. Production and innovation systems are considered in industrial systems, and firms are regarded as the network of firms with industrial systems. Such a schematic framework is useful in theoretically understanding the complex firm–region relationship. The present study extends the previous work of Wheeler by identifying the firm–region relationship through that between corporate and urban systems (Bagchi-Sen and Wheeler, 1989; Holloway and Wheeler, 1991; Mitchelson and Wheeler, 1994; Wheeler, 1986, 1988a, 1988b).

Exploring the relationship between corporate systems and urban systems is useful in identifying firm–region relationship relative to intangible assets because different firm units have different functions and are linked to different types of regions or cities. Corporate systems include both networks among the separate functional units of the firm and those with other external economic actors, such as suppliers, customers, competitors/cooperators, community, university, and the government (Figure 6.1). Networks include the flows of both tangibles and intangibles. Three hypotheses are set in the aspect of the interaction of corporate systems with urban systems.

First, we hypothesize that the hierarchy of a corporate system is related to that of an urban system in terms of the processes of the flows of intangible assets within the former (H1). A firm interacts with different functional units within the organization for both tangibles and intangibles; this relationship can be regarded as an intra-firm network. In this aspect, a corporate system can

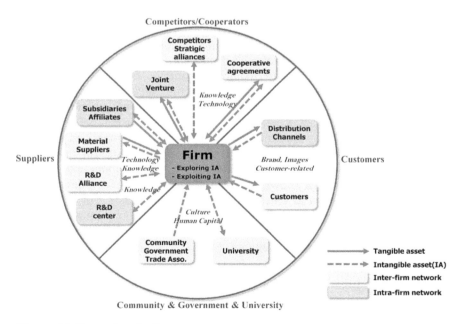

Figure 6.1 Networks of a firm

Source: Park, 2014.

be regarded as the interaction among diverse functional units of a firm in the economic space. In particular, the functional units of a firm, such as a headquarters, regional headquarters, production plants, R&D centers, and sales offices, are parts of a corporate system and interact with one another within the firm for the sharing, accumulation, and spillover of knowledge, as well as for networking the flows of tangibles. The flows of tangibles and intangibles, such as knowledge, technology, and brand, in joint ventures, subsidiaries and affiliates, as well as distribution channels can also be regarded as intra-firm networks. An MNF tends to locate its headquarters and regional headquarters in the capital region or in the largest metropolitan area because these areas are the hubs for the gathering and control of intangible assets within the corporate system. The gathering and flow of knowledge and information are important for R&D centers. Thus, R&D centers tend to locate their headquarters in the capital region or in the knowledge centers of a nation. The network of intangible assets may not be as important as that of tangible assets for production units, and manufacturing plants can be located even in peripheral cities. Firms consider the different external environments of cities based on their varying functions in gathering intangible assets in the interorganizational network. A firm interacts with the external environment through networks with customers, suppliers, competitors, universities, and other institutions located in diverse regions; this relationship can be regarded as an interorganizational network (Figure 6.1). However, network characteristics may differ depending on the types of operating units of a firm.

Second, we hypothesize that in seeking and exploiting intangible assets, agglomeration and clusters are important at the local level, whereas global cluster networks and temporary clusters are important at the global level (H2). Interorganizational networks are established at various spatial scales to seek and exploit intangible assets (Figure 6.2). Close interactions with suppliers,

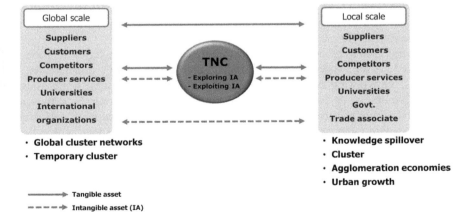

Figure 6.2 Local–global networks of tangibles and intangibles

Source: Park, 2014.

customers, competitors, producer services, universities, and the government within a local area are important in seeking and exploiting intangible assets and in reducing transaction costs. The interactions can be developed at international scales with various types of global networks comprising diverse economic actors (Figure 6.2).

Third, we hypothesize that most MNFs in a knowledge-based economy tend to explore and exploit intangible assets simultaneously (H3). We previously emphasized the exploiting behavior of MNFs in developing countries and their exploring behavior in advanced countries. However, most MNFs have corporate units in both advanced and developing economies, and such types of behavior can be observed simultaneously. The exploration and exploitation of intangible assets are continuous and complex cycles that can be observed simultaneously at a given time in the global economic space. Given this complexity, organizational ambidexterity has been emphasized in recent studies (Raisch et al., 2009).

The practical interaction of firms with regions in various spatial dimensions can be described in terms of urban systems because the individual units of a firm are actually located in diverse cities within regional, national, and global economic spaces. For example, the headquarters of a firm controls and interacts with all the functional units located in different locations over global economic spaces for intra-firm networks. The headquarters also interacts with its external environment. On one hand, firms tend to locate their headquarters in high-ranking metropolitan areas in the national urban system to perform efficient control activities and to interact efficiently with other actors within the city for intangible assets. Examples of such areas include Seoul in Korea, Tokyo in Japan, and New York in the USA. On the other hand, firms tend to locate their branch plants in peripheral cities or in developing countries, where production networks for both tangibles and intangibles can be efficiently established. Similarly, different units of corporate systems require different location factors. These units tend to locate in and interact with different cities within national urban systems of global economic spaces to accumulate and increase intangible assets.

The individual units of corporate systems interact with cities in urban systems to accumulate intangible assets, such as knowledge and technical bundles, networking bundles, marketing bundles, and cultural bundles of intangible assets. In corporate systems, the relationship among the different functional units of firms located in different regions and occupying different positions within the organizational structure of firms is embedded within the spatiality of such firms (Dicken and Malmberg, 2001). Cities or regions accumulate intangible assets through the interaction among actors in the local area to share knowledge within local areas, establish global networks, develop local social capital and local culture, and establish local innovation systems. Intangible asset accumulation in cities or regions can positively affect firms exploring intangible assets in the local area and those aiming to increase their intangible assets—that is, the exploration of intangible assets results in the

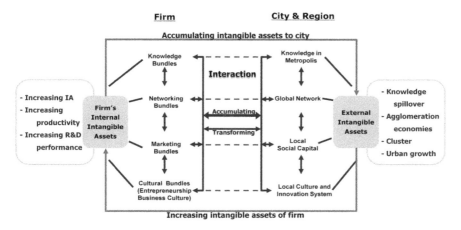

Figure 6.3 Accumulating intangible assets through interactions between a firm and a city

Source: Park, 2014.

accumulation of the intangible assets of firms, and vice versa, as shown in Figure 6.3, which presents the relationship between corporate and urban systems.

Cases of SEC and Lutronic corporation

To understand the relationship between corporate and urban systems in the process of intangible asset accumulation, two distinctive and contrasting global firms— namely, SEC and Lutronic—are selected for the case study. Globalization and knowledge-based societies are the major global megatrends. Thus, knowledge-intensive sectors, global firms, and the importance of intangible assets are considered in the selection of case firms. Firm size is also considered for comparison. As one of the leading global firms in the electronics sector, SEC understands the increasing importance of intangible assets in the process of firm growth. Lutronic is one of the leading small firms in the field of laser medical appliances but is a global actor in terms of market and investments. SEC and Lutronic are highly knowledge-intensive firms, and both show high ratios of R&D investment to total sales.

The two firms are selected because intangible asset accumulation is important in their competitiveness and because both are leading global actors despite their different sizes. SEC began producing electronic products in 1969. Over the last four decades, SEC has evolved from being a manufacturing firm of low-priced products to a leading global firm with high-value-added products. SEC has also transitioned from subcontracting manufacturing products to being an innovation flagship for producing world-first products. Currently, SEC is shifting its focus from innovation to the integration of innovation, marketing, and culture. Meanwhile, Lutronic was established in 1997 as a small high-tech firm, which is known as a venture firm in Korea when the country was confronted with a financial crisis. Over the last sixteen years, Lutronic has evolved into a leading innovator of aesthetic and medical advanced laser and related technology with investments in the USA and Japan. The general information on SEC and Lutronic is presented in Table 6.1.

The operating units of the two firms are historically analyzed in this chapter using various materials, such as corporate annual reports, newspaper materials, web materials, and statistics related to the spatial and structural growth strategies employed by the firms. In-depth interviews were conducted in January and October 2012 to clarify the interaction and the accumulation processes. The importance of intangible knowledge, the source and network of information and knowledge, and the importance of regions in the accumulation of knowledge and intangible assets were the major issues discussed in the interviews. The SEC interviews were conducted with the former president, executive director, and public relations director of the firm. The direct meetings with the former president and executive director required approximately two hours. The phone interview with the public relations director took approximately one hour. The Lutronic interviews, each of which took approximately two hours, were conducted with the president and executive director of the firm.

Table 6.1 SEC and Lutronic: brief information

SEC	Lutronic
Year established: 1969	**Year established**: 1997
Evolutionary stages:	**Evolutionary stages**:
1969–1971: Founding period	1997–1999: Founding period
1980s: Export and foreign-oriented development	2002–present: Focusing export
1990s: Advance for the new century	2006: KOSDAC listed
2000–2003: Leading digital convergence innovation	2007–present: Foreign subsidiaries and R&D center
2004–present: Building base of super first-class firm	**Sales and profits:**
	2011 total sales: About US$45 million
Sales and profits:	Continuous increase of sales since 1997
2011 Total sales: About US$140 billion	Continuous + profit since 2000
2011 Total profit: About US$14 billion	
	R&D expenditure and others:
R&D expenditure and others:	16–17% of total sales
About 6% of total sales: 10th in the world (2009)	10th in the aesthetic devise in the world
USA patent registration number: 2nd following IBM (2010)	3rd world market share in skin rejuvenation devise

Source: Gathered from the internal materials of SEC and Lutronic, websites, interview surveys, and newspapers.

To understand the relationship between corporate systems and urban systems, the evolution of the spatial corporate system and intangible asset accumulation through global networks and localized processes over time is initially examined. Intangible asset accumulation through global networks and localized processes over time, as well as the relationship of firms with urban systems, is then discussed. The three hypotheses identified in the previous section are investigated qualitatively, but not rigorously, by examining corporate data and reports, as well as the interview survey results.

Evolution of spatial corporate systems

SEC has grown remarkably since its establishment in 1969. Within ten years, SEC managed to join into a multinational corporation group with foreign investments. Located in the capital region of Korea, SEC started with the production of black-and-white TVs in 1970, after which it extended its products to refrigerators, air-conditioning units, washers, and color TVs. Since the 1980s, SEC has diversified to high-tech products, such as semiconductors, personal computers, mobile phones, tablets, and automobiles. SEC has been involved in FDIs since its first investment in the USA in 1978. For ten years beginning in 1978, SEC invested in foreign subsidiaries, such as branch offices in advanced countries, including the USA, Germany, the UK, Australia, and Canada. Thus, the 1980s are said to be the key period for foreign subsidiary investments. Since 1982, SEC has also invested in manufacturing plants and sales offices, with the key period being in the 1990s. The manufacturing invest-ments have been mainly greenfield investments. The production investments began in advanced countries, such as the USA and the UK, and then extended to industrializing countries, such as Thailand, Malaysia, India, and Brazil (Table 6.2). Foreign R&D investments from SEC started in 1987, with the key periods being the late 1980s and 2000s. These investments also started in advanced countries and then extended to industrializing countries (Table 6.2).

Lutronic started exporting its products four years after its establishment. The exports of the firm started in Asia and later extended to North America and Europe. With subsidiary investment in the USA in 2007, Lutronic began to accommodate foreign investments (Table 6.2). In 2010, Lutronic invested in an R&D center in the USA. Thus, despite its small size, Lutronic has already engaged in global activities and network expansion to seek knowledge and information. Thus far, the foreign investments of the company are mainly in advanced countries, but will soon be extended to China.

The evolution of the spatial corporate system of SEC suggests that corporate systems successively extend from foreign subsidiaries to manufacturing plants, sales offices, and R&D centers, as well as from advanced countries to industrializing countries, over time. Lutronic is considerably smaller than SEC in terms of sales and production because its history is relatively short. However, Lutronic has become one of the leading global firms in the skin-rejuvenation

Table 6.2 Evolution of spatial corporate systems through the global networks and localized processes over time

SEC	Lutronic
Foreign local subsidiary (1978–1988): Key period → 1980s: Advanced countries: USA, Germany, UK, Australia, Canada Foreign plant investment (1982–2011): Key period → 1990s: From advanced to industrializing Countries: Portugal, USA, UK, Thailand, Mexico, Malaysia, Brazil, Slovacia, India, Russia Foreign R&D Center (1987–2004): Key periods → late 1980s and 2000s: From advanced to industrializing Countries: USA, Japan, UK, Russia, Israel, China, India, Poland Foreign industrial complex (1995, 1996): Key period → 1990s: UK, Mexico	2001: Export to Asia 2004: Export to North America and Europe 2006: Listing KOSDAK (high-tech venture firm) 2007: USA Corporation 2008: Japan Corporation 2010: Global R&D Center

Source: gathered from the internal materials of SEC and Lutronic, websites, interview surveys, and newspapers.

device industry through high levels of R&D expenditure. In fact, the CEO said, "we want to continue R&D activities and technological development through keeping more than 15 percent of total sales allocated to R&D expenditure." Unlike SEC, Lutronic started exporting to Asia because penetrating the Asian aesthetic device market is relatively easy, given the similarities in the skin characteristics of Asians (i.e. skin sensitivity) compared with those of Koreans; such characteristics are different from those of Western people.[2] Overall, the two contrasting case firms suggest that spatial corporate systems evolve from subsidiary to R&D and then extend from advanced countries to industrializing countries.

Intangible asset accumulation through global networks and localized processes over time

With the evolution of spatial corporate systems, SEC and Lutronic have continuously accumulated intangible assets in the form of knowledge, technical know-how, marketing, brand, and so on. A firm can employ several methods to accumulate intangible assets. The two case firms reveal that formal and informal networks within clusters of local areas, continuous R&D investments, technology cooperation, and strategic alliances, as well as activities such as organizing and participating in temporary clusters, are the major mechanisms of intangible asset accumulation (Table 6.3). A recent study suggests that the

Table 6.3 Accumulation of intangible assets through the global networks and localized processes over time

SEC	Lutronic
Development of World New Products (1990 –): Key periods: 1999, 2004–2006, 2009–2010 Technology cooperation (1999–): Key periods: 2007, 2010 Technology strategic alliances (1995–): Key period: 2010–2011 Mergers and acquisitions (2010–): Key period: 2010–2011 Supporting sports team, Expo and Trade Show (2005–): Key period: 2010–2011 Continuous R&D investments (since 1980s): Key period: Since late 1990s Investing to new industry (2009–): Key period: 2010–: Medical sector: bio-similar, medical devise, health research	Important sources of knowledge and information for innovation: – External network and informal meeting of CEO – R&D, marketing, trade fair and exhibition Important regions as sources of knowledge and information for innovation: – Korea: Interactions in the capital region for all kinds of economic actors – USA, EU: for half of the sources (university, government, research manpower, customer, supplier) – Japan: for informal meeting of research manpower, customer Major partner of cooperative network – University, customer firm, competitive firms – All are in Seoul

Source: gathered from the internal materials of SEC and Lutronic, websites, interview surveys, and newspapers.

mobility of prominent scientists in the past has simultaneously increased knowledge flow and the creation of localized intangible assets (Schiller and Revilla Diez, 2012), thus suggesting that FDIs in the global economy influence the accumulation of regional intangible assets.

Formal and informal networks within local areas of foreign countries that are formed by individual corporate units are critical in the intangible asset accumulation of a firm. The accessibility of tangibles and intangibles is considered in the greenfield of manufacturing investments. As indicated in the interviews with officers of the two firms, the subsidiary and manufacturing investments made by both companies started in advanced countries because of their goal of gathering market information and technical knowledge, and because of the easy access to input factors. Initially, the R&D investments of SEC in innovation clusters in advanced countries, such as that in the Silicon Valley, were aimed at exploring knowledge and technology in the local cluster and collaborating with local specialists and firms. This objective demonstrates the behavior of exploring intangible assets accumulated in local clusters. In the early 1990s, SEC attempted to maintain close local networks to acquire knowledge and technology, as well as to cooperate with Silicon Valley firms in the early stage of its R&D investments (Park, 1994, 1996). On one hand,

SEC has practiced continuous and intensive R&D investments. On the other hand, the firm has maintained technical cooperation and strategic alliances with foreign firms in advanced countries to accumulate and explore new knowledge and technology that are needed in the development of new products. The asset-seeking or asset-exploring behavior of SEC is believed to have contributed to its continuous development of new products since the 1990s. Recently, SEC aggressively organized and participated in temporary clusters, such as expos and trade fairs, to enhance its innovative networks. Temporary clusters have significantly influenced the acquisition of new knowledge and product information, and the establishment of innovative networks (Bathelt and Glücker, 2011; Rinallo and Golfetto, 2011; Torre, 2008). Trade shows support firms in the development of their marketing capabilities into complementary assets, which are important in ensuring effective innovation and competitive advantage (Rinallo and Golfetto, 2011). The R&D investments of SEC suggest that clusters and agglomeration are important at the local level, whereas global cluster network and temporary clusters are important in seeking intangible assets (H2).

Sales network centers are outposts for exploiting marketing bundles of intangible assets in foreign countries. The interactions of SEC with other regions and markets within such foreign countries are good opportunities to accumulate marketing information and knowledge. SEC has extended its sales network centers globally to seek newly evolving information and knowledge, as well as to exploit global marketing information. Local networks in production centers contribute to savings in transaction costs and are helpful in accumulating intangible assets to be transmitted to regional headquarters. The interview results suggest that differentiating seeking and exploiting behavior is difficult. The operating units of different firms have recently demonstrated asset-seeking and asset-exploiting behavior simultaneously in one place and in different places through different operating units (H3).

In the case of Lutronic, the formal and informal relations of the CEO have served as important sources of knowledge and information for innovation. The CEO of Lutronic, Haelyung Hwang, establishes a strong external network with professors of medical schools, scientists connected with research labs, and engineers of high-tech firms, all of whom are excellent sources of knowledge of and information on new products and processes. In addition to conducting internal R&D activities, the CEO explores new knowledge and enhances the brand of Lutronic by periodically visiting institutions and arranging memorandums of understanding, as well as by exploring information on and knowledge of new technology. The CEO visits medical schools and hospitals in the USA and Europe several times a year, and explores knowledge related to aesthetic and medical laser technology and devices. Participation in temporary clusters also serves as an important resource in the acquisition of intangible assets. Staff members in the R&D sector participate in international scientific conferences, workshops, and meetings, where they present research articles and explore new knowledge.

As regards to temporary clusters, additional studies must be conducted to understand fully how knowledge creation, diffusion, and innovation may occur beyond regional boundaries. Nevertheless, trade fairs are good opportunities for small firms, such as Lutronic, to gain access to information on effective marketing and new products. Lutronic periodically participates in trade shows and conferences to establish new knowledge networks and to strengthen its existing knowledge networks with other scientists and firms continuously. The company also participates in trade shows and conferences to gather marketing information and investigate consumer behavior. Accordingly, Lutronic regards asset-seeking and asset-exploiting behavior as simultaneous actions, although the strength of each behavior might differ in different countries.

On one hand, Lutronic seeks intangible assets by closely interacting periodically with aesthetic service clinics and hospitals in the Capital Region of Korea. On the other hand, the company seeks knowledge and information for innovation through formal and informal networks with universities, governments, and research centers of advanced countries. Networks with customers and suppliers in the high-tech clusters of advanced countries are also important information sources for the improvement of new products and the acquisition of new information on production processes. Lutronic has designated major partners in the form of universities, customers, and supplier firms in Seoul, thus establishing cooperative networks. In addition, Lutronic promotes marketing activities in the emerging markets of Asia and Russia to exploit intangible assets related to product and market information. Given that Lutronic is a small firm, the role of its CEO in acquiring intangible assets, in addition to the formal and informal networks of the firm with major economic players, is critical.

Lutronic clearly maintains a close innovation network in the capital region of Korea and strong networks with major high-tech clusters in the USA. The company also actively participates in international trade shows, conferences, and workshops. Therefore, the interview results of Lutronic support H2 and H3. For intangible assets, agglomeration and clusters are important at the local level, whereas global cluster networks and temporary clusters are important at the global level (H2). The interview results also confirm that Lutronic seeks and exploits intangible assets simultaneously (H3).

Interactions with urban systems

Headquarters, regional headquarters, R&D centers, production plants, and sales offices can be regarded as the major units of corporate systems. To relate corporate systems to urban systems, cities are classified based on the country and the city levels within a country. Following the classification of the World Bank, we classify the countries in this work as follows: advanced country (A), industrializing country (B), and less industrialized country (C). Cities are classified as the capital or the largest metropolitan area, including suburbs (A);

large metropolises with a population of more than one million, including suburbs (B); and medium and small cities (C) (see the notes in Table 6.4).

As for the two firms in this study, we suppose that their headquarters should be located in the capital region of Korea to ensure easy communication with and control of diverse corporate units, access to the national government, close relations with financial firms, and close networks with leading universities and research labs. At present, the two headquarters are actually located in the capital region. Indeed, regional headquarters should be located in the major capital regions of divided global markets because of the control and management functions within such markets. SEC divides the global market into eight regions, as shown in the regional headquarters set-up in Table 6.4. The regional headquarters are all located in the capital region or in the largest metropolis of a leading country within the divisions of the global market (Table 6.4). The location of the regional headquarters clearly matches the capital region or the largest metropolis.

The locations of R&D centers show considerably diverse patterns. In particular, these locations match either capital regions or large metropolises with well-developed innovative clusters or regional innovation systems. Each division of the global markets has at least one R&D center. Examples of the so-called capital regions are London, Beijing, Moscow, and Tel Aviv, where high-tech clusters or clusters of knowledge-intensive services are well developed. Noncapital metropolises, such as San Jose, Dallas, Warsaw, Yokohama, Suzhou, Nangyung, Bangalore, and Delhi, are major innovation clusters or high-tech clusters of the corresponding divisions of the global market (Table 6.4).

Most production centers are located in industrializing countries, and this characteristic differs from the pattern of regional headquarters. For example, only one plant is located in an advanced country but is situated within small and medium cities. Two plants are located in a less industrialized country but is situated in a capital region. Most foreign plants (more than three-quarters) are located in the large metropolises of industrializing countries. Almost half of production centers are located in China, whereas one production center is located in the regional division of the Middle East and Africa, thus suggesting that production centers are closely related to industrial clusters, as well as to actual markets. Production centers are mainly located in cities with well-developed industrial clusters to make production networks efficient in local areas. The interview results suggest that for investments in production centers, the savings in transaction costs in the production networks of industrial clusters within industrializing countries are considered, and intangible assets are exploited in relation to production activities. Given the progress of the so-called information society, modern production centers today have long-distance networks for transactions despite being focused on such selected areas as industrial clusters or innovation clusters (Park, 2004).

Sales network centers show a highly diverse pattern that is considerably different from that of other corporate system units. Sales network centers are

Table 6.4 Corporate systems and urban systems

SEC		
	Regional HQs (4AA, 6BA) – North America: Ridgefield Park, NJ, USA: AA – Europe: Surrey, UK: AA – SE Asia: Singapore, Singapore: AA – China: Beijing, China: BA – Japan: Tokyo, Japan: AA – CIS and Baltics: Moscow, Russia: BA – Latin America: Sao Paulo, Brazil: BA – SW Asia: New Delhi, India: BA – Middle East and Africa: Dubai: BA – Africa: Johanesburg, South Africa: BA R&D Centers (2AA, 3AB, 3BA, 4BB) – North America: AB (San Jose); AB (Dallas); – Europe: AA (London); BA (Warsaw) – SE Asia and Japan: AB (Yokohama) – China: BA (Beijing); BB (Suzhou); BB (Nangyung) – CIS and Baltics: BA (Moscow) – Latin America: – SW Asia: BB (Bangalore); BB (Delhi) – Middle East and Africa: AA (Tel Aviv)	Production Centers (1AC, 2BA, 20BB, 7BC, 2CA) – North America: 1AC,1BB – Europe: 1BA, 2BC – SE Asia: 3BB, 2BC, 2CA – China: 12BB, 1BC – CIS and Baltics: 1BC – Latin America: 1BA 2BB – SW Asia: 2BB – Middle East and Africa: 1BC Sales Network Centers (14AA, 3AB, 29BA, 8CA) – North America: 2AA, 2AB, 1BA – Europe: 6AA, 1AB, 9BA – SE Asia, Japan and Australia: 4AA, 6BA – China and HK: 1AA, 1BA – CIS and Baltics: 2BA, 1CA – Latin America: 1AA, 4BA, 2CA – SW Asia: 1BA – Middle East and Africa: 5BA, 5CA	
Lutronic	HQ: Capital Region (AA) Regional HQ: New York (AA), Tokyo (AA) R&D Center: San Jose (AB) Sales Office: Birmingham (AB), Beijing (BA) Export to 60 countries Extending from Asia to Western countries – Export share of North America, EU, Japan: 22% in 2002 → 50% in 2010 4 Market differentiation for aesthetic device by skin color – Asia; North America; Europe; Latin America, China and Russia: emerging market		

Source: Gathered from the internal materials of SEC and Lutronic, websites, interview surveys, and newspapers.

Note: Corporate system: Regional HQ, R&D, production, and sales. Urban system: Considering both country and city level

Country level (first)	*City level (second)*
A: Advanced country	A: Capital/largest metropolitan area including suburbs
B: Industrializing country	B: Large metropolis (+million) including suburbs
C: Less industrialized country	C: Medium/small city

dispersed throughout the world from advanced countries to less industrialized countries. A considerable number of sales network centers are located in the less industrialized countries of the Middle East and Africa, Latin America, and CIS and the Baltic, although these centers are all in the capital regions. These sales network centers are located in either capital regions or large metropolitan areas. As a whole, approximately 94 percent of sales network centers are located in capital regions. Different functions are expected from the location of the centers based on the hierarchy of urban systems in the global economic spaces. First, sales network centers located in the capital regions of advanced countries seek various types of intangible assets in addition to marketing-related knowledge and product information. Second, sales network centers in the capital regions of industrializing countries pursue both asset-seeking and asset-exploiting activities simultaneously. Third, sales network centers in less industrialized countries gather information on local resources and suppliers to exploit intangible assets for the future development of the sales market and production activities beyond direct sales activities.

The location of operating units in the global space supports the first hypothesis— that is, the hierarchy of a corporate system is related to the hierarchy of an urban system in the processes of the flows of intangible assets within the corporate system (H1). The results of the interview surveys confirm that SEC primarily considers major capital regions in a continent when selecting locations for its regional headquarters to control operating units in the region, explore knowledge and information as well as innovative environments for R&D centers, identify markets for sales network centers, and access input materials as well as markets for production centers. Such consideration of different locations based on different functions confirms that high-tech MNFs consider the different external environments of cities based on different functions in gathering intangible assets in interorganizational networks.

Lutronic only has two regional headquarters, which are located in Tokyo and New York; these headquarters represent the firm's control centers in Asia and the West, respectively. The firm considers control and communication network functions in identifying the location of target regional headquarters in Eastern and Western countries to acquire diverse information on skin characteristics, medical information, and information on new technology development. The R&D center is located in Silicon Valley, which is the global innovation cluster for seeking and accumulating intangible assets, such as knowledge, marketing, and new product information. The sales offices are located in the capital region of China (Beijing) and in a large US metropolis (Birmingham). Although the operating units of Lutronic are few in number, the case still has the tendency to support the first hypothesis— that is, the hierarchy of a corporate system is related to the hierarchy of an urban system in the processes of the flows of intangible assets within the corporate system (H1). However, H1 is not fully supported because of Lutronic's lack of operating units.

Lutronic broadly differentiates four global markets—namely, Asia, North America, Europe, and Latin America, and pursues different strategies by region. In the interview, the representatives of Lutronic identify different skin characteristics, including sensitivity and color, in four global markets and then pursue different strategies in marketing and technical development. Chinese and Russian markets have recently been considered as emerging markets. On one hand, Lutronic has focused on asset-exploiting and asset-seeking activities in emerging and advanced markets, respectively. On the other hand, Lutronic simultaneously pursues asset-seeking and asset-exploiting behavior despite some differences in the emphasis of different economies. Accordingly, the relationship between corporate and urban systems in terms of seeking and exploiting intangible assets can be further clarified when Lutronic expands to a global market and establishes additional operating units in the future.

The examination of spatial corporate systems and urban systems relative to the intangible assets of the two contrasting firms suggests a strong relationship between corporate and urban systems in global economic spaces. Interactions between firm and region are mainly based on the hierarchies of corporate and urban systems. The results of the in-depth interviews and data analysis regarding the location of the units of corporate systems show that firms accumulate intangible assets through interactions with urban systems in global economic spaces. The case study also confirms the conceptual framework and the three hypotheses in general, and identifies the processes of intangible asset accumulation in terms of asset-seeking and asset-exploiting activities.

Concluding remarks

This chapter attempted to develop a conceptual framework of the relationship between corporate and urban systems in terms of intangible asset accumulation with the aim of extending J. O. Wheeler's work on corporate and urban systems relative to global spaces and intangible assets. Two distinctive and contrasting global firms were historically analyzed using various materials and statistics related to both firms' spatial and structural strategies for growth. In-depth interviews were conducted to clarify the interactions and accumulation processes that have occurred within each firm.

We formulated three hypotheses in this work: (H1) the hierarchy of a corporate system is related to the hierarchy of an urban system in the processes of the flows of intangible assets within the corporate system; (H2) agglomeration and clusters are important at the local level, whereas global cluster networks and temporary clusters are important at the global level in seeking and exploiting intangible assets; and (H3) most MNFs in the knowledge-based economy tend to explore and exploit intangible assets simultaneously. The results of the interview surveys and the analysis of the location of the operating units of the two cases support the three hypotheses. However, this study did not rigorously test the three hypotheses but rather attempted to examine overall trends in the relationship between corporate and urban systems relative to intangible assets.

The data analysis and the interview surveys suggest that firms' intangible assets are critical in ensuring their competitiveness within a knowledge-based information society. The intangible assets of firms can be increased through the accumulation of knowledge, technology, human capital, brand values, and so on. Such accumulation is possible through formal and informal interactions and networks with suppliers, customers, competitors, governments, and communities. In the process of intangible asset accumulation and interactions with urban systems, firms differentiate their strategies for cities through the level of the country's development and the status within the urban system. Intangible assets are also important in maintaining the competitive advantages of cities and regions. Accumulation of local intangibles results from the evolutionary development of the relationships between corporate and urban systems.

The accumulation of some intangible assets in a given region enables industrializing countries to attract FDIs. The externalities stemming from knowledge spillover from firms can influence the accumulation of regional intangible assets and result in a positive relationship between firm and region in a knowledge-based economy (Artis et al., 2012). However, policies devoted to the generation of regional intangible assets should consider the specificities of regions in terms of urban systems. This suggestion is based on the fact that accelerating intangible asset accumulation and the effects of such intangible assets are inhomogeneous over hierarchies of urban systems, as examined in this study.

The conceptual framework and the case studies presented in this work have limitations. Nevertheless, we hope that this study contributes to the efforts toward re-examining broad issues in the relationship between corporate and urban systems, especially with regard to intangible asset accumulation in a knowledge-based information society. The results of such works are very important in understanding dynamic global economic spaces, which have been relatively neglected in the field of geography.

Notes

1   This chapter is a revised version of Park, Sam Ock (2014). Interactions of corporate and urban systems: accumulation of intangible assets. *Urban Geography* (www.tandfonline.com/doi/full/10.1080/02723638.2014.934522).
2   According to the interview surveys on Lutronic and an aesthetic service firm, Asian skin is significantly more sensitive than that of Westerners. Moreover, Asians follow a more complex and difficult skin care regimen than Westerners.

References

Anson, W. (2007). *The Intangible Assets Handbook: Maximizing Value from Intangible Assets*. Chicago: American Bar Association.

Artis, M. J., Miguelez, E. and Moreno, R. (2012). Agglomeration economies and regional intangible assets: an empirical investigation. *Journal of Economic Geography*, 12(6), 1167–1189.

Asheim, B. T., Boschma, R. A. & Cooke, P. (2011). Constructing regional advantage: platform policies based on related variety and differentiated knowledge bases. *Regional Studies*, 45(7), 893–904.

Bagchi-Sen, S. & Wheeler, J. O. (1989). A spatial and temporal model of foreign direct investment in the United States. *Economic Geography*, 65(2), 113–129.

Bathelt, H. & Glückler, J. (2011). *The Relational Economy: Geographies of Knowing and Learning*. Oxford: Oxford University Press.

Bianchi, P. & Labory, S. (Eds.). (2004). *The Economic Importance of Intangible Assets*. Aldershot: Ashgate.

Birkinshaw, J. Brannen, M. & Tung, R. (2011). From a distance and generalizable to up close and grounded: reclaiming a place for qualitative methods in international business research. *Journal of International Business Studies*, 42(5), 573–581.

Dicken, P. & Malmberg, A. (2001). Firms in territories: a relational perspective. *Economic Geography*, 77(4), 345–363.

Dunning, J. H. (1995). Re-appraising the eclectic paradigm in an age of alliance capitalism. *Journal of International Business Studies*, 26(3), 461–491.

Dunning, J. H. & Narula, R. (1995). The R&D activities of foreign firms in the United States. *International Studies of Management and Organization*, 25(1–2), 39–73.

Fey, C. F. & Birkinshaw, J. (2005). External sources of knowledge, governance mode, and R&D performance. *Journal of Management*, 31(4), 597–621.

Gong, H. & Wheeler, J. O. (2002). The location and suburbanization of business and professional services in the Atlanta area. *Growth and Change*, 33(3), 341–369.

Holloway, S. R. & Wheeler, J. O. (1991). Corporate headquarters relocation and changes in metropolitan corporate dominance (1980–1987). *Economic Geography*, 67(1), 54–74.

Hymer, S. H. (1976). *The International Operation of National Firms: A Study of Direct Foreign Investment*. Cambridge, MA: MIT Press.

Kramer, J.-P., Marinelli, E., Iammarino, S. & Revilla Diez, J. (2011). Intangible assets as drivers of innovation: empirical evidence on multinational enterprises in German and UK regional systems of innovation. *Technovation*, 31(9), 447–458.

Kramer, J.-P., Revilla Diez, J., Marinelli, E. & Iammarino, S. (2009). Intangible assets, multinational enterprises and regional innovation in Europe (Working Paper 1.3.b.). IAREG, 1–69.

Kumar, N. (1998). *Globalization, Foreign Direct Investment and Technology Transfers: Impacts on and Prospects for Developing Countries*. New York: Routledge.

Lev, B. (2001). *Intangibles: Management, Measurement, and Reporting*. Washington, DC: Brooking Institution Press.

Lösch, A. (1952). *The Economics of Location (Die Räumriche Ordnung der Wirtschaft (1940))*. (W. Woglom, trans.). New Haven, CT: Yale University Press.

Makino, S., Lau, C.-M. & Yeh, R.-S. (2002). Asset-exploiting versus asset-seeking: implications for location choice of foreign direct investment from newly industrializing economies. *Journal of International Business Studies*, 33(3), 403–421.

Marrocu, E., Paci, R. & Pontis, M. (2012). Intangible capital and firms' productivity. *Industrial and Corporate Change*, 21(2), 377–402.

Mitchelson, R. L. & Wheeler, J. O. (1994). The flow of information in a global economy: the role of the American urban system in 1990. *Annals of the Association of American Geographers*, 84(1), 87–107.

O'Mahony, M. & Vecchi, M. (2009). R&D, knowledge spillovers and company productivity performance. *Research Policy*, 38(1), 35–44.

Park, S. O. (1994). High technology industrial development and formation of new industrial district: theory and empirical cases. *Journal of Korean Geographical Society*, 29(2), 117–136 (in Korean with English summary).

Park, S. O. (1996). Network and embeddedness in the dynamic types of new industrial districts. *Progress in Human Geography*, 20(4), 476–493.

Park, S. O. (2004). The impact of business to business electronic commerce on the dynamics of metropolitan spaces. *Urban Geography*, 25(4), 289–314.

Park, S. O. (2014). Interactions of corporate and urban systems: accumulation of intangible assets. *Urban Geography* (www.tandfonline.com/doi/full/10.1080/02723638.2014.934522).

Park, S. O. & Wheeler, J. O. (1983). The filtering down process in Georgia: the third stage in the product life cycle. *The Professional Geographer*, 35(1), 18–31.

Raisch, S., Birkinshaw, J., Probst, G. & Tushman, M. L. (2009). Organizational ambidexterity: balancing exploitation and exploration for sustained performance. *Organization Science*, 20(4), 685–695.

Regional Studies. (2012). Special issue: Intangible assets and regional economic growth. *Regional Studies*, 46(10), 1277–1416.

Revilla Diez, J. (2000). The importance of public research institutions in innovative networks—empirical results from the metropolitan innovation systems Barcelona, Stockholm and Vienna. *European Planning Studies*, 84(4), 451–463.

Rinallo, D. & Golfetto, F. (2011). Exploring the knowledge strategies of temporary cluster organizers: a longitudinal study on the EU fabric industry trade shows (1986–2006). *Economic Geography*, 87(4), 453–476.

Schiller, D. & Revilla Diez, J. (2012). The impact of academic mobility on the creation of localized intangible assets. *Regional Studies*, 46(10), 1319–1332.

Surinach, J. & Moreno, R. (2012). Introduction: intangible assets and regional economic growth. *Regional Studies*, 46(10), 1277–1281.

Taylor M. & Asheim, B. (2001). The concept of the firm in economic geography. *Economic Geography*, 77(4), 315–328.

Tommaso, M. R., Paci, D. & Schweitzer, S. O. (2004). Clustering of intangibles. In P. Bianchi & S. Labory (Eds.), *The Economic Importance of Intangible Assets* (pp. 73–102). Aldershot: Ashgate.

Torre, A. (2008). On the role played by temporary geographical proximity in knowledge transmission. *Regional Studies*, 42(6), 869–889.

Verspagen, B. & Schoenmakers, W. (2004). The spatial dimension of patenting by multinational firms in Europe. *Journal of Economic Geography*, 4(1), 23–42.

Weber, A. (1929). *Theory of Location of Industries (Über den Standort der Industrien (1909))* (C. J. Friedrich, trans.). Chicago: University of Chicago Press.

Wheeler, J. O. (1981). Effects of geographical scale on location decisions in manufacturing: the Atlanta example. *Economic Geography*, 57(2), 134–145.

Wheeler, J. O. (1986). Corporate spatial links with financial institutions: the role of the metropolitan hierarchy. *Annals of the Association of American Geographers*, 76(2), 262–274.

Wheeler, J. O. (1988a). The corporate role of large metropolitan areas in the United States. *Growth and Change*, 19(2), 75–86.

Wheeler, J. O. (1988b). Corporate activities and the urban hierarchy in Georgia. *The Southeastern Geographer*, 28(2), 97–109.

Wheeler, J. O. (1999). Local information links to the national metropolitan hierarchy: the Southeastern United States. *Environmental and Planning A*, 31(5), 841–854.

Website references

Lutronic: www.korea.lutronic.com/
SEC: www.samsung.com/sec/

7 Evolution of the industrial cluster and policy

The case of Gumi City, Korea[1]

Introduction

Korea has achieved remarkable economic growth during the last half-century. Korea was among the poorest countries in the world following the devastation of the Korean War (1950–1953). The country's per capita GNP was less than US$100 (in 1996) in 1960, but increased to US$20,000 in 2007. Such a remarkable achievement in economic growth is closely related to Korea's successful implementation of the government's export-oriented and sector-specific industrial development strategies, development of human resources, as well as innovation policies since the launch of the First Five-Year Economic Development Plan in 1962. The rapid economic growth within a half-century reflects the characteristic of "compressed economic growth" (Park, 2009).

This compressed economic growth has resulted in several spatial problems, such as the concentration of the population and industry in the capital region and subsequent regional disparity. However, the noncapital region has undergone economic growth and improvements contributed by the development of industrial clusters, which caused dynamic spatial patterns and processes to progress in Korea's economy. In the early industrialization phase, the spatial disparity of economic activities has increased with the bipolar industry concentration. Spatial disparity has persisted through continuous population concentration, creating a new spatial division of labor between the capital region and the rest of the country, as well as path-dependent trends of industrial development. Despite the persistent spatial disparity of economic activities, that of per capita gross regional domestic product (GRDP) has considerably decreased over the last two decades. In addition, a new path-creation trend has evolved in the cities of provincial and rural areas with the development of Information and Communication Technology (ICT). The development of high-tech industries, such as electronics, in the noncapital region and the development of ICT have contributed to the spatial dynamics of the Korean economy (Kim and Lee, 2009; Koo, 2010; Lee, 2011; Park, 2009).

Gumi city is a good example that has contributed to development in the noncapital region and the progress of dynamics in the Korean economic space.

Gumi city has evolved as a leading global electronics industry cluster in the last four decades, achieving an export value of US$33 billion in 2010. The Gumi industrial park has transformed and evolved from a branch plant agglomeration, with the co-location of many branch plants in the electronic sector, to an industrial cluster with progressive local networks. Recognizing government industrial policies is critical in understanding the evolution of Gumi electronics cluster.

This chapter aims to examine the evolution of Gumi industrial cluster in relation to the changes in regional industrial policy in Korea. In the following section, Korean industrial and regional policies are introduced to understand the process of the dynamics of Gumi city. The history of industrial development and industrial cluster evolution in Gumi city is then examined.

Changes in regional industrial policies in Korea

Government industrial policy before the late 1990s

The government's industrial policy has significantly affected the industrial development and changes during the last half-century. Regional industrial policy has continuously changed focus from industrial park development in the early industrial development phase to innovation for competitive industrial development in recent years. Accordingly, understanding this industrial policy is a prerequisite to understanding industrial transformation and innovation in Korea.

The Korean national government has led the promotion of sectoral and spatial industrial policies since the launch of the First Five-Year Economic Development Plan in 1962. Export-oriented industrialization has become a major strategy since the early 1960s and was fashioned to promote the most promising industries at a certain stage. Labor-intensive industries, such as textiles and apparel, were the key sectors for the expansion of industrial exports before the mid-1970s, whereas heavy and chemical industries, such as petrochemicals, shipbuilding, automobile, and consumer electronics, were the leading industries for export expansion in the late 1970s and early 1980s. The government's heavy and chemical industrial policy contributed to the evolution of the Chaebol system (conglomeration) in the Korean economy, because of the allowed borrowing of foreign capital and several incentives for investments in the heavy industrial sector (Park and Markusen, 1995). Since the mid-1980s, high-tech industries, such as semiconductors, have been increasingly favored. The shift of sectoral industrial policies has caused a shift in the industrial structure of Korea from labor-intensive to technology-intensive assembly type. Labor-intensive industries have dominated during the rapid industrialization phase in the 1960s and early 1970s, but have shown a continuous decrease in their share of total industrial production since the late 1970s. By contrast, assembly-type industries, which include high-tech industries, have continuously increased since the late 1970s (Park, 2009). Since the mid-1990s, especially following the foreign exchange crisis in November 1997, the Korean government has exerted considerable effort to promote the development of knowledge-intensive industries and services; to open the country fully in terms of trade and capital movements; to restructure the economy, including the financial sector; and to make the labor market flexible.

Along with sectoral industrial policies, the national government promoted spatial policy with the establishment of several large industrial estates, especially in the southeastern part of the country, to decentralize industries from the capital region in the 1960s and 1970s. The resulting major new industrial cities or production complexes include those of Ulsan, Changwon, Pohang, Gumi, Gwangyang, and Ansan. Free export zones in Masan and Iri have been constructed to attract foreign direct investments (FDIs). However, the role of FDIs was relatively insignificant in the 1970s and 1980s compared with that of imported technology and foreign capital borrowing used by Chaebols to establish large branch plants that significantly contributed to the development and growth of industrial cities. The industrial policy focusing on industrial park development can be regarded as a strategy to establish production systems in the nation. However, the idea of territorial production systems was unsuccessfully implemented in the earlier development stage because of poor local industrial linkages—that is, industrial parks initially had only limited local inter-firm linkages and were merely agglomerations of production activities without significant intra-regional production networks.

Sectoral and spatial industrial policies until the 1980s significantly affected the spatial structure of the Korean economy. On one hand, the government's spatial industrial policy has resulted in the spatial division of labor, concentrating Chaebol headquarters in Seoul while decentralizing production functions to the noncapital region (Park, 1993). On the other hand, high-tech industrial policy since the mid-1980s resulted in the reconcentration of industries in the capital region because of the locational advantages of high-tech industries. These advantages include easy access to skilled labor, knowledge, technology information, and finance. The concentration of high-tech industries and advanced services, including R&D activities, in the capital region has intensified the spatial division of labor in Korean production systems and the space economy (Park, 1993; 2009).

Several local governments have exerted significant effort to attract knowledge-based industries through the realization of local autonomy since the mid-1990s. However, such industries are still overwhelmingly concentrated in the capital region because of favorable locational factors, such as the availability of high-quality and skilled labor, advanced information infrastructure, easy access to financial centers, other advanced producer services, and so on—that is, although new industrial parks have developed in the noncapital region based on the regional industrial policy of the government, regional variation in the growth of knowledge-based industries has persisted in the Korean space economy (Park et al., 2009).

Government innovation policies

In the early industrialization phase in the 1960s, innovation issues have been relatively neglected because the main goal was the establishment of manufacturing production bases. In the 1970s, the science and technology policy has focused on expanding education in the technical and engineering fields, establishing several government-supported research institutes in the field of heavy and chemical industries, as well as promoting the heavy and chemical industrial development policy. Government-supported research institutes have assumed a leading function in the improvement of industrial technologies during this period. Most firms were more interested in technology transfer from industrialized countries, rather than the promotion of their own R&D activities. Through the establishment of these research institutes, the national systems of innovation began to evolve in relation to industrial development.

However, innovation systems in Korea have significantly changed since the early 1980s through the considerable growth of the in-house R&D investments of private firms. During this time, firms have begun to emphasize technological developments because of the national industrial development and severe competition in international markets. Chaebols aggressively established R&D centers. In 1981, the share of private firms in the national total R&D expenditure reached 56 percent, and the turning point came when the share of private firms overtook that of the government. Since then, the share of private firms rapidly increased and reached 81 percent in 1985 (MOST, 1991). The number of 54 firms, most of which belonged to Chaebols, that had their own R&D centers in 1980 increased to 2,226 in 1995 (KITA 1995, 1996). Kim (1997) identified three major characteristics of firm innovation activities. In the 1980s, (1) large firms of Chaebols established strategic alliances with global high-tech firms; (2) large firms, which mostly belong to Chaebols, were aggressive in establishing foreign R&D centers and labs; and (3) the difficulties in obtaining a license for leading-edge complex technology caused large firms to become actively involved in the merger/acquisition of high-tech firms in the developed countries to secure original technology.

In the 1990s, even small and medium-size enterprises (SMEs) have begun to establish R&D centers. More than two-thirds of the total number of R&D centers in Korea currently belongs to SMEs. Accordingly, beyond the national innovation systems, regional innovation networks have begun to evolve because of the development of regional clusters of SMEs in technology-intensive sectors. Such development was likewise contributed by the establishment of science and high-tech parks, in addition to the Daeduck Science Town, in the noncapital region during those times. According to Park's (2000) questionnaire surveys for SMEs, conducted when Korea began to obtain financial support from the IMF, the role of SMEs has become important in the development of regional innovation systems in the country. Based on the survey, SMEs have become more involved in R&D activities during the 1990s, especially as one of the strategies for industrial restructuring. Out of the 825 firms that replied to the survey, 20 percent conducted R&D activities in 1993. This figure increased to 34 percent in 1996. Overall, among these firms, larger SMEs participate more in R&D activities than smaller SMEs. However, smaller SMEs show a higher ratio of R&D expenditure to total sales than larger SMEs. This finding reveals that a considerable proportion of smaller SMEs conducting R&D activities can be regarded as venture businesses, even in the early 1990s.

Inter-firm networks between large contract firms and suppliers of SMEs within the local area, as well as collaborations with other firms and trade associations of the same industry, have become an important mechanism for the innovation of SMEs in Korea. Large firms belonging to Chaebols served a critical function in forming inter-firm networks by establishing cooperative suppliers of SMEs. For some SMEs, collaboration with universities, government-sponsored research institutes, and other public entities has also become an important contributor to their technological development and innovation. The importance of inter-firm networks for the innovation of SMEs was supported by the extended survey of 1999 (Park and Nahm, 2000). Moreover, since the financial crisis in 1997, even some of the Korean SMEs have been established as the focal point of the network in Silicon Valley, which suggests that global innovation networks are becoming important for SMEs.

Regional innovation and cluster policy in the Participatory Government (2002–2007)

The Participatory Government, which began in 2002, has strongly promoted balanced national development with emphasis on regional innovation and cluster policies (Park, 2007). The government's regional innovation policy can be regarded as essential for balanced national development, and the basic framework of the policy was intended for the integration of "talents," "technology," and "industry." Major policies for regional innovation provide the basis for the establishment of regional innovation systems, strengthening the innovation capacity of universities in provinces, promoting science and technology in provincial regions, and establishing industry–university–research center networks (PCBND, 2007).

The Participatory Government has strongly promoted the innovative cluster policy in relation to the regional innovation policy. Seven innovative clusters have been designated as models with the reorganization of selected national industrial parks. These clusters include the electronics and IT cluster in Gumi; machinery cluster in Changwon; automobile cluster in Ulsan; parts and components cluster in Ansan; parts and components of automobile and machinery cluster in Gunsan–Janghang; photonics cluster in Gwangju; and medical instruments cluster in Wonju (Kim and Lee, 2009; Lim and Park, 2009). Each innovative cluster has developed three to seven mini clusters, which focused on a specific technology or product, to promote collaboration and solve problems in production. Later, the Participatory Government designated six more innovative clusters, and thirteen innovative clusters have been supported outside Seoul.

In addition, the Daeduck R&D special district in Daejeon City has been supported under a special law to promote R&D commercialization and diverse innovations. The development of innovative clusters has been promoted through the support provided for strategic industries in each region. High-tech IT and local culture clusters have been similarly supported to strengthen local innovation through collaboration among diverse economic actors. Private firm development of clusters has also been promoted. Some clusters that benefited from this practice are Suwon IT cluster by Samsung, Paju's semiconductor cluster by LG-Phillips, and Pohang's material cluster by POSCO.

The regional innovation policies have certainly contributed to the increased density of regional innovation networks in the provinces. However, limitations in the development of high-quality manpower in these regions seemed to have aggravated innovation potentials. Such a strong promotion of balanced national development policies through regional innovation and clusters apparently affected the relative decrease in the GRDP share compared with the population share in the capital region (Park, 2007). The trend of decreasing spatial disparity in terms of per capita GRDP, however, could have resulted from the complex mechanisms of economic spaces in Korea.

Reshaping regional policy in recent years

Since the launch of the new government of President Lee Myung-Bak, the Presidential Committee on Regional Development (PCRD) has set up a new scheme of regional policy. Drastic changes in the global and domestic economic environments, resulting from the unexpected global financial crisis in 2008 and global climate change, have caused the incumbent government to alter its philosophy on regional development policy (Richardson et al., 2011). The PRCD regards this change as a paradigm shift, calling it "reshaping regional policy." The change can be considered as a reshaping because the boundary of a regional development plan is not limited to one administrative area and instead includes several administrative units comprising a larger economic region for the synergetic effects of cooperation with other regions. The new regional policies build a spatial foundation for each region to attract and develop new industries while ensuring their effectiveness and competitiveness (Choe, 2011; Park, 2011). The new policy has also emphasized both localization and decentralization for regional development. The PCRD suggests that the new government altered its policy direction from declaratory "balanced regional development" to "regional specialization and competition," which attempts to implement effective self-reliant localization policies (Choe, 2011).

The new regional policy comprises five key strategies (Choe, 2011). First, the new policy is framed on a three-tiered approach based on different geographical scales: (1) the Economic Region (ER) scheme regroups upper-tier local governments (sixteen metropolises and provinces) into seven ERs;

(2) the Local Area scheme provides quality-of-life services and income-earning opportunities for all residents in lower-tier local governments (163 cities and counties); and (3) the Supra-Economic Region (SER) scheme creates four SERs along the three coastlines and an Inland SER to promote cross-economic region and cross-border cooperation.

Second, the government will promote regional development by providing a new specialization-based regional growth engine. Two selected industries for each ER will be fostered to enhance global competitiveness. Interregional linkages and cooperation will be boosted to promote the synergetic effects of strategic industries.

Third, several tasks will be promoted to enforce decentralization, delegating power from the central government to local governments. These tasks are the devolution of the regional agencies of the central government, redistribution of taxes between central and local governments, integration of diverse national subsidies into block grants for regional development, and transfer of development authority to local governments for better planning and implementation.

Fourth, the symbiotic development of the capital region and the noncapital region is pursued through diverse channels. Some examples are the transfer of capital gains earned by developing land in the capital region to local governments in the noncapital region, reduced regulations and improved institutional environment to reinvigorate the regional economy, and the stepwise deregulation of the capital region concurrent with regional development in the noncapital region.

Fifth, existing regional projects inherited from the former administration will be continued. For example, the dispersal program of government offices and public institutions will progress because of the contribution to the creation of growth hubs in the ER. Incentive measures, such as tax exemptions and low-priced land, can be used to attract high-tech businesses to the noncapital region.

Overall, the Korean industrial policy has evolved from the industrial park development in the 1960s and 1970s, to high-tech industrial development in the 1980s, to industrial restructuring in the 1990s, to innovation and industrial clusters by the Participatory Government, and to the establishment of ER with emphasis on interregional networks and cooperation (see Figure 4.9 in Chapter 4). Along with the changes and reshaping of the industrial and innovation policies, space economy in Korea has shown several dynamic characteristics: spatial division of labor, development of ICT and spatial changes with the dominance of Seoul, and virtual innovation networks in peripheral areas (Park, 2009; 2011). More details will be examined through the case of Gumi, a specialized electronics cluster in Korea.

The historical development of Gumi industrial city

Gumi is an industrial park established in 1971. The city was designed as an electronics district. Gumi is approximately 267 km south of Seoul, located about a half-hour's drive north of Daegu, which is the third largest city in Korea (see Figure 4.6 in Chapter 4). In 1977, the erection of considerable numbers of factories and buildings began in the first industrial park. By the early 1990s, over 240 firms employed more than 70,000 workers, who resided in the complex. Since that period, the number of firms has continuously increased, reaching 1,177 in 2009. However, the number of employees has fluctuated in the range of 65,000 to 80,000 (Figure 7.1). Growth in industrial output and export has been impressive, with an annual growth rate of more than 18 percent in the 1980s and continuous growth until 2005, except during the financial crises in 1997 and 2001 (Figure 7.2). Of course, growth has fluctuated during the last half-century. A negative growth rate has been noted for the changes in production, export, establishment, and employment within a few years, especially during the financial crisis in East Asia in 1997, as well as the global economic crisis in recent years. During the last four or five decades, export growth rates were generally over 10 percent and over 20 percent for more than half the period (Figure 7.3).

The resident population of Gumi grew by almost four times from 105,000 in 1980 to 404,920 in 2010. Gumi fitted into the Park administration's economic strategy of a new round of export-oriented development in the 1970s, based on electronics in particular. The development of electronics was an obvious route for a resource-poor economy, an attempt to diversify away from South Korea's dependence on heavy industry (Park and Markusen, 1995). Building the Gumi industrial park and location owed more to the exercise of discretionary political power than a commitment to a regionally balanced industrial growth. Gumi was a personal project of President Park, whose military regime targeted new investments in the southeastern region of Korea. Although situated far from the coast, which formerly was a consideration that

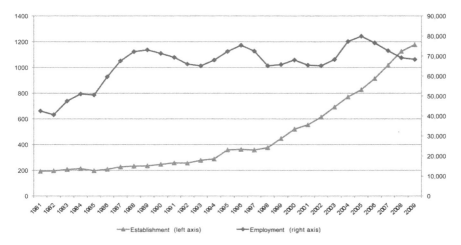

Figure 7.1 Number of firms and employees in Gumi

Source: Korea Industrial Complex Corporation, each year.

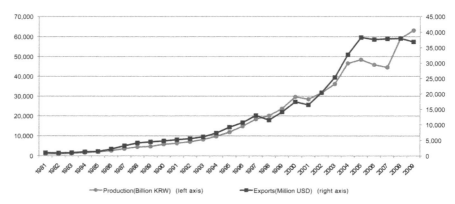

Figure 7.2 Production and export in Gumi

Source: Korea Industrial Complex Corporation, each year.

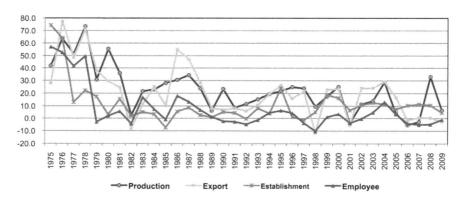

Figure 7.3 Annual growth rates of production, export, establishment, and
employees in Gumi, percent

Source: Park, 2010.

dictated the earlier export- and port-oriented selection of Pohang, Ulsan, and
Changwon as industrial cities for steel, chemicals, and machinery, respectively,
Gumi's countervailing asset was its good fortune in being the hometown of
President Park (Park and Markusen, 1995).

In 1969, when its fate was sealed, Gumi was a small agricultural village
where no significant economic changes had occurred for generations. The
industrial park was built by reclaiming land from the River Nakdong and by
building a 12 km embankment to rechannel the river's flow. Factories and
dormitories were rapidly erected, filling up the grid lines laid down on planners'
maps. The leading agent for Gumi's construction was the Korea Electronics
Industrial Corporation (KEIC), reorganized in 1974 as the Gumi Export Industrial

Corporation, to acknowledge the fact that the textile business was becoming as important a tenant as electronics in the complex. KEIC was an arm of the national government, under the Ministry of Trade and Industry, with its own special trust fund to finance land clearance and development. Over the years, the operations of KEIC have been increasingly funded out of proceeds from its land and energy activities, but the national government continues to oversee its policy development (Park and Markusen, 1995).

Government subsidies and incentives have served a major function in inducing companies to build plants in Gumi. Land clearance, site preparation, infrastructure, and water and energy supplies are ample and cheap, and efficient transportation links to Seoul and southern seaports are ensured. Tax breaks, worker education and training programs, as well as a modest level of business services have been provided. Although a plant is supposed to be "clean" to qualify as a Gumi resident, the government has tolerated water and air pollution, an advantage for firms that find restrictions tightening in Seoul. Initially, the principal input into the production process in Gumi was labor, the target labor force being young women from the 400 villages within 15 km of Gumi. KEIC actively helped to recruit the labor force by combing the high schools in rural areas. Larger plants have been required to set up their own in-house training facilities, and technical and vocational schools in Gumi supplement the labor supply. A major inducement to the immigration of very young women was the offer of a high school education in the factory itself, as part of the employment conditions. Meanwhile, managers and engineers were drawn from urban centers, such as Daegu, especially from the College of Engineering of Kyungpook National University. Job opportunities within the region have helped to staunch the flow of educated labor from such places as Daegu to the Seoul metropolitan area. Gumi has grown extremely fast as an industrial park. Manufacturing has served as the backbone of this growth.

Evolution of the Gumi industrial cluster

Gumi industrial park was created as an agglomeration of branch plants that could transform by generating spin-offs, spawning localized supplier networks, and creating governance structures that resemble those of industrial districts. Several questions were raised in studies during the early 1990s (Park and Markusen, 1995). Have the economies of Gumi continued to exhibit the features of a satellite industrial district? Over time, have there been signs of modernization, local entrepreneurship, vertical disintegration, increased networking among firms, or greater interest in flexible specialization? Or, do state management, branch plants, nonplace embeddedness, and exogenous decision-making still predominate?

This section examines the changing industrial specialization, and industrial and firm organization, as well as the prevalence of indigenous versus exogenous linkages in the context of industrial district evolution. The pressure to restructure these districts was intense in the early 1990s. Since the late 1980s, national factor advantages, such as cheap and abundant labor and cheap industrial land, have almost disappeared in Korea compared with other developing countries. As a result, industries in South Korea had to undergo significant restructuring to regain competitive advantage. The major triggers of this industrial restructuring were rapid wage increase, eruption of labor disputes, currency revaluation, and high financial costs (Park, 1994). Corporate strategies and regional characteristics, as well as the role of the state, were found to be important factors in the industrial restructuring at national level (Park, 1993). Overall, the current study suggests that Gumi industrial park originally started as a satellite industrial district, as defined by Park (1996). It confronted its difficulties and has evolved into an industrial cluster with continued diversification under the main trend of specialization in the electronics industry.

Changes in industrial specialization

Gumi was initially designed for high-level industrial specialization to encourage the localization of economies and inter-firm networking. Such specialization is a key feature of industrial districts in the New Industrial District literature (Park and Markusen, 1995). Gumi started with considerable sectoral specialization and was originally designed to host the electronics sector. In 1990, the electric machinery and electronics share accounted for 49.9 percent of the total employment (Park and Markusen, 1995). This share increased in the last two decades, reaching 60.2 percent in 2009 (Table 7.1). Along with the share increase of the electronics sector, the share of textiles continuously decreased from 38 percent in 1980, to 28.1 percent in 1990, and to 6.4 percent in 2009 (Park and Markusen, 1995; Table 7.1).

Initially, Gumi's success stood on two sectoral pillars— namely, textiles and electronics. The high incidence of textiles in the initial development of Gumi, which was not part of the original plan, is attributable to the strength of the industry in domestic and export markets, and to the early difficulties that the complex experienced in attracting the electronics industry. As the nearby older industrial city of Daegu specialized in the textile industry, textile firms that were looking to expand out of the Daegu area were eager to come to Gumi in the early 1970s. Furthermore, when the first Gumi complex was built in the early 1970s, the city encountered difficulty in attracting enough electronics plants to absorb the prepared industrial sites. Despite the official designation of Gumi Electronic Industrial Corporation, the management of the complex lowered its high-tech aspirations and built space for textile factories (Park and Markusen, 1995).

Three important trends emerged in the specialization changes in Gumi. First, despite the continuous increase in the degree of specialization in electronics, a continuous decrease was noted in the share of textiles, whereas shares in other sectors, such as machinery, increased. The textile industry in the Gumi industrial park significantly decreased its share since the 1990s because several

Table 7.1 Changes in the industrial structure of Gumi (percent)

Industry	1999	2002	2004	2006	2007	2008	2009
Textiles and clothing	16.19	14.21	11.47	8.51	8.75	6.28	6.44
Nonmetallic	13.00	14.94	12.49	11.34	11.84	13.80	9.04
Machinery	4.03	3.89	5.24	4.17	4.72	11.97	13.47
Electric and electronics	55.43	55.30	61.44	66.23	64.55	58.70	60.16
Others	11.35	11.66	9.36	9.75	10.14	9.25	10.89

Source: Park, 2010.

textile firms closed or relocated to foreign countries owing to the government's restructuring policy of labor-intensive industries in the 1990s. Meanwhile, new sectors, such as new energy industries, emerged in Gumi. For example, LG Electronics changed its plasma display panel production line to a solar battery and module production line in 2009; LG InnoTech established solar battery production facilities in 2007; and Seronics produced solar battery parts through a joint investment with a Japanese firm in 2009 (Chung, 2011). This development can be recognized as the diversification of the industry within the general trend of the intensification of specialization in the electronics sector.

Second, the diversification trend of products within the electronics sector emerged with the intensification of electronics specialization. TV was the major product in the early development of the district. However, since the mid-1980s, semiconductors, computers, and some electronics parts and components have been produced with the construction of a second district in Gumi (Chung, 2011).

Third, Gumi's economy has become more diversified with the remarkable increase in the service sector. The share of services to total employment increased from 3.7 percent in 1980, to 10 percent in 1990, 34.5 percent in 1995, and 46.1 percent in 2009 (Korea National Statistical Office, each year). The service sector has remarkably increased since the 1990s when the number of SMEs increased in Gumi. The increase in the number of SMEs changed the occupational structure of the city with the increase in managerial personnel, which required diverse services to be available. In the 1980s, most of the families of the managers and the white-collar workers in the large branch plants remained in Seoul because of children's education. Their monthly salary was sent to their families in Seoul, causing the Gumi local labor force to be mostly made up of production workers whose salary level is low. However, with the increase in the number of small firms headquartered in Gumi, several diverse service activities have developed since the 1990s.

Changes in firm size distribution and industrial linkages

The remarkable changes in industrial development in Gumi are exemplified in the distribution of firm size. Small, independent and locally headquartered firms are more likely to engage in and benefit from the potential for networking and cooperation in local areas. The proliferation of locally linked establishments will benefit an industrial district by insulating it from volatile external demand, thus enabling firms to be flexible and share the burden of restructuring during adverse times (Park and Markusen, 1995).

Approximately three-quarters of the establishments in Gumi employed less than 300 workers in 1992. These plants accounted for approximately 20 percent of total employment. Gumi's major plants are large branch plants headquartered mostly in Seoul, revealing a branch plant economy in the 1980s. Large plants predominated when new construction rates peaked from 1981 to 1986, resulting in the prevalence of smaller plants among the new additions. As shown in Figure 7.1, the remarkable increase in the number of establishments since the financial crisis in 1997 is mainly attributable to the addition of small independent firms. The increase in the addition of SMEs resulted in an increase in the share of a number of SMEs from 93.9 percent in 1999 to 96 percent in 2008, whereas the employment share increased from 34.8 percent in 1999 to 49.4 percent in 2008 (Chung, 2011). The employment share of SMEs to the total employment of Gumi is almost half. Thus, a reasonable assumption is that the new industrial structure has evolved from the specialization of large branch plants in Gumi. Changes in industrial structure can be realized from labor restructuring, as evidenced by the change in occupational structure. The share of managerial and administrative personnel increased from 2.6 percent in 1987, to 3.5 percent in 1992, and to 17.2 percent in 2010, whereas the share of production workers decreased from 82.3 percent in 1987, to 75.6 percent in 1992, and to 67.8 percent in 2010 (Park and Markusen, 1995; Chung, 2011).

The remarkable increase in the number of SMEs may give rise to growing local linkages between suppliers and buyers and among competitors, which might set off endogenous growth dynamics. In 1988, Daewoo Electronics, which had branch plants in Gumi, Chunan, Incheon, and Gwangju, had spatial linkages of input materials with the southeastern region of Korea by only 14 percent, revealing the limited linkages of the branch plant located in Gumi in the late 1980s (Park, 1990). The regional share of cooperative firms in the Gumi branch plant of SEC was 11.1 percent in the southeast region of Korea (Park, 2004), suggesting a low level of local linkages of branch plants in Gumi. Given the weak local linkages of large branch plants located in Gumi, the prospect of Gumi's economy was not optimistic in the late 1980s. In addition, considering that the small firms in Gumi are mostly subcontractors to the large branch plants in Gumi, the increase in the number of smaller firms reveals a growing subcontracting community in the city (Park and Markusen, 1995).

However, positive evidence has been identified in Gumi in recent years. According to Chung's survey (Chung, 2011), 54 percent of the firm respondents procured more than 75 percent of the total procurement from Gumi, and 55 percent of the firm respondents sold more than 75 percent of their total products to Gumi, revealing a high level of local input and output linkages. The strong local linkages are related to the restructuring strategy of large firms.

Large branch plants in Gumi encouraged employee spin-off to reduce the number of employees and establish a subcontracting relationship with the spin-offs. The senior workers of large branch plants can utilize their experiences and know-how to start new firms in a related industry, which is beneficial to large branch plants and to the local economy of Gumi. The subcontracting activities of the spin-offs fueled the atmosphere of the branch plant economy. However, a new trend emerged with considerable nonlocal linkages. Approximately 24 percent of the respondent firms procured less than 25 percent of the total procurement from Gumi, and 17 percent sold less than 25 percent of their total products to the city. This observation suggests that a considerable number of SMEs in Gumi have nonlocal industrial linkages and are not merely subcontractors of large branch plants. Several SMEs in the city are still subcontractors to large branch plants, and the subcontracting economy still exists. However, the trend of reshaping the economy has been concurrently evolving in recent years. Evidence from innovation can further explain the evolution of the Gumi electronics cluster.

Strengthening the innovation of SMEs

One of the most significant changes in the Gumi industrial cluster is the significant increase in innovation since the early 1990s. The number of registered patents in Gumi was negligible until the mid-1980s. This number has increased dramatically since the early 1990s. The number of patents decreased during the financial crisis in 1997, but continuously increased after 2004. An overall trend of diversification in innovation has clearly emerged in Gumi because the gap between the number of total patents with the number of patents of electricity and computing has continuously increased since the beginning of the twenty-first century (Figure 7.4). The rate of the increase in the number of patents is comparable with the average of Korea. Despite the concentration of innovation activities in the capital region, Gumi is now moving toward becoming an innovation cluster from being a branch plant economy (Figure 7.5).

The innovation cluster started to emerge in the early 1990s. Approximately 61 percent of the respondent firms of Park and Markusen's (1995) survey in 1992 introduced new technology in the last two years, and 43 percent of the firms responded to the introduction of new technology for production. The most important finding is that the major actors of innovation are moving from large firms to SMEs. In terms of the number of patents for electricity and computing, the share of large firms decreased from 95.1 percent before 2000 to 60.8 percent in 2009 to 2010, whereas the share of SMEs increased from 2 percent to 20 percent in the same period (Table 7.2). The innovation network has been growing because the share of joint patents significantly increased from 2 percent to 9.6 percent. In the electronics and communications sector, the expanding role of SMEs in innovation activity is remarkable. In the electronics and communications field, large enterprises had a 64 percent share, whereas

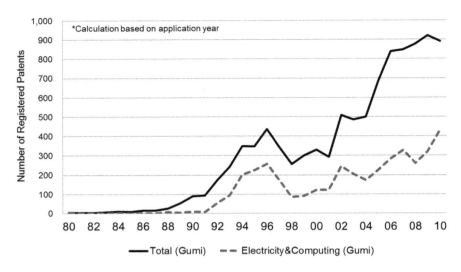

Figure 7.4 Changes in the number of registered patents in Gumi

Source: Korea Intellectual Property Rights Information Service (by September 29, 2013).

Note[1]: Electricity & Computing (Section H and G04–08 of the IPC).

Note[2]: Includes both registered and ended patents.

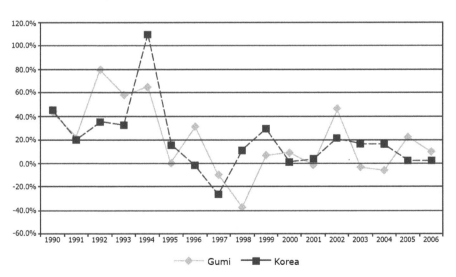

Figure 7.5 Growth rate in the number of registered patents: Gumi and Korea

Source: Chung, 2011.

SMEs had a 26.6 percent share of the registered patents before 2005. These values were completely reversed after 2005, in which large enterprises had a 24.2 percent share compared with the 57 percent registered patent share of SMEs (Table 7.3). After 2005, the shares of the individual and joint patents increased from 6.3 percent and 3.2 percent to 8.5 percent and 8.5 percent, respectively. Tables 7.2 and 7.3 show that the role of SMEs in the innovation activities in Gumi has proliferated in recent years, and collaboration with other actors showed a tendency to increase. Technology alliances with transacted firms and firm technology development were recognized as the most important factors in the introduction of technology and innovation (Chung, 2011). In the process of restructuring and specialization, large firms in Gumi have supported subcontracting SMEs to improve technology and promote R&D activities for the subsequent improvement of the quality of supplied parts and components. These firms believe that the technological progress of subcontracting SMEs is critical for retaining the competitive advantages of their final products in the global market.

Large customer firms are the most important original source of innovation information. However, small and medium customer firms, supplier firms, and competitive firms are also considered as vital sources of innovation information. Such knowledge and innovation networks of firms in Gumi suggest that the industrial park is now evolving toward becoming an innovative cluster from being an early satellite platform-type industrial district, despite the continuously significant role of large branch plants (Park, 2010).

Table 7.2 Changes in the number of electricity and computing patents[1] in Gumi, by firm size[2] (number, percent)

Period Applicant	Before 2000	2000– 2002	2003– 2004	2005– 2006	2007– 2008	2009– 2010	Total
Large firm	1,156 (95.1)	361 (73.8)	260 (69.0)	337 (66.2)	361 (61.6)	456 (60.8)	2,931 (74.7)
SMEs	24 (2.0)	81 (16.6)	70 (18.6)	115 (22.6)	136 (23.2)	150 (20.0)	576 (14.7)
Individuals	10 (0.8)	17 (3.5)	22 (5.8)	23 (4.5)	21 (3.6)	29 (3.9)	122 (3.1)
University and R&D centers	1 (0.1)	1 (0.2)	1 (0.3)	5 (1.0)	26 (4.4)	43 (5.7)	77 (2.0)
Joint patents	24 (2.0)	29 (5.9)	24 (6.4)	29 (5.7)	42 (7.2)	72 (9.6)	220 (5.6)
Total	1,215 (100.0)	489 (100.0)	377 (100.0)	509 (100.0)	586 (100.0)	750 (100.0)	3,926 (100.0)

Source: Korea Intellectual Property Rights Information Service (by September 29, 2013).
Note[1]: Electricity & Computing (Section H and G04–08 of the IPC).
Note[2]: Includes both registered and ended patents.

Table 7.3 Patent applications for electronics and communications in Gumi (number, percent)

Applicants	Before 2005		Since 2005		Total	
	Number	*%*	*Number*	*%*	*Number*	*%*
Large firm	101	63.9	40	24.2	141	43.7
SMEs	42	26.6	94	57.0	136	42.1
Individuals	10	6.3	14	8.5	24	7.4
University and R&D centers	0	0.0	3	1.8	3	0.9
Joint Patents	5	3.2	14	8.5	19	5.9
Total	158	100.0	165	100.0	323	100.0

Source: Korea Intellectual Property Rights Information Services (by August 31, 2010); Chung, 2011, p. 78.

Changes in the role of local government in recent years

Along with the previously examined innovation policies of the central government, changes in the role of the local government have also considerably contributed to the evolution of the Gumi industrial cluster. The local autonomy system in which city mayors and provincial governors are all directly elected by the people, was put into operation in Korea in 1995; thereafter, local governments have transformed themselves from mere administrators to active planners for their own development (Park, 2007; Choe, 2011).

Korea has adopted a two-tier local government system. Sixteen upper-level local governments (seven metropolitan and nine provincial governments) exist under the central government. Moreover, 230 lower-level local governments comprise 75 cities, 86 counties (rural local bodies), and 69 urban districts. Local governments have the authority to control all administrative affairs within their own jurisdiction. These affairs include policy formulation and implementation, personnel and financial management, organizational reengineering, and so forth. The revenue source of local governments is divided into two categories: self-generated revenue and grants from the central government.

Gyeongsangbuk Province is located in southeastern Korea and is the third largest province with a population of 2,600,032 (2010). The province is divided into 10 cities and 13 counties. The largest city in the province is Pohang, with a population of 517,088, and Gumi is the second largest city with a population of 413,446. The GRDP of Gyeongsangbuk Province is ₩79,444 billion (US$71.7 billion) in 2010, which accounted for 6.8 percent of GDP in Korea. The GRDP per capita in Gyeongsangbuk Province is ₩30.6 million (US$27.6 thousand) higher than the national average of ₩24.2 million (US$21.8 thousand). The annual budget of the province in 2011 was ₩18,054 billion (US$16.3 billion), but only 28.1 percent came from self-generated revenue.

Corresponding to the innovation policies of the central government, the Gyeongsangbuk provincial government and the Gumi City government cooperated to build local innovative capacity and cooperative relationship between firms in the Gumi industrial cluster. The Gyeongsangbuk provincial government has set up a blueprint for local industrial development with the aim of attracting supportive programs from the central government to bear some expenses for the project, whereas the Gumi City government has set up and operated R&D institutes and business associations (Chung, 2011).

The central government establishes key industries for each province considering the opinion of the provincial government and long-term national development. During the start of the Participatory Government in Korea in 2003, the central government, in collaboration with the provincial governments, selected promising local strategic industries for each province and fostered them intensively. Gyeongsangbuk Province selected electronics and information technology as a strategic industry in 2004. The Korean government also tried to select and nurture leading industries for each economic region. Gyeongsangbuk Province selected IT and new energy as its leading industries. The central government provides financial support to promote the strategic or leading industries in the province. In addition, based on the Korean government's action plan for regional development, the "Revised 4th Comprehensive National Territorial Plan (2008–2020)," Gyeongsangbuk Province set up the "Revised 3rd Comprehensive Provincial Territorial Plan (2008–2020)." Based on the 3rd Comprehensive Provincial Territorial Plan, Gyeongsangbuk Province established plans for restructuring its electronics industry and for the development of the new energy industry while suggesting the continuous development of the Gumi industrial cluster (DGDI, 2010; Gyeongsangbukdo, 2011).

Local governments have focused on increasing their local R&D capacity and promoting the new industry because the central government has set up a general scheme of development direction. As part of this local government policy, a complex of R&D facilities for the electronics industry was built within the Gumi industrial cluster in 2002, and the Gumi Electronics & Information Technology Research Institute (GERI) was established through a joint investment of the central government, Gyeongsangbuk Province, and Gumi city in 2007 (DGDI, 2010). GERI supports the R&D activities of SMEs, R&D of the electronics industry, expert training and education, the incubation of high-tech industry, and the development of a new renewable energy industry. Gumi city is in charge of operating GERI (Chung, 2011).

Meanwhile, Gyeongsangbuk Province and Gumi city tried to attract foreign firms to the Gumi industrial cluster by designating the Gumi Foreign Investment Zone within the Gumi industrial cluster and then attempting to agglomerate the new industries, such as LED and new energy, through several subsidies and incentives (DGDI, 2010). Unlike the early stage of the Gumi industrial complex development, business networks were established between the existing electronic firms and the newly entered energy sector firms to restructure the existing industries and enhance the local R&D capacity. These practices were undertaken in addition to the relocation of large facilities to Gumi. For example, the photovoltaic device industry, a kind of new energy industry, requires intermediate goods that are also utilized in the semiconductor and display industries. This condition enables SMEs in the electronics sector to expand their business scope to the new industry. Thus, GERI operates a technical assistance team for the promotion of the photovoltaic device industry in Gumi. The team constructs test-beds that are useful for problem-solving experimentation in the business conversion of electronic firms. Moreover, the team supports networking for cooperative R&D among SMEs in photovoltaic devices and electronic industries (Chung, 2011).

The Gumi city government also supports the formation of cooperative relations among SMEs by supporting the establishment and operation of business associations of SMEs. Previously, cooperative relations in Gumi mainly consisted of subcontracting activities from the large branch plants located in the Gumi industrial complex (Park and Markusen, 1995). The increase in the proportion of SMEs in the region and the change of government industrial policy into an innovation-oriented one highlighted the importance of diverse cooperative relations among firms (Chung, 2011). The Gumi Small and Medium Business Association (GSMBA) was set up through the voluntary participation of local SMEs in 2002. A similar association cannot be found in other cities in Korea. GSMBA serves as a channel agency in the performance of the central and local governments' support program for SMEs, undertaking such tasks as providing joint research activities for product development and process innovation, business support services, and so on. Gumi city furnishes the GSMBA with an operation fund and authorizes the group as an independent SME support institution through a Gumi city ordinance. A total of 758 SMEs have participated in the GSMBA since 2007. This number is equivalent to 65 percent of the total SMEs in Gumi (Chung, 2011). Such changes, as well as strengthening the role and function of the local government for R&D-focused policy and SME support, have significantly contributed to the evolution of the local economy and industrial cluster in Gumi.

Conclusion

Gumi was a typical satellite platform-type new industrial district until the early 1990s. In a previous study on Gumi, Park and Markusen drew the following conclusions:

> In Gumi, large branch plants predominate, surrounded by a growing number of smaller subordinate firms with captive subcontracting relationships. Gumi's branch plants have maintained significant intra-organizational but nonlocal linkages to other establishments of their parent firms located in other regions. Most establishments, with the exception of captive subcontractors, have extensive relationships with firms headquartered

outside the region, even outside the country. In other words, they are non-locally rather than locally embedded, and embedded within the vertically integrated structure of their parent firms, rather than among a set of vertically disintegrated firms. Most continue to operate with mass production processes and little local R&D, with the more customized and innovation-intensive work remaining in Seoul. They fit the depiction of 'global Fordism' more closely than they do that of 'flexible specialization'.

(1995, p. 100)

In the last two decades, however, Gumi underwent considerable changes and consequently evolved into an industrial cluster with significant local linkages and innovation activities despite the continuously significant role of branch plants in shaping the city's industrial and economic atmosphere. The government's industrial policies significantly influenced the changes in the Gumi industrial cluster. The state was the developer and locator of business activities within the confines of the Gumi industrial complex, both in terms of origin and contemporary operation, as demonstrated in the case of Changwon (Markusen and Park, 1993). The state initiated the development of several national industrial complexes in the late 1960s and 1970s. These complexes included those in Ulsan (petrochemical and transportation equipment), Changwon (machinery), and Pohang (steel). The state likewise initiated the industrial decentralization policy.

The promotion of the innovative cluster policy during the Participatory Government (2002–2007) contributed to R&D activities, and the formation of local knowledge and technology networks. Before the 1990s, local universities were not important actors in industrial cluster formation and R&D activities, although the capability of a region to supply university-educated engineering labor facilitated the development of Gumi. However, the recent emphasis placed on innovative clusters caused the Kumoh National Institute of Technology in Gumi to strengthen its participation in R&D activities and technology networks with local firms.

The role of the state during the initial development of Gumi industrial complex was critical and important for the evolution of the industrial cluster. However, the provincial and city governments have had a progressive function in supporting the innovative activities of SMEs during the last decade. The role of the state in creating a broader picture of industrial development remains important, and large branch plants share more than half of Gumi's production and export. In addition, the local government, local universities, and SMEs are becoming important agents in reshaping Gumi's local economy. An increasing trend of cooperation has recently been observed among the local government, local universities, and local firms. In some fields, such as electronics and communication, the share of SMEs in the number of registered patents surpassed that of large firms in the last five years, revealing the significant role of SMEs in reshaping Gumi's future industrial environment. Local inter-firm networks among SMEs for input and output material linkages, information and knowledge networks, as well as cooperation for technological development with other local actors have evolved in the Gumi economy. Notably, despite the hub-spoke hierarchical relationship between the large firms and SMEs in the industrial linkages, large branch plants have significantly contributed to the emergence of local SME networks with technology transfer, management consulting, and collaborative research.

The case of Gumi suggests the important aspects of industrial cluster evolution in developing countries. The mere agglomeration of establishments without significant local networks during initial development can possibly facilitate the formation of local networking and cooperation. The initial momentum of industrial development is based on entirely exogenous rather than endogenous phenomena induced by government policy and the investments of large firms. However, in addition to material linkages, the industrial cluster with the formation of local innovative networks for information, knowledge, and technology have evolved over time. Firms co-evolve with industries and networks in a cluster over time (Ter Wal and Boschma, 2011). The time period, however, should be carefully noted. In the case of Gumi, more than a quarter of a century was required to enable local cooperative networks of knowledge and technology to emerge beyond the hub-spoke relationships between large branch plants and SMEs.

Given the considerable resilience with sustained growth after the financial crisis in 1997 and the recent global economic crisis, the case of Gumi can be regarded as a successful Korean model for industrial specialization and development. However, the future prospects of the Gumi electronics cluster may depend on innovative activities and cluster formation with the concurrently intensification of local and global networks, as well as industrial networks, with diverse related sectors. In addition, the supply of qualified labor and knowledge-intensive advanced services is also important for the future competitiveness and sustainability of Gumi.

Note

1 This chapter is a revised version of an article: Park, Sam Ock and Chung, Dochai (2012) Evolution of industrial cluster and policy: the case of Gumi City, Korea. *The Journal of Korean Geographical Society*, 47(2), 226–244.

References

Choe, S. C. (2011). Introduction: reshaping regional policy in Korea. In H. Richardson, C.-H. C. Bae & S. C. Choe (Eds.), *Reshaping Regional Policy* (pp. 3–18). Cheltenham: Edward Elgar.

Chung, D. C. (2011). *Evolution of industrial cluster through overcoming the lock-in effect of branch plant agglomeration*. Ph.D. dissertation, Department of Geography, Seoul National University (in Korean with English summary).

Daegu Gyeongbuk Development Institute (DGDI). (2010). *New Design Daegu Gyeongbuk*. Daegu: DGDI (in Korean).

Gyeongsangbukdo. (2011). *The Provincial Administration of Gyeongsangbukdo in 2011*. Daegu: Gyeongsangbukdo Provincial Government (in Korean).

Kim, H. S. (1997). Innovation systems and science and technology policies in Korea. In K. Lee et al. (Eds.), *Technology Capacity and Competitiveness of Korean Industry* (pp. 123–166). Seoul: Kyungmungsa (in Korean).

Kim, H. & Lee, J. H. (2009). Multi-scalar dynamics of cluster development: the role of policies in three Korean clusters. *Journal of the Korean Geographical Society*, 44(5), 634–646 (in Korean with English summary).

Koo, Y. (2010). Agglomeration patterns of advertising industries and spatial networks of advertisement production. *Journal of the Korean Geographical Society*, 45(2), 256–274 (in Korean with English summary).

Korea Industrial Technology Association (KITA). (1995). *Statistics of Industrial Technology*. Seoul: KITA (in Korean).

Korea Industrial Technology Association (KITA). (1996). *Directory of Korea Technology Institute 95/96*. Seoul: KITA (in Korean).

Markusen, A. & Park. S. O. (1993). The state as industrial locator and district builder: the case of Changwon, South Korea. *Economic Geography*, 69(2), 157–181.

Lee, K. (2011). Firm-activity networks in the context of the value chain of regional resources-based industries: a case study of fermented soy product industry in Sunchang. *Journal of the Korean Geographical Society*, 46(3), 351–366 (in Korean with English summary).

Lim, Y. H. & Park, S. O. (2009). The spatial structure of the production of technological knowledge in the Korean photonics industry. *Journal of the Korean Geographical Society*, 44(3), 355–371 (in Korean with English summary).

Markusen, A. & Park, S. O. (1993). The state as industrial locator and district builder: the case of Changwon, South Korea. *Economic Geography*, 69(2), 157–181.

Ministry of Science and Technology (MOST). (1991). *Science and Technology Annual*. Seoul: MOST (in Korean).

Park, S. O. (1990). Corporate growth and spatial organization. In M. Smidt & E. Wever (Eds.), *The Corporate Firm in a Changing World Economy: Case Studies in the Geography of Enterprise* (pp. 207–233). London and New York: Routledge.

Park, S. O. (1993). Industrial restructuring and the spatial division of labor: the case of the Seoul metropolitan region, the Republic of Korea. *Environment and Planning A*, 25(1), 81–93.

Park, S. O. (1994). Industrial restructuring in the Seoul metropolitan region: major trigger and consequences. *Environment and Planning A*, 26(1), 527–541.

Park, S. O. (1996). Network and embeddedness in the dynamic types of new industrial districts. *Progress in Human Geography*, 20(4), 476–493.

Park, S. O. (2000). Innovation systems, networks, and the knowledge-based economy in Korea. In J. H. Dunning (Ed.), *Regions, Globalization, and Knowledge-Based Economy* (pp. 328–348). Oxford: Oxford University Press.

Park, S. O. (2004). The impact of business to business electronic commerce on the dynamics of metropolitan spaces. *Urban Geography*, 25(4), 289–314.

Park, S. O. (2007). Regional innovation policies for maximizing endogenous regional development capabilities. In *Balanced National Development Policy in Korea: Theory and Practice*. Seoul: Presidential Committee on Balanced National Development (PCBND).

Park, S. O. (2009). A history of the Republic of Korea's industrial structural trans-formation and spatial development. In Y. Huang & A. M. Bocchi (Eds.), *Reshaping*

Economic Geography in East Asia (pp. 320–337). Washington, DC: World Bank Publications.

Park, S. O. (2010). Regional resilience and path dependence: examples of four Korean industrial clusters. Paper presented at the 57th Annual North American Meeting of RSAI, Denver, USA. November 10–13.

Park, S. O. (2011). Long-term strategies for regional development policies. In H. W. Richardson, C.-H. C. Bae & S. C. Choe (Eds.), *Reshaping Regional Policy* (pp. 302–320). Cheltenham and Northampton, MA: Edward Elgar.

Park, S. O. & Markusen, A. (1995). Generalizing new industrial districts: a theoretical agenda and an application from a non-Western economy. *Environment and Planning A*, 27(1), 81–104.

Park, S. O. & Nahm, K. B. (2000). Development of regional innovation systems and industrial districts for the promotion of small and medium enterprises. *Journal of Korean Planners Association*, 35(3), 121–140 (in Korean with English summary).

Park, S. O., Yang, S.-M., Yoon, Y.-K., Lee, K. & Lim, H.-C. (2009). *The Sustainable Development Model and Growth Engines for Korea*. Seoul: Seoul National University Press (in Korean with English summary).

Presidential Committee on Balanced National Development (PCBND). (2007). *Balanced national development policy in Korea: theory and practice*. Seoul: Presidential Committee on Balanced National Development.

Richardson, H. W., Bae, C.-H. C. & Choe, S. C. (Eds.). (2011). *Reshaping Regional Policy*. Cheltenham: Edward Elgar.

Ter Wal, A. L. J. & Boschma, R. (2011). Co-evolution of firms, industries and networks in space. *Regional Studies*, 45(7), 919–933.

Website references

Korea Industrial Complex Corporation: www.kicox.or.kr/

Korea Intellectual Property Rights Information Service: www.kipris.or.kr/khome/main.jsp

Korea National Statistical Office (KOSTAT): http://kostat.go.kr/

8 Restructuring, innovation, and the global networks of Samsung

Introduction

The framework of the dynamics of economic spaces in the global knowledge-based information society can be examined through the role of firms as actors in economic spaces. This chapter explores how a global firm interacts with economic spaces relative to innovation systems, contrasting spatial processes, and evolving the dynamic features of economic spaces introduced in Chapter 2. Samsung has been selected as a case study to examine the dynamics of economic spaces based on the role of firms. Through the evolution of Samsung in the context of firm and space over time, we attempt to consider the framework of the dynamics of economic spaces. We can also consider the notions of service innovation and path dependence discussed in Chapters 3 and 4 in the analysis of the restructuring and innovation of Samsung.

Over the last two decades, global economic spaces have been significantly reshaped by the progress of global megatrends, such as globalization, knowledge-based economy, and information society. Manufacturing firms have pursued diverse strategies and interacted with economic spaces to sustain growth under the diverse environments brought about by global megatrends. Innovations of new products and processes have been critical in sustaining competitiveness. Networking with other firms and stakeholders has become important for the accumulation of intangible assets beyond the tangibles, as emphasized in traditional industrial location theories. Innovation is important for both manufacturing and service firms (Bryson and Daniels, 2007). The boundary between services and manufacturing has been considerably blurred by the importance of intangible assets in manufacturing.

The dramatic progress of industrialization and economic development in Korea during the last four decades is embedded in the evolution of large Korean conglomerates. Samsung's growth has also progressed in relation to the overall changes in the Korean economy. Consequently, Samsung, as a leading enterprise, has contributed to the development of modern Korea in terms of the development of ICT and high-tech industries. Accordingly, Samsung can be regarded as both a shaper and a product of the Korean economy (Michell, 2010). Samsung has grown as a leading conglomerate with total sales of

₩274.3 trillion and profit of ₩20.3 trillion in 2011. Samsung has transformed from being a low-cost manufacturer to being a world leader in production, marketing, R&D, and design, ranking eighth in brand value globally in 2013. The core company of Samsung Group is Samsung Electronics Corporation (SEC), with sales of ₩165 trillion and shares of more than 60 percent of the entire Samsung Group in 2011 (SEC, 2012b). SEC has evolved from a subcontractor to a manufacturer and then to a leading innovator of electronic products through the proper mobilization of a talented team.

The role of intangible assets has been critical in the evolution of the Korean economy and of Samsung. The accumulation of intangible assets by firms and by regions has become an important factor for gaining competitiveness, as examined in Chapter 6. In the processes of a firm's intangible asset accumulation, regions outside the internal organization of the firm become important for acquiring and integrating external knowledge beyond the internal knowledge base of the firm. These processes reflect the firm's interaction with diverse regions and global networks to access region-specific knowledge; as such, the importance of regions as the key drivers of innovation is undeniable (Asheim et al., 2011). However, the relationship between corporate system and region in the global economy relative to the accumulation of intangible assets to increase the competitiveness of both firm and region is yet to be sufficiently examined and remains in the early stage of theoretical development.

Given the evolution of SEC in relation to the development of Korea in the era of globalization and knowledge-based information society, SEC is an appropriate example to understand contemporary ideas and debates regarding the manufacturing industry. This chapter thus aims to examine Samsung, focusing on SEC, as a case study in terms of corporate evolution and restructuring, brand development, innovation and firm strategy, and global networks. This chapter emphasizes SEC's global network in terms of firm and region relationships in the accumulation of intangible assets. Various materials and firm statistics are examined, and in-depth interviews with managers, executive directors, and former CEOs are conducted to clarify the interaction and accumulation processes of intangible assets.

Evolution of Samsung: path dependence, restructuring, and new path creation

Samsung's history can be described in terms of path dependence, restructuring, and new path creation. In broad terms, Samsung Group has evolved from a small commercial firm to a global conglomerate through four stages of development: early group formation stage, diversification of manufacturing industries, reorganization and restructuring, and global-leading innovation organization.

Before the launch of SEC in 1969, Samsung was in the early group formation stage. Samsung Group originated from Samsung Sanghoe, a small commercial firm, established in 1938 in Daegu, Korea, by the late Byung-Chul Lee, the former chairman of Samsung Group. Before the independence of Korea in 1945, Samsung's business mainly focused on trading, textiles, and food. In 1948, Samsung established Samsung Moolsan, a commercial trading company. Samsung expanded its activities to the processing, apparel, and life insurance industries in the 1950s. During the First Five-Year Economic Development Plan launched in 1962, Samsung expanded into more diverse business activities, including a paper mill, hospital, newspaper, culture center, and real estate. In this initial group formation stage, business activities mostly focused on the service sector.

In the late 1960s to the early 1980s, manufacturing became the major business of Samsung. The new stage of the evolution of Samsung Group started with the emergence of Samsung's core business, SEC, which was established in 1969. In the early industrialization of Korea, the government controlled certain industries into which firms can enter by limiting permits. However, the government encouraged firms to participate in the electronics industry by establishing the Electronics Industry Cooperative Association in 1967 and Electronics Industry Promotion Law in 1969 (Park, 1991; SEC, 2010). Samsung's founding Chairman Lee established a development project at Samsung Moolsan to prepare for the establishment of an electronics firm. The establishment of SEC was the result of the founding chairman's vision for the future of Samsung as well as the Korean government's promotion of electronics industrial development. The late founding chairman Lee concluded that the "electronics industry is perfectly fitted to Korea's economic development stage in all aspects of technology, labor, value added, the prospect of domestic demand and export and so on" (SEC, 2010, p. 22). Samsung-Sanyo Electronics was established in 1969, and was renamed Samsung Electro-Mechanics (SEC) in 1975, which then merged with Samsung Electronics in 1977.

Starting with the electronics industry, Samsung entered a new era of its history. In the 1970s, the Korean government enthusiastically promoted heavy and chemical industrial development, resulting in the emergence of many large firms and Chaebols in the heavy and chemical industries (Park, 1991). Samsung Group established diverse firms in the heavy and chemical industries in the 1970s and early 1980s, such as Samsung Petrochemical, Samsung Heavy Industry, Samsung Precision, Samsung Shipbuilding, Samsung Semiconductor, and Samsung Semiconductor and Communication. Samsung also invested into producer services, such as Jaeil Planning, Korea Engineering, Samsung Integrated Construction, Dongbang Training Center, Samsung Integrated Training Institute, and Samsung Data System.

Starting with black-and-white TV, Samsung entered the production of diverse household electric appliances, such as color TVs, washing machines, refrigerators, microwave ovens, air conditioners, VCRs, and personal computers. SEC became a major manufacturer in the Korean market and began to export color TVs for the first time in this period. Samsung and all the other Korean large firms benefited from Korea's economic development policy that focused on heavy and chemical industries during the 1970s and early 1980s

(Park, 1991). Samsung successfully prepared strategic foundations for entering global markets and its future growth with investments in the heavy and chemical industries, including the electronics industry. In the early to mid-1980s, Samsung diversified its activities into information technology services, such as system integration, system management, consulting, and network services.

The late 1980s to the late 1990s served as the reorganization and restructuring period of Samsung with an emphasis on technological development and the global market. This period is important in the history of Samsung because of two aspects: opening the era of the new chairman, Kun-Hee Lee, son of founding chairman Lee after the latter passed away in 1987, and emphasis on technological development and innovation to compete in a changing world. On one hand, the new chairman, Kun-Hee Lee, continued to focus on talented human resources, following the vision of the founding chairman. On the other hand, he created the vision for leading global products and market through R&D activities and innovation in the field of ICT and electronics. In this aspect, the new chairman manifested leadership with the creation of a new path, as well as a path-dependent vision. Samsung Semiconductor and Telecommunications Co. merged with SEC in 1988, with SEC selected home appliances, telecommunications, and semiconductors as its core business lines.

New chairman Lee declared a "New Management" initiative, which was the first management innovation that shifted the focus from quantity to quality to enhance competitiveness and to accomplish the new vision of becoming a leading global corporation in the twenty-first century. The "New Management" initiative integrated Western best practices related to strategy formation, talent management, and compensation into Samsung's existing model (Khanna et al., 2011). "World Best," "World First," and "World Wide" were emphasized in the new management for its goal of becoming a leading global corporation in the twenty-first century (SEC, 2010, p. 128). Samsung was confronted with tremendous challenges in the high-tech sector in the 1990s and invested continuously in R&D to overcome such challenges. The title of "world's first" products began to appear in the 1990s.

The other important change in this period is the restructuring of the Samsung Group amid the financial crisis in Korea in 1997. The financial crisis caused the bankruptcy or dissolution of 16 out of 30 conglomerates in Korea, following the government's strong restructuring strategy (SEC, 2010). Samsung faced its most serious crisis since its foundation. However, Samsung initiated its second management innovation in 1996, one year before the financial crisis. Management innovation in 3P (Product, Process, and Personnel) was emphasized under the motto of independent, speedy, and simple managements (SEC, 2010). The strategies of the first and second management innovations were helpful for overcoming the serious crisis in the late 1990s.

Despite its management innovation, SEC was confronted with serious loss of parity exchange in addition to a large loan. Actually, at the end of 1997, Samsung's financial structure deteriorated with loans amounting to ₩13 trillion and a debt of ₩6 trillion (SEC, 2010). Samsung decided to enforce strong restructuring based on the result of the task force team meeting of CEOs. Highlights of the restructuring process were the disposal of unnecessary parts of business that resulted in securing ₩1.2 trillion, 28 percent reduction in global manpower (23,000 employees), and concentration on the core business by cutting off 120 marginal units. Samsung promoted six restructuring strategies: disposal of nonprofit assets; decreasing stocks and reduction of debenture; bold curtailment of nonessential costs; slimming down manpower and organization; selection of and concentration on profitable business; and improving financial structure with focusing on cash flow and profit and loss. With the strategy of improving financial structure, debt ratio decreased from 300 percent to 8 percent within two years. This restructuring made remarkable changes possible, enabling Samsung to open up new opportunities.

Since the beginning of twenty-first century, Samsung has moved toward being the world's best by pioneering the digital age. In overcoming the challenges from the Asian financial crisis, Samsung leaped into the world's best enterprises in the twenty-first century by finding and creating new business opportunities in the existing group enterprises and in new businesses. New businesses were unrelated to the existing businesses but fell within Samsung's core capabilities, such as the Internet and digital businesses (Michell, 2010). Such new businesses can be regarded as the creation of a new path, along with path-dependent improvement or reorganization of existing paths. Product and process innovations were continuously emphasized, and new businesses were developed. Strategic alliances for new businesses and new projects, such as healthcare sectors, as well as green management strategy, have been promoted for continuous restructuring and the search for new opportunities. Samsung has emphasized speed, talents, design, brand power, and soft value of technology in its "creative management," which is related to the line of "creation-innovation-challenge." With strategies for pioneering the digital age, Samsung exhibited a successful performance during the first decade of the twenty-first century. The case of SEC in the twenty-first century is related to the resilience and alternative path-dependent evolution discussed in Chapter 4 (Figures 4.5a and 4.5b). Samsung became resistant to the financial crisis through restructuring, reinforcing the solid path, and promoting the dynamic process of innovation and renewal.

Samsung currently has 18 companies in the 3 major fields of electronics, finance, as well as heavy and chemical industries. It also has 11 other affiliates that are relatively independent, as seen in Table 8.1. Samsung has managed to hold its group structure together in a synergistic manner, emphasizing the fusion and compounding of its affiliates. Michell (2010) highlighted that this complex structure suffered from internal threats of cross-holding of Korean systems, as well as external threats caused by systemic risks among Korean financial institutions. However, the strong leadership and fusion of speed with teamwork, inherited from historic ethnic characteristics, are regarded as the strengths of its Korean-style management (Kim and Kim, 2013). Samsung's

Table 8.1 Samsung's affiliates

Electronics industries	Samsung Electronics
	Samsung SDI
	Samsung Corning Precision Materials
	Samsung SDS
	Samsung Techwin
	Samsung Mobile Display
	Samsung Digital Imaging
Financial services	Samsung Life Insurance
	Samsung Fire & Marine Insurance
	Samsung Card
	Samsung Securities
	Samsung Asset Management
	Samsung Venture Investment
Heavy and chemical industries	Samsung Heavy Industries
	Samsung Total Petrochemicals
	Samsung Petrochemicals
	Samsung Fine Chemicals
	Samsung BP Chemicals
Other affiliated companies	Samsung C&T Corporation
	Samsung Engineering
	Cheil Industries
	Samsung Everland
	The Shilla Hotels & Resorts
	Cheil Worldwide
	S1 Corporation
	Samsung Medical Center
	Samsung Human Resources Development Center
	Samsung Economics Research Institute
	Samsung Lions
	The Ho-Am Foundation
	Samsung Foundation of Culture
	Samsung Welfare Foundation
	Samsung Life Public Welfare Foundation

Source: Samsung Group webpage (www.samsung.com/us/aboutsamsung/corporateprofile/affiliatedcompanies.html).

New Management initiative aimed to improve marketing, R&D, and design while retaining core strength in manufacturing, resulting in Samsung's hybrid management system that sought the best of traditional Japanese and Western systems (Khanna et al., 2011). More details on Samsung's rise are discussed in the following sections with a focus on SEC.

Innovation and evolution of SEC's product development

In understanding the tremendous success of Samsung during the last two decades, SEC should be more closely examined in terms of innovation, as SEC has been the core of Samsung with a share of approximately 60 percent of the total sales of Samsung Group. Sales have continuously grown since the late 1990s, even after the Asian financial crisis in 1997 and after the global financial crisis in 2008 (Figure 8.1). Before SEC's innovation is discussed, SEC's global spatial strategy is briefly examined.

SEC, the core company of Samsung, has grown remarkably since its establishment in 1969 and has become a global leading innovator. SEC initially joined a multinational corporation group in 1979, ten years after its establishment. The global headquarters of SEC, located in Suwon city in the capital region of Korea, started with the production of home appliances, such as black-and-white TVs, refrigerators, washers, and others, in the early 1970s. The company started the production of color TVs in 1977. With the development of the first VCR in the nation, SEC began to initiate product development and innovation. Since the 1980s, SEC has diversified into more high-tech-oriented products. SEC has been involved in foreign direct investments (FDIs) since its first investment in the USA in 1978. For ten years beginning in 1978, SEC invested in foreign subsidiaries in advanced countries, such as the USA, Germany, the UK, Australia, and Canada (Table 8.2). SEC's FDIs can be differentiated with several stages over time: foreign subsidiary; foreign manufacturing and sales; and foreign R&D activities. From the late 1970s to the late 1980s, SEC's FDIs focused on the establishment of foreign subsidiaries, with the key period being the 1980s. The 1980s saw the transition from foreign subsidiary investment to production investment. SEC has invested in manufacturing plants and sales offices since 1982, with the key period being the 1990s. Production investments began from advanced countries, such as the USA and UK, and then extended to industrializing countries, such as Thailand, Malaysia, India, Brazil, and so on (Table 8.2). SEC started foreign R&D activities from 1987, with the key periods being the late 1980s and 2000s.

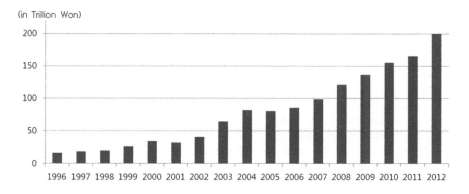

Figure 8.1 Growth of SEC's sales

Source: SEC, 2012b; Internal materials of SEC.

Table 8.2 SEC's major stages of global networks over time

Major stages	Period	Key period	Major countries
Foreign local subsidiary	1978–1988	1980s	Advanced countries: USA, Germany, UK, Australia, Canada
Foreign plant investment	1982–	1990s	From advanced to industrializing countries: Portugal, USA, UK, Thailand, Mexico, Malaysia, Brazil, Slovacia, India, Russia
Foreign R&D center	1987–2004	Late 1980s and 2000s	From advanced to industrializing countries: USA, Japan, UK, Russia, Israel, China, India, Poland
Foreign industrial complex	1995–1996	1990s	UK, Mexico

Source: Gathered from SEC's internal materials, websites, interview surveys, and newspapers. (Revised from Park, 2012.)

The R&D investments also started from advanced countries and extended to industrializing countries.

The evolution of SEC's spatial corporate system suggests that corporate systems successively extend from foreign subsidiaries to manufacturing plants and R&D centers, and from advanced countries to industrializing countries over time. Overall, SEC's investments suggest that spatial corporate systems evolve from subsidiary to R&D investments and then extend from advanced countries to industrializing ones. On one hand, investments in advanced countries in the earlier period seem to be related to the exploration of knowledge, whereas investments in developing countries in the later period seem to be related to the exploitation of knowledge. On the other hand, accumulation of intangible assets through both exploring and exploiting knowledge over time is critical for SEC.

Innovation has been the most important factor for SEC's successful growth. Continuous innovation activities have been the underlying forces of restructuring, resilience, and creating new paths for Samsung. Innovation strategy comes from SEC's headquarters and Samsung Group as a whole, according to the vision and major strategies of Samsung. Several important aspects in the innovation of SEC are discussed as follows.

First, to overcome crises and the highly competitive global market, SEC emphasized R&D activities for product and process innovations. SEC's R&D investment has been continuously rising, reaching ₩10.3 trillion in 2011, which accounted for 6.2 percent of total sales. Overall, the ratio of R&D investments fluctuates from 5.6 percent to 6.8 percent of total sales, with a decreasing ratio during the global economic crises in 2008 and 2009. However, the amount of R&D investments has continuously increased (Table 8.3). R&D

Table 8.3 SEC's R&D investment

	2011	2010	2009	2008	2007	2006	2005
R&D investment (trillion won)	10.3	9.4	7.6	7.1	6.1	5.7	5.5
Ratio of R&D to total sales (%)	6.2	6.1	5.6	5.8	6.2	6.7	6.8

Source: SEC, 2012b.

manpower has also continuously increased, reaching 55,320 in 2011, accounting for a quarter of SEC's total manpower (Figure 8.2). With intensive R&D investments, SEC has ranked second in the number of patents registered in the USA since 2006.

Second, the foreign R&D investments of SEC in recent years are related to both seeking and exploiting knowledge concurrently through diverse interactions with regions and cities, as discussed in Chapter 6. Cantwell and Piscitello (2005) suggest that the location of foreign R&D centers tends to consider different sources of spillovers and externalities, such as

> (1) the presence of industry-specific spillovers and specialization externalities; (2) the breath of local technological activities in the region, i.e. the opportunity to enjoy diversity externalities and to capture inter-industry spillovers; and (3) the presence of external sources of knowledge and science-technology spillovers.
>
> (p. 11)

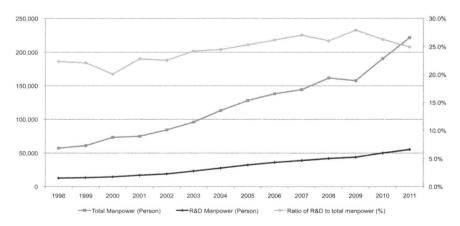

Figure 8.2 Growth of SEC's R&D manpower and ratio to the total number of employees

Source: SEC, 2010, 2012b.

The three types of externalities and spillovers can be observed in the seeking and exploiting of knowledge by SEC's foreign R&D centers.

Third, the SEC's foreign R&D centers are mostly located in large metropolitan areas or high-tech clusters with strong intra- and inter-industry externalities. R&D centers in foreign countries closely cooperate with local institutes to secure regionally strong or specialized technologies. For example, SEC emphasized local R&D cooperation of the cloud, next-generation web, OS, and next-generation UX in Silicon Valley; communication, RF/antenna, and server in Dallas; and security and recognition in Israel. In Bangalore, the thrust is on cooperation for system S/W, web browser, and B2B solution, whereas in Russia and Ukraine, SEC focuses on collaboration for algorithm, system S/W, and H/W enabling. In Beijing, cooperation for Chinese DTV/ communication standard is the key area of cooperation because China controls its own technology standard. Recent R&D activities in foreign countries suggest that SEC also pursues exploring and exploiting knowledge concurrently in both advanced and developing countries.

Fourth, SEC has cultivated strategic alliances with global leading firms, such as IBM, Intel, HP, Sony, Nokia, Discovery, Charter, and so on, for joint technological development and cooperation. Strategic alliances clustered from 2003 to 2007, which coincided with the cluster of the world's first product development. Strong drives for global technology alliances with global leading firms surely contributed to the establishment of the global standard of technology and successful innovations. To strengthen patent defense, SEC participated in cross-licensing agreements with global IT firms, such as Toshiba in 2009, Qualcomm, Kodak, International Ventures, Rambus, and Sharp in 2010, and IBM, Microsoft, and Spansion in 2011. In January 27, 2014, Samsung and Google signed a global patent cross-license agreement covering a broad range of technologies and businesses. This agreement forged a long-term cooperative partnership for mutual benefits. Samsung and Google can access each other's industry-leading patent portfolios with deeper collaboration on R&D activities of current and future products and technologies (Samsung Village, www.samsungvillage.com/blog/2014/01). The long-term (for ten years) cross-license will contribute to saving risk costs and concentrate on innovation. Such strategic alliances facilitate the clustering of technology and innovation through science-technology spillovers and externalities, as suggested by Cantwell and Piscitello (2005).

Fifth, Samsung expanded transactions in local areas through an open innovation system. In addition to internal R&D activities and cooperation networks with subcontractors, Samsung supports diverse activities for SMEs in terms of manpower, funds, technology, marketing, and so on. SEC has also introduced open sourcing systems for the joint development of parts and facilities with innovative SMEs, despite the latter being excluded as official subcontractors. In 2011, 651 technology-consulting projects existed through open sourcing, and 23 projects were adopted through peer reviews (SEC, 2012a). Samsung has also cooperated with universities, R&D institutes, and leading small and medium high-tech firms with future technology that complements SEC's technology. R&D centers in foreign countries closely cooperate with leading universities and research institutes in relevant regions. Samsung has spearheaded major cooperative activities within local areas, such as investments for start-ups in Silicon Valley, national projects with govern-ment research centers and the operation of future technology consulting committee in Dallas, and joint lab establishment with Tsinghai University in Beijing. The open innovation group at Samsung Advanced Institute of Technology, Samsung Group's R&D hub, offers two specific collaboration programs: Global Research Outreach program for academic collaborations and Collaborative Open Research Expert Network program to promote communication and interaction with global science and technology leaders (Samsung Advanced Institute of Technology, www.sait.samsung.co.kr/ saithome/). In building research partnerships with academic communities, Samsung implemented three future technology promoting programs in conjunction with creative economy: basic science, which is fundamental to future technology; material science, which is a basis for advanced manu-facturing; and ICT convergent creative projects, which build added value into innovation.

Sixth, SEC has also endeavored to foster a creative organizational culture. The Creative Development Institute has recently been opened to support the personnel in actualizing their creative ideas into commercial products. SEC personnel with creative ideas on diverse fields, such as product development, business, operation of organization, and so on, can apply for a one-year stint in the task force team of the Creative Development Institute. The first fruit of the Institute was an eyeball-mouse called "eyeCan," through which a user with total paralysis can operate the cursor and computer by moving his/her eyeballs.

With its intensive investment in R&D, global technology alliances, and other internal and external cooperative activities, SEC has evolved as a global leader in product development (Table 8.4). The development of products with the nation's first brand started from 1979, with the development of the VCR. Several products were first developed in the nation in the early 1980s, and then in 1986, the initiative advanced to the first product development worldwide for the 4 mm VTR. In the 1990s, two products were developed for the first time in the firm, and two other products were the first in the world. After the Asian financial crisis, SEC achieved successful product development results with five of the world's first product developments related to TFT-LCD, NAND flash, and DRAM process from 2001 to 2004. From 2005 to 2007, as many as seven of the world's first products related with NAND flash, touch screen, mobile DRAM, and DTV were developed, representing a cluster of the world's first new products development in the early and mid-2000s (Table 8.4). After the global financial crisis in 2009, SEC developed four of the world's first products. In 2012, despite the lack of development of the world's first products, SEC developed several new products.

Table 8.4 SEC's major products development

Year	First at firm level	Nation's first products	World's first products
1970s		VCR, 1979	
1980s	Semiconductor1M SRAM	64K DRAM, 1983 256K DRAM, 1983 1M DRAM, 1986	4mmVTR, 1986
1990s	16M DRAM, 1990 1G DRAM, 1996		256M DRAM, 1995 1G alpha chip, 1999
2000–2004	70N Semicon. Process, 02		40"TFT-LCD, 01 54"TFT-LCD, 02 70N 4G NAND Flash, 03 70N DRAM Process, 04 60N 8G NAND Flash, 04
2005–2007		70N DRAM, 05	50N 8G NAND Flash, 05 CTF NAND Tech, 06 16 step MCP, 06 DDI Touch Screen, 06 1G Mobil DRAM, 06 65N Receive Chip of DTV, 07 30N 64G NAND Flash, 06
2008–2012	Green Server Solution, 12 1.5Mb STT-MRAM, 12 Graphin Semicon, 12 QC Application Process, 12	30N 4Gb DDR4 Dram,12	4G DDR3 DRAM, 09 40N DRAM, 09 3mm thick LED TV, 09 0.6mm 8 step Chip, 09 30N DRAM, 10

Source: SEC, 2012a; various newspapers for 2012.

Continuous evolution of new products has surged in the area of DRAM, which represents the accumulation of technology with continuous integration and cycle of path-dependent evolution, and the creation of new paths with newly created technology (Table 8.4). TV products are also continuously evolved from black-and-white TV, to color TV, to digital TV, and to LED TV. This process is certainly a path-dependent evolution of new products. Strong investments in R&D activities, even amid the financial crisis of 1997, and numerous world-first developments of new products in the early and mid-2000s caused SEC to mass produce new products during the global financial crisis in the late 2000s and early 2010s. SEC began to mass produce many products in the world's first mass production during the global financial crisis. These products include 50 Nano 1G DDR2 DRAM in 2008, 40 Nano DDR3 DRAM in 2009, 4G DDR3 DRAM in 2010, 30 Nano DRAM in 2010, DRAM module for server in 2011, 46" LCD panel in 2012, and 20 Nano LPDDR2 4Gb mobile DRAM in 2012. SEC has also introduced several new products to the global market as first in the world since 2008. Such pioneering mass production and the introduction of new products to the global market imply that SEC has significant advantages with premium price in the world market. In 2012, the premium price enabled Samsung to record a new high of "200 to 20" trillion, which indicated a first record of more than ₩200 trillion in sales and more than ₩20 trillion in profit.

The restructuring and new path creation of Samsung can be expected from the announcement of the new catch phrase by Samsung Group's chairman. In 1993, chairman Lee announced the catch phrase "New Management" with emphasis on "change from quantity-focused consciousness, institution, norms and habits to quality-focused system" (SEC, 2010, p. 123). The new management supplied the momentum for restructuring Samsung into a worldwide and world-best enterprise through innovation. chairman Lee's new year's message in 2014 required another change with strong emphasis on "awareness of crisis and innovation" (Chosun-Ilbo, January 29, 2014, p. C2). This message emphasized the dignity and value of products, services, and businesses beyond the emphasis of quality. Samsung has been successfully restructured from a quantity-focused system to a quality-focused system under the catch phrase of "New Management" for the last two decades. Samsung prepares for another leap forward by overcoming a new crisis by securing new technology and a new growth engine. Three major innovation directions of Samsung are technological innovation for future uncertainties, innovation of business structure to lead industry trends, and system innovation to accomplish a global management system. Samsung planned to invest more than ₩23 trillion until 2020 into five new businesses—namely, solar battery, automobile battery, LED, bio-medicine, and medical equipment, to develop new future industries. Samsung has restructured and evolved continuously through the chairman's vision and continuous innovations.

Branding Samsung

Before the early 1990s, Samsung did not consider branding as seriously as innovation and production. The majority of Samsung's products sold in foreign countries were with other companies' brands or with parts and components inside other firms' products. In the mid-1990s, however, Samsung wanted to build a brand, not only a product, shifting from low-end products to a premium brand strategy. Samsung's global brand campaign started in 2001, and Samsung's sports marketing initiatives through sponsorship during the Winter Olympic Games in Salt Lake City in 2002 provided critical momentum for the successful future brand campaign of the company (Michell, 2010). SEC is convinced that increased marketing will benefit sales and profit margins. SEC has strongly supported global brand marketing since the late 1990s. With Eric Kim's joining SEC in 1999 as head of responsibility for global marketing,

Samsung's investments in marketing activities exceeded $900 million in 2002. The global campaign has had a successful result, as seen in Figure 8.3. Before 2000, Samsung's brand was not included in Interbrand's top 100 list. However, in 2000, the brand value of Samsung leaped to US$5.22 billion, ranking 43rd. During the early 2000s, the brand value and rank of Samsung increased significantly. SEC's brand value has again increased sharply since 2010, resulting in a US$32.89 billion value and ranking 9th in 2012.

The dramatic increase in Samsung's brand value is not solely the result of the global brand campaign or sports marketing, but is the integrated result of innovation and marketing. The strength of the brand grows as a company introduces new products against competition and as the products grow in sophistication (Michell, 2010). SEC has practiced diverse brand marketing strategies for securing global leadership in the twenty-first century as follows (SEC, 2010).

First, SEC has promoted market-driven change for marketing innovation and invested approximately 3–4 percent of total sales into marketing since 2000. Samsung enhanced the emotional benefits of digital convergence through campaigns that combined communication, entertainment, and information. They also focused on producing competitive products with the development of leading-edge technology and improvement of design manpower. The key marketing strategies were the construction of brand leadership by enhancing the competitiveness of outstanding digital products, promotion of a systematic brand strategy, creation of high value-added services from premium products, and promotion of a single master brand that integrated the product brand into the corporate image.

Second, SEC increased brand value through design management. Samsung began to regard design as a primary management factor after the declaration of "New Management" in 1993. Since the announcement of the design revolution in 1996, however, SEC has plunged into the design management

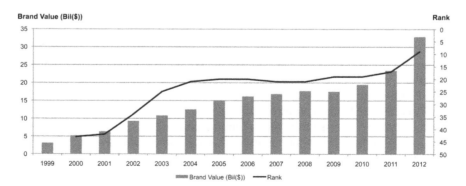

Figure 8.3 Samsung's brand value

Source: SEC, 2010; Samsung Group webpage (www.samsung.co.kr/samsung/outcome/brand.do).

system in earnest. SEC recognizes the necessity of the transformation of product sensitivity beyond superior function and technology to establish a global premium brand, which has been the motivation behind the strategic meeting of major CEOs at the global design core, such as that in Milan in 2005. In this strategy meeting, Samsung announced the "Four Milan Design Strategies"—namely, the construction of original design and User Interface (UI) identity, securing excellent design talents, fostering a creative and new organizational culture, and strengthening the infrastructure of mold technology (SEC, 2010). SEC also emphasized the construction of design infrastructure. SEC operates global design research centers in San Francisco, Los Angeles, London, Milan, Tokyo, and Shanghai for market-driven design activities. SEC has produced several hundred designers and operates global design membership in the USA, UK, Italy, China, and Japan.

Third, since 2005, SEC has promoted the second brand strategy for premium brands and a cultural marketing strategy. The focus is on enhancing the premium image of the brand, with the aim of transforming the existing Sensible Brand Buyer to a High-Life Seeker. The first brand strategy was the campaign of "DigitAll" with the slogan "SAMSUNG DIGITall, everyone's invited," promoted during from 1999 to May 2005, whereas the second brand strategy was the campaign "Imagine" promoted in June 2005. In the second strategy, target customers have been reestablished as "High-Life Seekers" with an increase in high value-added products. High-Life Seekers pertain to customers who feel that the product and brand speak for their own identity and style, and positively seek mixed values of functional excellence, emotional fulfilment, and aesthetic experience in the products (SEC, 2010). Accordingly, SEC emphasized cultural marketing for premium brand and marketing in gate cities and noted places.

Fourth, SEC has promoted sports marketing to strengthen its brand. Samsung participated as an Olympic partner in the Nagano Winter Olympic Games in 1998, Sydney Olympic Games in 2000, Salt Lake City Winter Olympic Games in 2002, Athens Olympic Games in 2004, and so on. SEC's official sponsorship of the Athens Olympic Games in 2004 and Torino Winter Olympic Games in 2006 contributed to the establishment of Samsung's brand image among Europeans. SEC also promoted football marketing. Samsung contracted official sponsorships with the Asian Football Federation (AFC), Chelsea FC of the UK, and Corinthians FC of Brazil. In addition, SEC has driven diverse sports marketing campaigns to be aligned with diverse regional characteristics. In the Sochi Winter Olympic Games in 2014, SEC was among the top ten enterprises in terms of official sponsorship. SEC has the responsibility to sponsor mobile communication for the Olympic Games. In addition, SEC also participated in individual sponsorship for Yuna Kim in figure skating. Such sports marketing through official sponsorship in the Olympic Games has a significant effect on increasing the brand value of an enterprise.

The brand value of Samsung has been continuously increasing, further achieving US$39.6 billion and ranking eighth in the world in 2013. Considering its value of only US$3.1 billion in 1999, we find that the brand value of Samsung has overwhelmingly increased. The continuous and rapid increase in Samsung's brand value resulted from the integrated effects of marketing, management innovation, technological innovation, and sports marketing. Accordingly, the increase or change in a firm's brand value is strongly related to the evolution of the firm and processes of branding over time. In addition, brands and branding are economic and geographic because they produce geographic differentiation over time and space (Pike, 2013).

SEC's global networks

Along with the restructuring, path-dependent evolution, and new path creation, SEC has continuously accumulated intangible assets in the form of knowledge, technology, brand, and so on. SEC reveals that formal and informal networks within clusters of local areas, continuous R&D investments, technology cooperation, and strategic alliances, as well as such activities as organizing and participating in temporary clusters are the major mechanisms of knowledge accumulation and global networks, as examined in Chapter 6.

Networks within local areas of foreign countries formed by individual corporate units are critical in a firm's knowledge accumulation. In the early stage, larger firms' R&D investments in the innovation cluster of advanced countries have been clearly regarded as activities relevant to seeking or exploring knowledge. SEC maintained close local networks to acquire knowledge and technology, as well as cooperated with Silicon Valley firms in the earlier stage of R&D investments (Park, 1994, 1996). This asset-seeking or exploring behavior through global networks resulted in the continuous development of new products, beginning in the 1990s. More recently, SEC aggressively organized or participated in temporary clusters, such as expos and trade fair events, to enhance its innovative networks. As examined in Chapter 2, temporary clusters have significantly influenced the acquisition of new knowledge and product information and the establishment of innovative networks (Bathelt and Glücker, 2011; Rinallo and Golfetto, 2011; Torre, 2008). Temporary clusters, such as trade shows, are among the important avenues of global networks that support firms in the development of marketing capabilities in addition to securing new ideas and knowledge, which are important for effective innovation and competitive advantage. Sales network centers are outposts of global networks for exploiting marketing information in foreign countries. Interactions with other regions and markets within such foreign countries are excellent opportunities for accumulating marketing information and knowledge. Local networks of production centers within local clusters in foreign countries contribute to savings in transaction costs and are also helpful in accumulating technological knowledge to be transmitted to the R&D centers and headquarters in Korea.

SEC currently operates 206 global bases of diverse functional units, such as regional headquarters, production centers, sales centers, R&D centers, design centers, and others within seventy-five countries in the world. Among the different functional units, the headquarters, regional headquarters, R&D centers, production plants, and sales offices can be regarded as the major units of the corporate system that interact differently with diverse regions and cities to establish global networks according to their hierarchical function in the corporate system, as examined in Chapter 6.

The global headquarters of SEC should be located in the capital region of Korea to ensure easy communication with and control over diverse global corporate units, access to the Korean national government, close relations with financial firms, and close networks with leading universities and research labs in the capital region. In fact, SEC is based in the famous area of Gangnam in Seoul. Despite the emphasis on the dispersion of power to individual corporate units, the global headquarters of SEC makes major decisions for investments and long-term strategies.

Regional headquarters (RHQs) support SEC affiliates for shared services in finance, tax, legal issues, risk management, and logistics. These headquarters plan and introduce local-oriented products through market surveys and deliberation of customer lines. Promoting sports marketing and conducting local-oriented cultural and CSR activities, such as "Hope for Children," has also been recently included in the role of RHQs. RHQs accumulate regional intangible assets through these diverse activities, whereas local firms and institutes accumulate knowledge and technology through interaction with SEC. SEC divides the global market into ten regions, as seen in the RHQ set-up discussed in the SEC section of Table 6.4. The RHQs are all located in the capital region or the largest metropolis of a leading country within the divisions of the global market (SEC part of Table 6.4). The location of RHQs clearly matches with the capital region or the largest metropolis in the urban hierarchy, which is meaningful, given the role of RHQs in the global networks.

The major roles of R&D centers in foreign countries are cooperation with local areas in the field of local superior technologies, the promotion of open innovation with local leading universities and institutes, and the development of local-oriented products and solutions to respond to the regional technology standard. In the development of local-oriented products, SEC considers local culture, tradition, and characteristics to generate different strategies by region. For example, SEC emphasizes sensing or asset seeking for technology at Silcon Valley or London, and exploiting and exploring specialized technologies by region in other areas. Accordingly, R&D centers accumulate knowledge through exploring and exploiting local-specific intangible assets. The locations of R&D centers match with either capital regions or large metropolises, where innovative clusters or regional innovation systems are soundly developed. London, Beijing, Moscow, and Tel Aviv are the examples of R&D center locations in the capital region, where high-tech clusters are well developed. Several noncapital metropolises also serve as locations of R&D centers. These areas are mostly major innovation clusters or high-tech clusters of the global market.

For the location of production centers, SEC considers diverse factors, such as lead time, transportation and utility infrastructure, labor costs, commercial environment, market merits, and government incentives. Industrializing countries, especially China, have significant advantages in terms of the location of production centers, which is different from the pattern of R&D centers. Only one plant is located in an advanced country, but in a low-level city. Meanwhile, two plants are located in less industrialized countries, but are both in the capital region. More than 90 percent of the foreign plants are located in industrializing countries, among which approximately 76 percent are located in larger metropolises. More than 40 percent of the production centers are located in China, whereas the regional divisions of the Middle East and Africa have only one production center each, suggesting that production centers are closely related to industrial clusters, as well as to actual markets. Production centers are mainly located in cities where industrial clusters are well developed to make the production networks efficient in local areas. This set-up suggests that production centers consider savings in transaction costs within production networks of industrial clusters, as well as in exploring and exploiting intangible assets with relation to the production activities.

Sales network centers (SNCs) focus on local marketing and interactions with local areas for developing local-oriented strategies in global networks. In some aspects, the role of SNCs is similar to that of RHQs for global networks, albeit at a significantly smaller spatial scale. As such, SNCs are all located in either the capital region or large metropolitan areas regardless of the level of the countries. SNCs are relatively dispersed throughout the world, from advanced to less industrialized countries, which is considerably different from the case of other corporate units. A considerable number of SNCs are located in the less industrialized countries of the Middle East and Africa, Latin America, and CIS and Baltic areas, although these units are all in the capital region. SNCs located in major cities of advanced countries explore various types of intangible assets in addition to marketing-related knowledge and product information, whereas those in the capital region of industrializing countries attempt to explore knowledge as well as exploit intangible assets. SNCs in less industrialized countries exploit intangible assets for the future development of the sales market and production activities. This observation suggests that the function of SNCs in the global networks differs by location type.

Overall, the global networks of operating units of SEC reveal two aspects. First, the locations of different operating units of SEC have different characteristics of local environment in terms of the hierarchy of national urban systems and externalities, and spillovers of knowledge. Second, SEC's diverse global networks of different functional units contribute to the accumulation of intangible assets through exploring and exploiting knowledge in regions and cities of foreign countries. Continuous activities for exploring and exploiting knowledge enable SEC to pursue innovation and create new paths for development. Examples of knowledge spillovers from collaborations with foreign firms and R&D investments in the USA and Europe are the important processes of learning and knowledge acquisition for most Asian firms (Poon et al., 2006). Such examples in Asian firms confirm that SEC has advanced to the stage of new knowledge creation from the stage of learning and knowledge acquisition from knowledge spillovers in advanced countries.

Conclusion

The case of Samsung reveals that global manufacturing firms are closely related to the activities of product and process innovation, marketing, branding, diverse services, and society in the global space economy. SEC has evolved from being a manufacturing firm of low-priced products to a global leading firm of high value-added products over the last four decades. SEC has also transformed from subcontracting manufacturing products to being an innovation flagship for producing world-first new products. Currently, SEC also moves to transform from innovation to integration of innovation, marketing, and culture. SEC also has evolved toward organizational ambidexterity, balancing exploration and exploitation behavior in the global networks.

In its evolution, SEC has displayed the processes of path dependence, restructuring, and new path creation. Continuous improvement of technology and upgrading innovation in semiconductor technology can be attributed to the historical inheritance of a strong leadership and speedy management. Restructuring and new path creation are related to the adoption of global standards and a Western management system. Successful restructuring during the Asian financial crisis in the late 1990s and during the recent global financial crisis conferred SEC with resilience against the external crises. Management innovations and restructuring contributed to the creation of new paths for SEC. The processes of path dependence, restructuring, and new path creation are not completely separated, but rather overlapping in a continuous complex process. Production and process innovations were previously regarded as critical for a firm's competitiveness. However, design innovation, brand marketing, and network with society are currently regarded as important for a firm's competitiveness, reflecting the need for complex processes and strategies. Through these dynamic processes, SEC evolved into a global technology and market leader.

SEC displays the important role of the CEO and Samsung Group chairman for designing visions and expanding global management. The decision-making power of SEC's headquarters is very important despite the independent role of RHQs and SNCs in some aspects. The regional dimension is important not only for production networks, but also for R&D activities and marketing. Beyond the physical infrastructure and environment, regional tradition and culture are important for determining the specialty of R&D activities and marketing.

During its evolution, SEC promoted diverse strategies for the accumulation of intangible assets. Firms' intangible assets are critical in ensuring competitiveness within a knowledge-based information society. The intangible assets of firms can be increased through the accumulation of knowledge, technology, human capital, brand values, and so on. Such accumulation is possible through formal and informal interactions, and networks with suppliers, customers, competitors, governments, and communities (see Park, 2012 and Chapter 6 of this book). In the process of intangible asset accumulation and interactions with regions, firms differentiate their strategies with cities through the level of the country's development and the status within the urban system. Intangible assets are likewise important in maintaining the competitive advantages of cities and regions. Accumulation of local intangibles results from the evolutionary development of the relationships between the corporate and urban systems. The case study also suggests the processes of intangible asset accumulation in terms of asset-exploring and asset-exploiting activities through the interaction of firms and regions. The observations are consistent with the notion of organizational ambidexterity in management science (Raisch et al., 2009). Notably, the interaction of firms with regions is progressing in multiple levels of the spatial scale from local, regional, global, and virtual by operating diverse functional units in the global space.

Some challenges remain for Samsung in the future. In recent years, especially during the period of the global economic downturn attributed to the global financial crisis, Samsung began to emphasize corporate partnership and symbiotic development with the global society. SEC opted for investment in a production center in Africa in 2012 and participated in diverse activities for education and training programs in Africa, in addition to supporting handicapped persons. SEC is moving toward emphasizing corporate social responsibility (CSR). Symbiotic development and CSR cannot be successful without serious consideration of the global society beyond the declaration of responsibility. In a similar vein, SEC has emphasized green management and tried to apply a green management system throughout its production chains. Considering the serious problems brought about by global climate change, SEC should move one step forward to formulate a pro-environmental management strategy in all value chains of economic activities. SEC has recently shown interest in investments in Africa not only for global network or regional development strategies but also for reconsideration of CSR, which is a positive sign for change. SEC has accumulated immeasurable intangible assets throughout its global networks. Moving forward, SEC will be confronted with the challenge of contributing to the accumulation of regional intangible assets in the peripheral areas of the global economy.

References

Asheim, B. T., Boschma, R. A. & Cooke, P. (2011). Constructing regional advantage: platform policies based on related variety and differentiated knowledge bases. *Regional Studies*, 45(7), 893–904.
Bathelt, H. & Glückler, J. (2011). *The Relational Economy: Geographies of Knowing and Learning*. Oxford: Oxford University Press.

Bryson, J. R. & Daniels, P. W. (Eds.). (2007). *The Handbook of Service Industries.* Cheltenham and Northampton, MA: Edward Elgar.

Cantwell, J. & Piscitello, L. (2005). Recent location of foreign-owned research and development activities by large multinational corporations in the European regions: the role of spillovers and externalities. *Regional Studies*, 39(1), 1–16.

Chosun-Ilbo. (2014). Aggregating power to five new businesses such as a secondary cell, bio-medicine after smart-phone. *Chosun-Ilbo*, page C2, January 29 (in Korean). Available at: http://biz.chosun.com/site/data/html_dir/2014/01/28/2014012802621.html

Khanna, T., Song, J. & Lee, K. (2011). The paradox of Samsung's rise. *Harvard Business Review*, 89(7/8), 142–147.

Kim, S. S. & Kim, K. J. (2013). Fusion of nomadic speed with classic leadership . . . "Korean style" management has the hope of future. *Weekly BIZ of Chosun Daily*, January 12–13 (in Korean).

Michell, T. (2010). *Samsung Electronics and the Struggle for Leadership of the Electronics Industry.* Singapore: Wiley.

Park, S. O. (1991). Government management of industrial change in the republic of Korea. In P. Rich & G. Linge (Eds.), *The State and Spatial Management of Industrial Change* (pp. 74–87). New York: Routledge.

Park, S. O. (1994). High technology industrial development and formation of new industrial district: theory and empirical cases. *Journal of Korean Geographical Society*, 29(2), 117–136 (in Korean with English summary).

Park, S. O. (1996). Network and embeddedness in the dynamic types of new industrial districts. *Progress in Human Geography*, 20(4), 476–493.

Park, S. O. (2004). The impact of business to business electronic commerce on the dynamics of metropolitan spaces. *Urban Geography*, 25(4), 289–314.

Park, S. O. (2012). Interaction between firm and region in the accumulation of intangible assets. Paper presented at the 2012 Annual Meeting of AAG, New York, February 24–28.

Pike, A. (2013). Economic geographies of brands and branding. *Economic Geography*, 89(4), 317–340.

Poon, J. P. H., Hsu, J.-Y. & Jeongwook, S. (2006). The geography of learning and knowledge acquisition among Asian latecomers. *Journal of Economic Geography*, 6(4), 541–559.

Raisch, S., Birkinshaw, J., Probst, G. & Tushman, M. L. (2009). Organizational ambidexterity: balancing exploitation and exploration for sustained performance. *Organization Science*, 20(4), 685–695.

Rinallo, D. & Golfetto, F. (2011). Exploring the knowledge strategies of temporary cluster organizers: a longitudinal study on the EU fabric industry trade shows (1986–2006). *Economic Geography*, 87(4), 453–476.

Samsung Electronics (SEC). (2010). *Forty Years of Samsung Electronics: The History of Challenge and Creation.* Suwon, Gyeonggi, Korea: Samsung Electronics (in Korean).

Samsung Electronics (SEC). (2012a). *43rd Business Report* (2011.1.1–12.31). Seoul: SEC (in Korean).

Samsung Electronics (SEC). (2012b). *Global Harmony with People, Society & Environment.* Seoul: SEC (in Korean).

Torre, A. (2008). On the role played by temporary geographical proximity in knowledge transmission. *Regional Studies*, 42(6), 869–889.

Website references

Samsung Advanced Institute of Technology: www.sait.samsung.co.kr/saithome/
Samsung Electronics (SEC): www.samsung.com/sec/
Samsung Group: www.samsung.co.kr/
Samsung Village: www.samsungvillage.com/blog/2014/01/

9 Future perspectives for the dynamics of East Asian economic spaces and policy implications

Introduction

The spaces of human life can be considered as the spaces where economic activities transpire. Accordingly, these spaces change along with changes in economic spaces and vice versa. Economic spaces and spaces of human life are closely related with the changes in society. The changes in regions or countries have been influenced by megatrends that drove economic or social changes in the world. Therefore, studying regions and spaces requires a thorough understanding of the changes and contents of global megatrends that result in social changes. The evolution of global megatrends, however, renders economic spaces complex as they evolve in time.

In consideration of its dynamic and evolving aspects, developing a single model of the dynamics of economic space can be dangerous. This book has attempted to integrate various aspects of economic spaces under global megatrends. However, the theoretical framework and integrated models proposed in this book do not represent complete theoretical aspects of the dynamics of economic spaces. Numerous aspects should be considered to explain the dynamics of economic spaces in a global knowledge-based economy. Furthermore, the theoretical framework of the dynamics of economic changes discussed in Chapter 2 is closely related to four global megatrends since the 1990s. The newly added megatrends shown in Figure 1.2 of Chapter 1 have not been fully considered in the theoretical models of the dynamics of economic changes. Accordingly, this final chapter focuses on the dynamics of economic changes in relation to climate change.

Smith (2011) identified population change, resource demand, globalization, and climate change as the four global forces that change the world and shape our future. In addition, he described technology as an essential force that is related to all four global forces. Smith's three global forces—namely, population change, globalization, and climate change—are included in the global megatrends in the twenty-first century, as discussed in Chapter 1. Among these trends, population change and climate change are new megatrends that emerged in the twenty-first century. Climate change and the rapidly aging society as new global megatrends have engendered cooperation among actors, regions, and nations in the global economy and transcended competition. In addition, the importance of sustainability and resilience in organizing economic spaces has been demonstrated. Finally, creativity and open innovation based on cooperation have become vital concerns in global economic spaces, as well as regional sustainability and resilience during economic and natural crises.

In this chapter, the most significant aspects in the dynamics of economic spaces in the next two decades are examined, with a focus on climate change and changes in energy systems in East Asia. Future perspectives in reshaping global economic spaces are discussed, particularly with regard to climate change in a knowledge-based information society. Finally, policy implications in Korea and East Asia are briefly discussed.

Climate change and changes in energy systems

Climate change is different from other global megatrends in that its effect can be overwhelmingly destructive if we do not appropriately respond to it. The results of numerous studies on climate change indicate that by the end of the century, the average temperature of the earth will increase by more than 3°C (Rifkin, 2011). Scientists assert that within the century, the average temperature of the earth will increase from 1.5°C to 3.5°C, which can result in the extermination of various plant and animal species. Simulation findings show that the extermination ratio of plants and animals ranges from 20 percent to 70 percent (Pachauri and Reisinger, 2008). The greenhouse effect significantly affects the circulation of water in the earth because it increases atmospheric moisture retention potential by 7 percent along with a temperature increase of 1°C (Solomon et al., 2007). Therefore, without prudent policy and practice, a large-scale disaster can be expected by the end of the twenty-first century.

During the Climate Conference at Copenhagen in December 2009, the EU proposed that all countries in the world should limit their respective carbon dioxide emissions by less than 450 ppm until 2050 (Rifkin, 2011). The International Energy Agency (IEA, 2012) enacted special measures to keep the carbon dioxide discharge less than 450 ppm to maintain an average temperature increase of less than 2°C toward the end of the present century. However, Hansen et al. (2008) argued that the EU miscalculated the increase in temperature under the 450 ppm rule and that the climate change resulting from the increase in carbon dioxide emissions can result in a shocking increase in the average global temperature of up to 6°C by the end of the century. If Hansen et al.'s assertion is correct, the entire human civilization can be annihilated within the century. Moreover, the increase in global temperature can be higher than what EU scientists expected because they did not consider positive feedback loop effects, which induce the effect of temperature increase (Rifkin, 2011).

Despite some disagreements in the rate of temperature increase caused by carbon dioxide emissions, we can agree that without a concrete plan of action that will limit carbon dioxide emissions, we will soon be facing a large-scale climate disaster. For the long term, we should therefore replace fossil fuel with an alternative form of energy to reduce carbon dioxide emissions, the principal source of climate change. In this regard, the EU has enforced several policies and has moved to develop alternative energy forms, such as solar, wind, geothermal, and hydrogen energy. To reduce carbon dioxide emissions, the EU committed to reducing its dependence on fossil fuel, such as coal and petroleum, and increasing the ratio of alternative energy use. For example, the EU plans to increase the ratio of new energy in the supply of electricity through the 20–20–20 targets set in EU2020. These 20–20–20 targets represent a commitment to a minimum of 20 percent reduction in greenhouse gas (GhG) emissions by 2020 compared with that by 1990, a 20 percent saving in the EU's energy consumption compared with projections for 2020, and a 20 percent share of renewable energy in the overall energy consumption in the EU (European Commission, 2010). This plan to increase the ratio of new energy implies the systemic changes that will be introduced in manufacturing production, transportation system, and service industries to improve energy efficiency and promote new energy systems to reduce carbon dioxide emissions. Despite the weakening of measures to reduce carbon dioxide emissions in the last few years because of the European financial crisis, significant long-term changes in energy systems will be seen.

Laughlin (2011), a winner of the Nobel Prize in Physics in 1998, predicted that with the present rate of consumption, fossil fuels will run out within two centuries. He argued that market forces will drive the development of new energy forms because consumers and providers alike eagerly adopt the cheapest products, in accordance with the laws of economics— that is, in the next two centuries, market forces, particularly low prices, will be the driver of innovation in the development of alternative energy forms. According to Laughlin, the potential for alternative energy forms will emerge from unexpected sources, such as geothermal energy in the deep sea, animal waste, trash, or solar energy. Although Laughlin remains optimistic about solving the energy crisis in the future, the successful development of alternative energy forms can only be possible when we can appropriately respond to the disasters that result from climate change.

As discussed in Chapter 1, the global force of climate change is one of the most important forces that will alter global economic spaces in the next two decades. If every country in the world agrees to reduce its carbon dioxide emissions and cooperate to develop alternative energy forms, the future of the global economy will be significantly restructured. IEA predicts that renewable energy (hydro, biomass/MSW, wind, and other renewable energy forms) will account for more than 40 percent of global electricity generation in 2030 under the 450 ppm scenario (Rogner, 2012). Current policy scenario indicates that the renewable energy share will only be 21 percent of the global electricity generation in 2035 without the 450 ppm scenario considered (Figure 9.1). At present, the global energy map is changing, with potentially far-reaching consequences for energy markets and trade, because of large-scale energy developments in the USA, energy efficiency technology development and investment, increase in natural gas demand, and increase in renewable energy. Evidently, the changes in energy systems in response to greenhouse effects will result in a reduction of the share of fossil fuel in the energy supply and an increase in the use of new, renewable energy forms. The IEA described the increasing share of renewable energy as follows:

> A steady increase in hydropower and the rapid expansion of wind and solar power has cemented the position of renewable as an indispensable part of the global energy mix; by 2035, renewable will account for almost one-third of total energy output. Solar grows more rapidly than any other renewable technology. Renewable will become the world's second largest source of power generation by 2015 (roughly half that of coal) and, by 2035, they approach coal as the primary source of global electricity. Consumption of biomass (for power generation) and biofuels grow fourfold, with increasing volumes being traded internationally. Global bioenergy resources are more sufficient to meet our projected biofuels and biomass supply without competing with food production, although the land-use implications have to be managed carefully. The rapid increase in renewable energy is underpinned by falling technology costs, rising fossil-fuel prices and carbon pricing, but mainly by continued subsidies: from $88 billion globally in 2011, which will rise to nearly $240 billion in 2035. Subsidy measures to support new renewable energy projects need to be adjusted over time as capacity increases and as the costs of renewable technologies fall, to avoid an excessive burden on governments and consumers.
>
> (IEA, 2012, p. 6)

Such a rapid increase in the supply of renewable energy and the decline in the cost of renewable technology caused by the expanded capacity of renewable energy supply will inevitably transform the global energy landscape. Because of the global economic crisis and the European financial crisis in recent years, investments toward the development of renewable energy and technology in developed nations have slowed down. Successive editions of the IEA's World Energy Outlook have shown that "the climate goal of limiting warming to 2°C is becoming more difficult and more costly with each year that passes" (IEA 2012, p. 3). Worldwide agreement to cut carbon dioxide emissions and engage in the development of energy-efficient technologies is crucial to attain the 2°C goal.

Notwithstanding the difficulties in attracting investments for renewable energy development during the global economic recession, considerable changes in the energy structure must be achieved within two decades. As the IEA predicted, "coal remains the largest source of electricity generation globally, but renewable and nuclear power account for more than half of

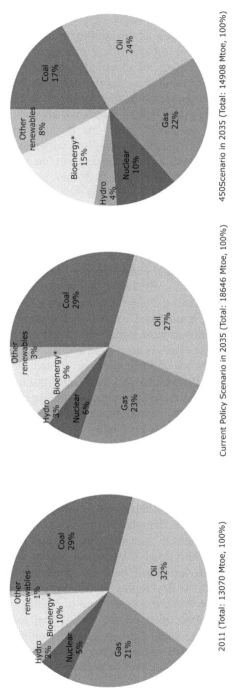

2011 (Total: 13070 Mtoe, 100%)   Current Policy Scenario in 2035 (Total: 18646 Mtoe, 100%)   450Scenario in 2035 (Total: 14908 Mtoe, 100%)

Figure 9.1 World primary energy demand by scenario

Source: Data from IEA (2013).

all new capacity added through to 2035" (Birol, 2011, p. 8). In addition to structural changes in the global electricity supply, the development of new energy forms and the construction of an intelligent electricity network can result in significant changes in industries and economic spaces. The establishment of an intelligent network of electricity or smart grid through the integration of energy and communication systems can contribute to the creation of millions of employment opportunities. The construction of energy-efficient houses, buildings, shopping malls, offices, industrial clusters, and technology districts will create new industries and jobs through the boom in the construction industry (Rifkin, 2011). In addition, diverse R&D activities, services, and new industries will emerge; these are related to direct products and sectors associated with the development of new energy. Rifkin (2011) stated that the integration of new energy systems with communication systems generates new technology, products, and services in broad areas. This integration results in significant changes in the industrial structure and the generation of numerous jobs.

In the next two decades, society will undergo considerable changes. In the era of fossil fuels, vertical or hierarchical power structures with centrally concentrated power will prevail. However, the emergence of new energy systems along with the weakening of centrally concentrated power focused on fossil fuel will reveal the importance of the civil society, while centrally concentrated power will shift toward horizontal civil power (Rifkin, 2011). Such changes have already begun, as seen in examples of information spread through the horizontal network of Facebook, the spread of game industries through smartphones, and the spread of knowledge through Wikipedia, an online encyclopedia, which is developed through the direct participation of readers. Therefore, technological development and innovation can lead us to live in complex and dynamic economic spaces.

However, although technological development can be a driver of changes, it can only weaken the problems that result from global forces, such as climate change. Smith (2011) stated that the changes brought about by global forces of demographic changes, resource demands, globalization, and climate change cannot be stopped despite new technologies, which can only contribute to slowing down the speed of such changes.

Advances in biotech, nanotech, and material science affect demand for different resource stocks. Smart grids, solar panels, and geoengineering might combat climate change. Modern healthcare and pharmacology are shifting population age structures in the developing world, and so on. However, under our "no silver bullets" rule these and other vital technological advances are evaluated as enablers or brake-pads on the four global forces, rather than somehow preempting them (Smith, 2011, p. 25). Therefore, considering the global megatrends in our global knowledge-based economy, we need new policy directions that will sustain economic activities.

Future perspectives for the dynamics of economic spaces in East Asia

Climate change and the emergence of new industries

The transformation in technologies, industries, and lifestyle with regard to sustainability concerns (i.e. sustainability transitions) has been widely investigated in the field of innovation studies. Research on sustainability transitions has disregarded spatial aspects (Truffer and Coenen, 2012). However, an increasing number of cities and regions, such as Curritiba, Gothenburg, and Hamburg, have reinvented themselves in recent years as sustainable centers or green-technology leaders (Carvalho et al., 2011). These initiatives aim at "implementing integrated programmes for sustainable urban living, encompassing broad range of new technologies such as energy-efficient housing, renewable energies, the efficient use of water, and green public transport policies" (Truffer and Coenen, 2012, p. 14). Such initiatives for sustainability transition in cities and regions can serve as an impetus in the intensification of spatial innovation systems as a part of the development of environmental technologies in response to climate change. In particular, by building innovative systems, cities and regions can effectively promote sustainability transition because diverse actors in the region provide crucial resources for innovation processes through intensive local and global networks.

In light of climate change, environmental industries, even the service sector, therefore need to be significantly developed. For example, the carbon financial service industry has emerged as a new service industry that influences the shaping and reshaping of economic spaces in the global economy. Knox-Hayes (2009) stated that new carbon markets are composed of social and economic networks that rely on social connectivity and proximity. As such, established financial centers, such as London and New York, will find the task of developing new carbon markets easy. Although existing centers can be reinforced as suggested by Knox-Hayes (2009), the role of secondary financial centers will expand over time and thus make global economic spaces dynamic.

The emergence of carbon markets reshapes the financial market and results in dynamic economic spaces. Knight (2011) suggested that the carbon market can serve as a means to understand the economic geography of financial markets. He argues that "certain national factors (market structure) and institutional factors (regulatory phase) better explain how carbon markets operate than company level differences" (p. 817). The results of Knight's study illustrate the dynamics of economic spaces with respect to the carbon market:

> Aggregating our findings on timing and market structure, we believe there may be important implications for corporate innovation and investment in new technologies. If companies operate in a context in which they are able to pass through the cost of carbon then they may have little genuine incentive to invest new technologies and production processes. While

economic theory may suggest that over the long term this problem may correct itself as electricity demand corrects to short-term price spikes, the episodic and time-sensitive nature of carbon market development suggests that such long-term consistency may be currently lacking. It appears that investors do not yet regard carbon as a long-term price point upon which to make their decisions. Rather the price of carbon and its financial implications are closely tied to the institutional (time) and market structure (space) characteristics of the particular carbon market phase in play.

(Knight, 2011, p. 837)

Zheng et al. (2011) suggested that household carbon dioxide emissions vary across major Chinese cities and that regional economic development and household carbon dioxide emissions are strongly correlated. They also stated that currently, the standard household greenhouse gas emission in the dirtiest city in China (Daqing) is only one-fifth of the greenest city in America (San Diego). However, if we consider China's population size and rapid economic development, we can expect that its carbon dioxide emissions and energy demand will account for a significant proportion of those of the rest of the world. The IEA projects that China and India will account for more than half of the increase in global energy demand from 2011 to 2035 (Figure 9.2).

This production-based carbon accounting, however, should be complemented by consumption-based carbon accounting. Carbon emissions from emerging economies, such as China and India, can be regarded "as far more implicated in the supply chains that satisfy the demands of European and American consumers than has been recognized" (Bergmann, 2013).

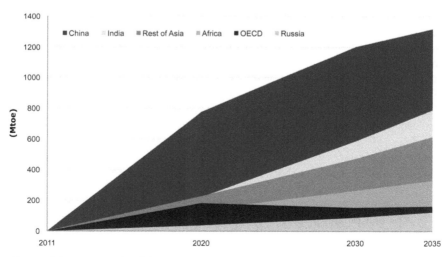

Figure 9.2 Increases in global energy demand
Source: Data from IEA (2013).

Considering the chains of carbon in international trade and consumption-based carbon accounting, Bergmann (2013) argued that the majority of carbon emissions in the world can support capital accumulation in countries other than where the emissions originated. In this regard, the era of climate change demands global cooperation for us to develop environmental technologies that can be transferred to emerging industrializing countries.

Several significant challenges in human health and well-being have also emerged in this era of climate change. Curtis and Oven (2012) suggested key dimensions of health and climate change for geography as issues of adaptation and resilience, sustainability, and environmental justice, and the socially unequal effects of climate change. The effects of climate change on health indicate socially and geographically unequal effects that often exacerbate existing health disparities (Curtis and Oven, 2012). Issues on the health risks of climate change are complex processes that operate at various spatial scales from local to global and demand global cooperation and a global governance system. In particular, we should collaborate to deliberate on the needed transformation as a response to global environmental change that results from climate change (O'Brien, 2012). Cooperation at the level of multiple spatial scales, as well as interdisciplinary collaboration, is necessary to respond to climate change. At present, East Asian countries are cooperating to mitigate desertification in northwestern China, which results in sandy dusts blowing from the Gobi Desert to eastern China, Korea, and Japan.

Spatiality of learning, knowledge, and innovation

Howells and Bessant (2012) suggested three areas that are significant for the coevolution and intertwined trajectory of economic geography and management studies: "the shifting geographical and organizational boundaries of the firm; the role of knowledge and innovation interactions over space and time; and lastly, how changing geography (and responses to it) will shape future patterns of firm development and growth" (Howells and Bessant, 2012, p. 936). From these three arenas in the era of globalization, the shifting boundaries of firms can be regarded as the most crucial factor in reshaping the innovation system over space with the rise of "open innovation." Innovation and knowledge interactions vary across sectors, communities, and places. In addition, technological development in soft innovations, such as mobile phones and ubiquitous shopping, will inevitably redefine the spatiality of innovation.

With the increasing complexity of innovation, innovation networks, and management, "open innovation" has been regarded as a new imperative in creating and generating profit from technologies (Chesbrough, 2003; Chesbrough et al., 2006; Teirlinck and Spithoven, 2008). In the open innovation model, firms prefer to conduct R&D activities and innovation externally. Teirlinck and Spithoven (2008) summarized the features of the open stage-gate process of innovation as follows:

(1) the centralized in-house R&D laboratory is no longer the main source of ideas or knowledge and is being complemented by other enterprises, new technology based start-ups, universities, and public research centers;

(2) commercialization also occurs outside the traditional markets of the enterprise through licensing, spin-offs, and research joint ventures;

(3) the role of the first mover advantage becomes more important than the development of a defensively oriented system of knowledge and technology protection.

(p. 690)

In their empirical studies, Teirlinck and Spithoven (2008) found that firms in less urbanized areas conduct open innovation with an increase in the presence of outsourcing and codeveloping innovations. With these results and the concept of temporary clusters considered, innovations can be achieved not only in peripheral areas in developed countries but also in emerging countries in Asia to reshape the spatial organization of innovation. Social, cultural, and environmental features that allow easy access to external knowledge and information can likewise be important for innovation, apart from the large cities that enjoy the advantage of having an external knowledge network for innovation in terms of urbanization and localization economies.

In East Asian countries, however, innovative activity remains highly concentrated in major metropolitan areas. In particular, the top three regions in China—namely, Guangdong, Beijing, and Shanghai—share about 73 percent of all patents in the country. The overwhelming concentration of Chinese innovation in these areas seems to be related to the traditional agglomeration effects with increasing spatial disparity. In particular,

> the geography of innovation in China is akin to what could have been predicted under a 'new' economic geography framework. It is a traditional agglomeration story: richer regions with an intense agglomeration of activities, good infrastructure endowments, and a greater degree of industrial specialization not only have higher patenting rates, but also absorb innovative potential from neighboring areas. When agglomeration effects are taken into account, the R&D spillovers become negative and significant, generating what is known as the 'Krugman shadow effect' (McCann and Ortega-Argilés, 2011), that is, the agglomeration of innovation in core areas leads to ever greater concentration of innovation by promoting further outflows of knowledge from neighboring regions. This drawing of resources from surrounding areas is a sign of the presence of what can be considered as a less mature innovation system.
>
> (Crescenzi et al., 2012, p. 1075)

The issue of related variety is also important in the innovation and growth of regions in East Asia. In the two largest Chinese cities, Beijing and Shanghai, replication and diversification of related variety affect the locational dynamics of the emerging Internet industry (Zhang, 2013). In Gangnam District, which is located in the southern part of the River Han in Seoul, diverse related service activities are important for emerging, new high-technology start-ups. However, significant differences exist in the generation and evolution of related variety among the regions in terms of institutional embeddedness. Transnational entrepreneurship is important in China, whereas localized venture firms are vital in Seoul, a result suggesting differences in the evolution of regional innovation and related variety by region in East Asia. Along with the importance of related variety in regional innovation and growth, regions should be understood in terms of "relational complexity," as suggested by Healey (2006), beyond self-contained closed identity. Aside from the self-contained entity of a region, the relational position of this region as a node in a wide economic and cultural environment is also important (Paasi, 2013).

Beyond local cluster and regional innovation systems in East Asia

In the last two decades, studies in economic geography and policy have emphasized the local cluster and regional innovation systems. Beginning in the Marshallian and Italian industrial districts, spatial proximity has been considered in the local organization of production and innovation. However, clusters and innovation systems can be developed because other proximities can be found in global economic spaces. These proximities are as follows (Faulconbridge, 2006, p. 520):

- *Organizational proximity* (common approaches, language, and job roles specific to a firm);
- *Relational proximity* (shared ethos, language, and approach to work everyone in an industry shares);
- *Institutional proximity* (shared "rules of the game" specific to a firm or industry); and
- *Temporal proximity* (a shared vision of how things should be in the future and where the industry is at present and ultimately heading).

Accordingly, transferring and creating tacit knowledge over space can be done in many ways. Faulconbridge (2006) asserted that globally stretched learning and the generation of new knowledge with social practice and interactions are possible. Tacit knowledge can be transformed into face-to-face contact through travel, migration, and temporary cluster, among others. However, beyond the transfer of knowledge, new knowledge can be produced with social networks and practices; collaborations of universities, firms, and R&D centers; joint R&D activities, and temporary clusters. Multiple spaces of knowledge transfer and creation with global stretching can be found beyond local boundaries.

Morrison et al. (2013) argued that global pipelines are beneficial to the accumulation and acquisition of knowledge only when a high quality local buzz exists in a cluster or when the cluster is small and weakly endowed in terms of knowledge base. A small cluster in developing areas has a significant implication because in this cluster, access to external knowledge that comes from the outside is important to improve cluster performance (Morrison et al., 2013). Both external and internal interactions contribute to increasing knowledge in a cluster, but the effective mix of the two can be different by region and type of cluster, as suggested by Morrison et al. (2013):

> In our simulation model, actors who are experts (i.e., more knowledge-able than the average actors in the cluster) and externally connected spontaneously behave as external stars rather than knowledge gatekeepers. Therefore, the existence of global pipelines is not per se a guarantee of the better performance of a cluster in terms of the acquisition of knowledge. A condition for global pipelines to behave as knowledge gatekeepers is the existence of a high-quality local buzz; that is, when external knowledge reaches the cluster it is important that its diffusion mechanisms function efficiently. Moreover, our model underlines that global pipelines are particularly important when the cluster is small and weakly endowed in term of its knowledge base because, in this case, access to knowledge coming from outside is key to improving the cluster's performance.
>
> (Morrison et al., 2013, pp. 92–93)

In consideration of the above findings, small clusters in developing countries or in the peripheral areas of advanced countries should strengthen global pipelines and internal networks to contribute to the emergence of knowledge gatekeepers. However, in the large clusters in the core areas of developing countries or in advanced countries, diverse strategies to form high-quality local knowledge networks should be supported to bring about knowledge gate-keepers with the use of global pipelines. With the importance of temporary clusters beyond territory considered (Bathelt et al., 2011), the role of knowledge gatekeepers should specifically be strengthened. Encouragement and the support of firm participation in small clusters in trade fairs and international conferences are vital because the knowledge bases of these firms are relatively weak.

In this global stretching of learning, the ambidexterity of knowledge exploiting and exploring behavior has become increasingly important, as examined in the case of Samsung in Chapter 8. In recent years, knowledge sourcing in multiple spaces beyond the local buzz and global pipelines has been evident in some sectors, such as software industries (Trippl et al., 2009). The case study on the software sector in Vienna suggests a different typology of knowledge network as distinguished from market relations, formal networks, spillovers, and informal networks (Trippl et al., 2009). Knowledge spillovers and informal networks are evident in all spatial scales beyond the local buzz and the global pipeline. Korea has had a clear tendency of having a local cluster of software industries and producer services. Nevertheless, the diverse networks of producer services in terms of knowledge sourcing and interactions indicate the emergence of multiple spaces of innovation and knowledge sourcing in recent years (Kim, 2012). The recent dispersion trend under the overall concentration of knowledge-intensive industries in Korea suggests the possible trend of multiple spaces of innovation and knowledge sourcing in East Asian countries. The ambidexterity of the knowledge exploiting and exploring behavior of Samsung Electronics in Chapter 8 also suggests the importance of multiple spaces in learning and innovation.

The global stretching of learning beyond a specified local scale is related to the broad view of a relational approach to explain learning in a socio-spatial context. The relational approach considers the diverse dimensions of proximity beyond spatial proximity and "takes agents and their relations as objective of analysis rather than regions as bounded territories and allows an understanding of the relation between space and learning from the perspective of the agents involved in the process of learning" (Rutten and Boekema, 2012, p. 990). Therefore, learning in space can be regarded as a knowledge exchange process between agents at several spatial scales affected by cultural and relational factors (Hassink and Klaerding, 2012) on one hand and producing new knowledge through social practice and interactions on the other hand. However, note that the relational approach and global stretching of learning do not disregard the significance of the "learning region" concept or geographical proximity in the explanation of dynamic economic spaces.

The concept of learning region and innovation is increasingly conceived to be too narrow to address the challenges in the age of climate change. In this era, sustainable forms of development must be considered to deal with issues of learning and innovation (Healy and Morgan, 2012). Sustainability with regard to climate change requires reconsidering the space of learning and innovation because "conventional notions of space as a bounded territorial entity are compromised by the fact that GhG emissions have the same global effect whatever their local source" (Healy and Morgan, 2012, p. 1048). Sustainability requires open innovation and a democratic model of innovation, which is far from the bounded model of innovation in the past, as suggested by Chesbrough (2003) and von Hippel (2005).

The active role of the state as a coproducer of environmental technologies and innovation with respect to finance, regulation, and public procurement has become important, especially in less favored regions. However, local and regional governments, as well as the state government, must design innovation and development strategies on sustainability issues. Examples of these strategies are the

> new solar energy technology in Austin, Texas; carbon capture and storage in New Haven, West Virginia; clean technology in general in California;

renewable energy in the home in Marburg, Germany; urban congestion charging in London (UK) and Stockholm (Sweden); urban food security in Belo Horizonte, Brazil; peasant-owned food cooperatives in Henan Province, China; and zero emission buses in Helsinki, Finland (Morgan, 2008).

(Healy and Morgan, 2012, p. 1049)

Cities and regions can be regarded as the facilitator and implementer rather than the innovator or inventor. These examples of technological progress can be regarded as the results of the open and democratic pattern of innovation in practice with regard to the issue of sustainability.

Creative economy and creative regions

The last two decades have seen an increasing interest in a creative economy that focuses on creativity to promote economic development. The Australian report *Creative Nation: Commonwealth Cultural Policy*, which was published in October 1994, addresses the cultural policy in Australia. It presents the beginning of how the creative industry and the creative economy were considered in the nation. Since the adoption of the creativity concept by Florida (2002) and Cunningham (2002), the importance of creative class, creative industries, and creative region has permeated Europe, Asia, and recently, the world (Chapain et al., 2013). The policy implications of creativity have been given much attention, with many conferences and seminars conducted in both advanced and developing countries in the last decade. However, the concept possesses different aspects with regard to the application of creativity in Europe and the USA as follows:

More and more cities and regions around the world have been focusing on the 'creative class' and/or on the 'creative industries' in their economic development or regeneration strategies as part of this now globally fashionable discourse (for example, see Evans, 2009, who discusses an international survey of such strategies). On one hand, the concept of creative class from Richard Florida in the United States (Florida, 2002) focuses on how individuals working in a broad range of 'creative' occupations in the economy contribute to local economic growth, and can themselves help foster an open and dynamic environment in which to work and live; by doing so, Florida highlighted the importance of attracting talent in today's highly mobile world. On the other hand, the creative industries discourse in Australia and then in the UK focuses on how firms in these industries can be helped and supported, on the assumption that they are highly innovative and are new motors of economic growth (for a review, see Flew and Cunningham, 2010). Interestingly, these two concepts represent two sides of the same coin: one looking at individuals and the other looking at firms or, as expressed by Comunian et al. (2010), one looking at the demand side of the labor market and other looking at its supply side.

(Chapain et al., 2013, p. 131)

Despite debates on the definition of the creative industry and creative class with regard to artistic and cultural activities as well as the knowledge economy (Chapain et al., 2013), the promotion of local and regional economic development has gained growing policy interest. In general, a trend of expansion in the location of artistic and cultural industries has been emerging in Europe from the core of the metropolis to far suburban areas to represent the interconnected conglomerate of creative activities (Bertacchini and Borrione, 2013). However, note that the location of creative industries and the creative class shows diverse patterns by country. In Korea, for instance, artistic and cultural activities are mostly concentrated in the central cities of major metropolises. Some attempts have been made to develop the cluster of creative industries in the suburban areas, but this is still in the initial stage of development.

Currently, Korea emphasizes creative industries for economic development in three aspects: the application of information and communication technology (ICT) and scientific technology to cultural activities, the creation of new jobs, and fostering regional development. The development of a creative economy is the grand policy of the Park G. H. administration. Some cases in which creative industries are being developed in provincial regions are also apparent. However, despite the trend of suburbanization of creative industries in the capital region, this development has yet to flourish in provincial areas because of the concentration of the creative class in the capital region. Accordingly, the policy issue in Korea should focus on the fusion of ICT with other industries to improve productivity and develop new industries in provincial regions.

In consideration of the significant development of ICT in most East Asian countries, the fusion of ICT with other industries, such as cultural industries and environment-related industries, promises to create new industries and new jobs. In this aspect, the creative economy in East Asia has a broader spectrum than that in Europe or the USA. However, the development core of the creative economy is in the capital region of East Asian countries or in a few major metropolitan areas. Decentralization to the suburban areas of major metropolitan regions and dispersion to provincial regions are possible in the long term. A rapid progress of spatial expansion of the creative region can be realized with strong support from both local and national governments.

Population aging and changes in economic spaces in East Asia

Population aging is rapidly progressing in East Asia. Japan has already entered the super-aged society, and most of the newly industrialized and industrializing countries in East Asia are now in the aging society and moving rapidly toward the aged society. In particular, Korea is expected to move toward the aged society soon and to the super-aged society by 2026 (Park et al., 2007). Economic spaces in East Asia will inevitably undergo abrupt changes because of such rapid population aging. Several important aspects of changes in economic spaces will occur in East Asia.

First, overall economic growth rate in East Asia will decline because of the decreasing number of the population aged between 15 to 65 who can actively participate in economic activities, especially after the 2020s. Government expenses for pensions and medical services for the elderly will rapidly increase, which will cause financial distress to governments in East Asia in the future, similar to that experienced in Europe in recent years. East Asian countries will restructure the pension and medical insurance systems to mediate the burden from the aging population. Accordingly, the roles of governments as facilitators, mediators, and active agents will continue to be important in East Asia in the next two decades.

Second, new elderly-friendly industries and services will be created for the increasingly aging population in East Asia. Governments will continuously support the creation of elderly- friendly industries and the improvement of such existing industries and services through the application of new technologies, such as information and communication technology and biotechnology. Clusters of elderly-friendly industries and services can be developed in the suburban areas of major metropolitan regions in East Asia. Japan and newly industrialized economies such as Korea, Singapore, Hong Kong, and Taiwan will have advantages in the development of elderly-friendly industries and services. China will soon catch up with the development of elderly-friendly industries because of the knowledge transfer from multinational corporations and its large market of aged population. However, Japan and the newly industrialized economies will take a leading role in the development of new elderly-friendly services because of their active innovation and technology fusion using new ICT.

Third, significant changes in economic structure are expected because of the increasingly aging population in East Asia. The demand for medical services and tourism for elderly people will rapidly increase in the next two decades because of the increasing number of the elderly and the increasing level of income. In China, the rapid increase in per capita income will result in tourism being one of the most rapidly growing services in the country. In newly industrialized economies such as Singapore and Korea, complexes or clusters for the combined services will be developed in the major metropolitan areas and tourist cities. Such combined complexes and clusters will have strong international networks by connecting the international demand for the services to the service suppliers in newly industrialized and industrializing economies. A service world will be realized in the newly industrialized economies in East Asia because of the increasing demand for medical services and tourism. Advanced economies will have advantages because of the increasing demand for such combined activities.

However, the unification of the Korean peninsula will mediate the problems of the aging population in Korea for one or two decades. Unification will result in overwhelming changes in transportation networks, material and service flows, flows of capital and labor, and so on. Currently, South Korea is like an island because the demilitarized zone between the south and north is a great barrier for interaction. The unification of the Korean peninsula may have a greater impact on East Asian economic spaces than the effect that the unification of Germany had on European economic spaces because there has been negligible interaction between South and North Korea for more than sixty years. Economic landscapes will significantly change because of direct intercontinental transportation connections from South Korea to the major cities of Russia and Europe; direct gas pipelines between Russia and South Korea; the rapid economic development of North Korea with significant FDIs; and significant flows of labor, capital, knowledge, and technology within the Korean peninsula, among other factors. Unification will mediate the problems of decreasing economic activities in South Korea as a result of the rapidly aging population. Complementarities between South and North Korea in terms of capital, technology, natural resources, and economic structure will have significant effects on the growth of the Korean peninsula as a whole. Despite the numerous barriers to unification and the many serious problems that will occur after the unification because of the significant gap in economic levels between the North and the South, unification will certainly reshape the economic landscapes in East Asia.

Policy implications in East Asia

Policy issues for regional development in East Asia involve diverse aspects. In this section, only two broad policy issues are briefly discussed because several policy implications have been discussed in previous chapters of this book. The two policy issues are sustainability with regard to climate change, and innovation and regional development in developing countries.

Sustainability and climate change

Sustainability will remain an important issue in the next two decades. Sustainability "relates to the analysis of the consequences of socioeconomic development on regions and cities, on one hand, and the role that specific places and scales play in the actual formation of socio-technical configurations, on the other hand" (Truffer and Coenen, 2012, p. 16). Sustainability transitions will certainly affect city and regional policies beyond those in Western countries. Sustainability has already become an important issue in regional and industrial policies in most newly industrialized countries despite the slow-moving practice of spatial policy. However, many cities and regions should emphasize strategies, such as energy-efficient housing, green public transportation systems, and the development of renewable energy (Morgan,

2008). These strategies will definitely extend to most East Asian countries. With regard to less favored regions in East Asian countries, the public sector should be innovative in becoming an enabler or a facilitator of collective learning and innovation to sustain society in the era of climate change. Local, regional, and state governments should consider business incentives and public–private partnerships, in addition to appropriate regulations, to create and diffuse environment-friendly technologies for a sustainable economy in less favored regions.

The concept of sustainability has inspired a number of policy approaches from the global to the local scale (Krueger and Gibbs, 2008). In the last two decades, the concept of sustainable development has been increasingly applied to local and regional development strategies. Since the mid-1990s, many European countries have adopted Local Agenda 21 as a key element in European sustainable development (Van Begin, 2004). In the USA, instead of Local Agenda 21, "smart growth" is regarded as a set of policy approaches to sustainable development. The smart growth approach is "built on two key themes: tripartite concerns for community, environment and economy; and regulatory reforms that enable the market to promote these concerns" (Krueger and Gibbs, 2008, p. 1266). However, Krueger and Gibbs (2008) stated that smart growth in the USA represents a "third wave" in the ongoing shift in local and regional development toward market-oriented policy approaches. The smart growth approaches of the USA, however, may not be appropriate for East Asian countries because of their high population density. Rather, energy-efficient community building, transportation systems, and integration of the energy system into communication systems, such as intelligent energy management systems (smart grid), are appropriate for East Asian countries.

The current problems that result from climate change and the environment have led to increased calls for a green economy, which is promoted as "a means to develop a 'win–win' for the economy and the environment" (Davies and Mullin, 2011, p. 793). However, marginalizing the social dimensions of sustainability involves some concerns—how social needs can be affected by the greening processes of the economy should be considered. Specifically, supporting the structure of small and medium enterprises should extend to environmentally focused social enterprises. Consumption-based carbon emissions in global carbon emission accounting, the progress of global cooperation for development, and the transfer of environmental technologies to emerging industrialized countries should also be considered.

Innovation and regional development in developing countries

The basic forces that shape the space of innovation in developing countries in Asia are similar to those that mold the geography of innovation in developed countries; however, these factors operate differently from one country to another (Crescenzi et al., 2012, p. 1078). General policy strategies to promote innovation consist of R&D investments, attracting foreign direct investments

(FDIs), improving human capital, and innovating infrastructure, among others. However, the USA and Europe (Crescenzi et al., 2007) significantly vary in their geographical foundation of innovation, and so do China and India (Crescenzi et al., 2012). Therefore, innovation policy should consider the differences in geographic foundations of innovation by country to promote innovation and regional development in East Asian countries. Doing so is more than what is called for in the general strategy to foster innovation. The absorptive ability of foreign technologies in these regions must depend on regional innovation, as suggested in a case study on the effect of FDIs in China (Huang et al., 2012), to obtain regional development and knowledge spillover from FDIs in these regions. The case study finds clear evidence of the double-threshold effects of regional innovation on productivity spillovers from FDI. This finding implies that the absorptive ability to enhance regional innovation and improve productivity should gain substantial benefits from the knowledge spillover from FDIs in emerging regions. Accordingly, government support to improve regional innovation in less favored regions is necessary to derive benefits from foreign investments. In consideration of the lack of large innovative firms in emerging regions, the "gatekeeper function" of public research institutions in the knowledge-exchange process is important (Kauffeld-Monz and Fritsch, 2013). The role of universities in emerging regions as a broker in knowledge-exchange and spillover processes should be considered and supported in East Asia.

Brain circulation should be strongly considered in regional development in East Asia. Innovation is a crucial driver of regional and national economic success, but the potential negative spatial consequences of innovation should also be considered in the development policy of less favored regions in East Asia. Low-level migration and less flexible labor markets in China can increase spatial inequality among regions because of spatial disparity in innovation activities. Lee and Rodriguez-Pose (2013) suggested that less flexible labor markets and low-level migration seem to be at the root of the association between innovation and spatial income inequality in Europe compared with the case in the USA. Various ways of brain circulation from advanced regions to less favored ones should be implemented to promote regional development in the less favored regions of East Asia in the era of the knowledge-based economy. With the significance of related variety in regional growth considered, as suggested by Boschma et al. (2012), brain circulation and labor flows between related industries should be taken into account in the regional development policy of less favored regions in East Asia. With the rapid development of new communication channels in developing regions, a pool of talented workers can be connected with the growth of less favored regions in East Asia.

Given the importance of skilled migration in the era of globalization in knowledge transfer and economic performance, brain circulation at the national and international levels significantly affects emerging regions in East Asia. Even in advanced countries, international flows of skilled migration positively affect regional development, as follows:

The widespread migration of highly skilled individuals is increasingly central to the process of globalization and can have a positive impact on the economic performance of receiving countries because of the diffusion and international dissemination of knowledge. This central idea has been informed by the literature on management and economic geography on the ability of corporate actors to transfer and use tacit knowledge (in the form of practice) across countries and institutional divides.

(Hatch, 2013, p. 280)

The importance of knowledge spillover and brain circulation in the development of Hsinchu Science Park in Taiwan and Zhongguancun Science Park in China also suggests the need for brain circulation strategies at the national and international levels in East Asia (Filatotchev et al., 2011; Saxenian, 2006). Filatotchev et al. (2011) stated that Chinese returnee entrepreneurs contribute to a significant knowledge spillover effect that promotes innovation in other local high-technology firms. Aside from capitalizing on the knowledge spillover of returnee entrepreneurs, emerging regions should develop strategies to enhance the absorptive capacity of technology and knowledge from the R&D activities of multinational enterprises. In consideration of climate change and the rapidly aging society, brain circulation within a country should also be fostered to improve the productivity and innovation potential of developing areas in East Asia. Along with the continuous progress of global megatrends, spatial restructuring, resilience, and spatial reorganization are expected to occur in the new creative economy under climate change. Global environmental issues and regional problems that arise from new global trends suggest the reconsideration of a regional policy that accords with changes in global megatrends for the next two decades.

References

Bathelt, H., Feldman, M. P. & Kogler, D. F. (Eds.). (2011). *Beyond Territory: Dynamic Geographies of Knowledge Creation, Diffusion, and Innovation*. London: Routledge.

Bergmann, L. (2013). Bound by chains of carbon: ecological–economic geographies of globalization. *Annals of the Association of American Geographers*, 103(6), 1348–1370.

Bertacchini, E. E. & Borrione, P. (2013). The geography of the Italian creative economy: the special role of the design and craft-based industries. *Regional Studies*, 47(2), 135–147.

Birol, F. (2011). *World Energy Outlook 2011, IEA*. Retrieved from www.iaea.org/OurWork/ST/NE/Pess/assets/WEO_FBirol_Nov2011.pdf (accessed August 14, 2013).

Boschma, R., Minondo, A. & Navarro, M. (2012). Related variety and regional growth in Spain. *Papers in Regional Science*, 91(2), 241–256.

Carvalho, L., Mingardo, G. & van Haaren, J. (2011). Green urban transport policies and cleantech innovations: evidence from Curitiba, Göteborg and Hamburg. *European Planning Studies*, 20(3), 375–396.

Chapain, C., Clifton, N. & Comunian, R. (2013). Understanding creative regions: bridging the gap between global discourses and regional and national contexts. *Regional Studies*, 47(2), 131–134.

Chesbrough, H. (2003). *Open Innovation: The New Imperative for Creating and Profiting from Technology*. Boston, MA: Harvard Business School Press.

Chesbrough, H., Vanhaverbeke, W. & West, J. (2006). *Open Innovation: Researching a New Paradigm*. Oxford: Oxford University Press.

Comunian, R., Faggian, A. & Li, Q. C. (2010). Unrewarded careers in the creative class: the strange case of bohemian graduates. *Papers in Regional Science*, 89(2), 389–410.

Crescenzi, R., Rodriguez-Pose, A. & Storper, M. (2007). The territorial dynamics of innovation: a Europe–United States comparative analysis. *Journal of Economic Geography*, 7(6), 673–709.

Crescenzi, R., Rodriguez-Pose, A. & Storper, M. (2012). The territorial dynamics of innovation in China and India. *Journal of Economic Geography*, 12(5), 1055–1085.

Cunningham, S. D. (2002). From cultural to creative industries: theory, industry, and policy implications. *Media International Australia Incorporating Culture and Policy: Quarterly Journal of Media Research and Resources*, 54–65.

Curtis, S. E. & Oven, K. J. (2012). Geographies of health and climate change. *Progress in Human Geography*, 36(5), 654–666.

Davies, A. R. & Mullin, S. J. (2011). Greening the economy: interrogating sustainability innovations beyond the mainstream. *Journal of Economic Geography*, 11(5), 793–816.

European Commission. (2010). *Europe 2020: a strategy for smart, sustainable and inclusive growth*. Brussels: European Commission.

Evans, G. (2009). Creative cities, creative spaces and urban policy. *Urban Studies*, 46(5–6), 1003–1040.

Faulconbridge, J. R. (2006). Stretching tacit knowledge beyond a local fix? Global spaces of learning in advertising professional service firms. *Journal of Economic Geography*, 6(4), 517–540.

Filatotchev, I., Liu, X., Lu, J. & Wright, M. (2011). Knowledge spillovers through human mobility across national borders: evidence from Zhongguancun Science Park in China. *Research Policy*, 40(3), 453–462.

Flew, T. & Cunningham, S. D. (2010). Creative industries after the first decade of debate. *Information Society*, 26(2), 113–123.

Florida, R. (2002). *The Rise of the Creative Class*. New York: Basic Books.

Hansen, J., Sato, M., Kharech, P., Beering, D., Berner, R., Masson-Delmotte, V. & Zachos, J. C. (2008). Target atmospheric CO_2: Where should humanity aim? *Open Atmospheric Science Journal*, 2(1), 217–231.

Hassink, R. & Klaerding, C. (2012). The end of the learning region as we knew it; towards learning in space. *Regional Studies*, 46(8), 1055–1066.

Hatch, C. J. (2013). Competitiveness by design: an institutionalist perspective on the resurgence of a "mature" industry in a high-wage economy. *Economic Geography*, 89(3), 261–284.

Healey, P. (2006). Relational complexity and the imaginative power of strategic spatial planning. *European Planning Studies*, 14(4), 525–546.

Healy, A. & Morgan, K. (2012). Spaces of innovation: learning, proximity and the ecological turn. *Regional Studies*, 46(8), 1041–1053.

Howells, J. & Bessant, J. (2012). Introduction: innovation and economic geography: a review and analysis. *Journal of Economic Geography*, 12(5), 929–942.

Huang, L., Liu, X. & Xu, L. (2012). Regional innovation and spillover effects of foreign direct investment in China: a threshold approach. *Regional Studies*, 46(5), 583–596.

International Energy Agency (IEA). (2013). *World Energy Outlook 2012—Executive Summary.* Retrieved from www.iea.org/publications/freepublications/publication/English.pdf (accessed August 15, 2013).

Kauffeld-Monz, M. & Fritsch, M. (2013). Who are the knowledge brokers in regional systems of innovation? A multi-actor network analysis. *Regional Studies*, 47(5), 669–685.

Kim, Y.-L. (2012). Spatial network structure of scientific research collaboration in Korea. MA thesis, Department of Geography, Seoul National University.

Knight, E. R. W. (2011). The economic geography of European carbon market trading. *Journal of Economic Geography*, 11(5), 817–841.

Knox-Hayes, J. (2009). The developing carbon financial service industry: expertise, adaptation and complementarity in London and New York. *Journal of Economic Geography*, 9(6), 749–777.

Krueger, R. & Gibbs, D. (2008). "Third wave" sustainability? Smart growth and regional development in the USA. *Regional Studies*, 42(9), 1263–1274.

Laughlin, R. B. (2011). *Powering the Future: How We Will (Eventually) Solve the Energy Crisis and Fuel the Civilization of Tomorrow.* New York: Basic Books.

Lee, N. & Rodriguez-Pose, A. (2013). Innovation and spatial inequality in Europe and USA. *Journal of Economic Geography*, 13(1), 1–22.

McCann, P. & Ortega-Argilés, R. (2011). Smart specialization, regional growth and applications to EU cohesion policy. Working papers 2011/14. Institut d'Economia de Barcelona (IEB).

Morgan, K. (2008). Greening the realm: cities and regions as laboratories of innovation and sustainable development. Plenary presentation to The Greening of Industry Network Conference. Leeuwarden, the Netherlands, June 26–28.

Morrison, A., Rabellotti, R. & Zirulia, L. (2013). When do global pipelines enhance the diffusion of knowledge in clusters?. *Economic Geography*, 89(1), 77–96.

O'Brien, K. (2012). Global environmental change II: from adaptation to deliberate transformation. *Progress in Human Geography*, 36(5), 667–676.

Paasi, A. (2013). Regional planning and the mobilization of "regional identity": from bounded spaces to relational complexity. *Regional Studies*, 47(8), 1206–1219.

Pachauri, R. K. & Reisinger, A. (Eds.). (2008). *Climate Change 2007: Synthesis Report.* IPCC Fourth Assessment Report. Geneva: IPCC.

Park, S. O., Park, S. C., Choi, S. J., Lee, J. J., Han, G. H., Lee, M. S., Kwak, C. S., Song, G. U. & Jeong, E. J. (Eds.). (2007). *Long-lived Persons and Areas of Longevity in Korea: Changes and Responses.* Seoul: Seoul National University Press (in Korean with English summary).

Rifkin, J. (2011). *The Third Industrial Revolution: How Lateral Power is Transforming Energy, the Economy, and the World.* New York: Palgrave Macmillan.

Rogner, H.-H. (2012). *World Energy Demand and Supply.* Vienna: International Atomic Energy Agency (IAEA).

Rutten, R. & Boekema, F. (2012). From learning region to learning in a socio-spatial Context. *Regional Studies*, 46(8), 981–992.

Saxenian, A. (2006). *The New Argonauts: Regional Advantage in a Global Economy.* Cambridge, MA: Harvard University Press.

Smith, L. C. (2011). *The World in 2050.* New York: Plume.

Solomon, S., Qin, D., Manning, M., Chen, Z., Marquis, M., Averyt. K. B., Tignor, M. & Miller, H. L. (Eds.). (2007). *Climate Change 2007: The Physical Science Base: Contribution of Working Group I to the Fourth Assessment Report of the Intergovernmental Panel on Climate Change.* Cambridge and New York: Cambridge University Press.

Teirlinck, P. & Spithoven, A. (2008). The spatial organization of innovation: open innovation, external knowledge relations and urban structure. *Regional Studies,* 42(5), 689–704.

Trippl, M., Tödtling, F. & Lengauer, L. (2009). Knowledge sourcing beyond buzz and pipelines: evidence from the Vienna software cluster. *Economic Geography,* 85(4), 443–462.

Truffer, B. & Coenen, L. (2012). Environmental innovation and sustainability transitions in regional studies. *Regional Studies,* 46(1), 1–21.

Van Begin, G. (2004). Aalborg ten years later. *Local Development,* 9, 210–213.

Von Hippel, E. (2005). *Democratizing Innovation.* Cambridge, MA: MIT Press.

Zhang, J. (2013). Related variety, global connectivity and institutional embeddedness: Internet development in Beijing and Shanghai compared. *Regional Studies,* 47(7), 1065–1081.

Zheng, S., Wang, R., Glaeser, E. L. & Kahn, M. E. (2011). The greenness of China: household carbon dioxide emissions and urban development. *Journal of Economic Geography,* 11(5), 761–792.

Index

266 *Index*

Japan 19, 144, 149, 153–159, 163–164, 251
Jeju Special Province 123
Johanesburg 185

Kaldor, M. 38
Kanbur, R. 142
Karlsson, C. 2, 50
Kauffeld-Monz, M. 255
Kenney, M. 9
Khanna, T. 218, 220
Kim, H. 192, 196
Kim, H. S. 195
Kim, K. J. 219
Kim, S. S. 219
Kim, W. B. 7, 117, 144, 151
Kim, Y.-L. 249
Klaerding, C. 249
Kloosterman, R. C. 50
Knight, E. R. W. 243
knowledge base 47–48, 248; three types of 47
knowledge-based economy 4, 6
knowledge-based information society 11, 26, 39, 169
knowledge economy 9
knowledge gatekeeper 248
knowledge sourcing 249
knowledge spillover 8–9, 37, 51, 173, 175, 177, 188, 232–233, 255; effects of 8
Knox-Hayes, J. 62, 243
Koo, Y. 55, 59, 126, 192
Korea 3, 15, 19, 21, 144, 153–160, 163–165, 192, 251–252
Korea Electronics Industrial Corporation 200
Korea Export Promotion Complex 138
Korea Industrial Complex Corporation 133, 136–137, 199–200
Korea Medical Hub 84
Korean peninsula 253
Kramer, J.-P. 37, 171, 173
Krueger, R. 61–62, 254
Krugman shadow effect 246
Krugman, P. 42
Kumar, N. 172
Kun-Hee Lee 218

labor dispute 126–127, 151, 202
Labory, S. 170–171
laser medical appliance 177
Laughlin, R. B. 239
layering 108, 111, 116–119
Lazzeretti, L. 18
Le Heron, R. 5, 17
Leaders Dermatology Clinic 72, 84–88, 92, 97, 100; spatial aspects of 88
leading industrial sector 131
learning 247; collective 254; global stretching of 248–249; in space 249; process of 249; region 249
learning-by-doing 8
learning-by-interacting 8
Lee, J. H. 192, 196
Lee, K. 192
Lee, N. 54, 255
Leinbach, T. R. 9
Lester, B. 112
Lev, B. 170
Levinthal, D. A. 8
Levitte, Y. M. 46
LG InnoTech 203
LG-Phillips 197
Li, F. 147
Lille School 76–77, 80
Lim, Y. H. 196
Liu, W. 36
Local Agenda 21 254
local buzz 39, 40, 145, 248
localization 6, 197; economy 53
lock-in 41, 105–106, 109; technological 41
London 184, 229, 243, 250
Los Angeles 229
Lösch, A. 171
Lundvall, B. 46
Lutronic 85–86, 100, 170, 177–180, 182–183, 186–187

MacArthur Foundation 15, 103, 112
MacKinnon, D. 103
Makino, S. 172
Malaysia 154
Malecki, E. J. 1–2, 10–11, 144, 146
Malmberg, A. 8, 43, 51, 173, 176
Mansvelt, J. 38

Marburg 250
Markusen, A. 1, 47, 129, 143, 193, 199, 201–202, 204–205, 210–211
Marrocu, E. 170–171
Marshall, A. 42–43, 50, 53–54
Martin, R. 41–42, 51–52, 82, 103–110, 112–114, 116, 119–120, 131, 136–137, 142, 164
Masan 194
Maskell, P. 43, 46, 51
Massey, D. 54
McCann, P. 246
Menzel, M. 51
Michell, T. 215, 219, 227–228
Milan 229
Miles, I 71, 74–75, 83
mini cluster 196
Mitchelson, R. L. 174
Monnoyer, M. 75, 81, 86
Moreno, R. 169–171
Morgan, K. 249–250, 253
Morrison, A. 50, 248
Moscow 184
MOST 195
Mullin, S. J. 254
multinational firms (MNFs) 172
Murphy, J. T. 57

Nadvi, K. 36
Nahm, K. B. 196
Nangyung 184
Narula, R. 37, 171
national innovation system (NIS) 46, 49, 83, 195
Negroponte, N. 10
Neill, J. 114
neoclassical model 142
network 41; global 180, 216, 222, 230–233, 243; global cluster 175; global knowledge 145; innovation 137–138, 173, 183, 205; innovative 182; intelligent electricity 242; inter-firm 174, 196, 211; intra-firm 174–176; local innovative 212; local-global 175; virtual innovation 165, 198
network externality 105, 111
networked dermatology clinics 83
networking 17, 39, 145

new economic geography 3, 42
New Haven 249
new industrial space 143
new international division of labor 54
New Management 227; initiative 218, 220
New York 176, 243
Nooteboom, B. 109
North Korea 253
North, D. 105

O'Brien, K. 60, 245
O'Mahony, M. 170
OECD 7, 12, 46, 144, 151–153, 165
Ohmae, K. 5
oil crises 151
Oinas, P. 1, 10, 144
open innovation 49, 231, 238, 245, 249; system 224
open sourcing system 224
organizational ambidexterity 176, 233–234
Ortega-Argilés, R. 246
Oven, K. J. 60, 62, 245
Owen-Smith, J. 40

Pachauri, R. K. 238
Page, S. E. 138
Paju 197
Park G. H. administration 251
Park, S. O. 1–2, 5–7, 9, 11, 15–18, 33, 43–44, 46, 49–51, 54–55, 59, 61, 82–84, 106, 108–109, 117, 120, 126, 129, 143–144, 146, 160, 163, 165, 170, 181, 184, 192–202, 204–205, 207–208, 210–211, 217–218, 230, 234, 252
Passi, A. 247
path as dynamic process 118–119
path as movement to stable state 119
path creation 41–42; new 216, 227, 230, 233
path creation phase 118–119, 131; new 134
path dependence 41–42, 103–105, 107, 109, 111–112, 116, 136–137, 215–216, 233; alternative model of 107

For Product Safety Concerns and Information please contact our EU
representative GPSR@taylorandfrancis.com
Taylor & Francis Verlag GmbH, Kaufingerstraße 24, 80331 München, Germany